Developing Web 2.0 Applications with EGL for IBM i

Joe Pluta

MC PRESS

MC Press Online, LP

Lewisville, TX 75077

Developing Web 2.0 Applications with EGL for IBM i
Joe Pluta

First Printing—October 2009

Every attempt has been made to provide correct information. However, the publisher and the author do not guarantee the accuracy of the book and do not assume responsibility for information included in or omitted from it.

IBM is a trademark of International Business Machines Corporation in the United States, other countries, or both. All other product names are trademarked or copyrighted by their respective manufacturers.

MC Press offers excellent discounts on this book when ordered in quantity for bulk purchases or special sales, which may include custom covers and content particular to your business, training goals, marketing focus, and branding interest.

For information regarding permissions or special orders, please contact:
MC Press
Corporate Offices
125 N. Woodland Trail
Lewisville, TX 75077 USA

For information regarding sales and/or customer service, please contact:
MC Press
P.O. Box 4300
Big Sandy, TX 75755-4300 USA

ISBN: 978-158347-089-3

To download the code referenced in this book, go to

http://tinyurl.com/egl-exch

Or go to this book's page on the MC Press store site at

http://www.mc-store.com/5108.html

To my Mom

You believed in me until I did, too. Thank you for always being there.

Acknowledgements

If you want the definition of a moving target, a book on a brand new technology is as close as you're likely to come. When I first started this project, EGL was a brand new just-past-beta release of a powerful thin-client technology with a pretty darned good IDE.

As I was doing my research and developing the application which is the root of the book, a completely revolutionary change occurred in the product. Right before my eyes EGL spawned an entire new technology, the first WYSIWYG Rich UI development environment. I still don't think there's a tool that matches it. This new technology became the focus of the book and thus the title.

Trying to draw a line in the sand where the book would still be relevant when it was released but yet contain enough of the new technology to be helpful was a neat trick. Luckily, I had the unflagging support of some of the best technical minds in the business, who also are the best professional associates a writer could ask for. It was a humbling experience. Start with the unflappable teaching of Jon Sayles who brought me up from a young grasshopper, add the indefatigable technical advances of Chris Laffra, and then throw in some serious doses of the audacious technical vision of Tim Wilson, and I was constantly reminded of the sheer magnitude of this thing called EGL. And I don't speak lightly—EGL is indeed a great and unprecedented step forward in application development.

There were a lot of other brilliant folks who were willing help me and listen to my trials and tribulations and especially made me feel comfortable that the tool would take care of the people I care about, the IBM i developers, whether it was putting in i-specific features or just making sure the tool made sense to us old green screen dinosaurs. Folks like Justin Spadea and Scott Pecnik and Joe Vincens and Will Smythe—no matter how many stupid questions I asked, they were willing to help, and once in awhile they even let me believe I helped make the tool a little better.

I can't forget to mention the help I got from Kou-Mei Lui whenever I couldn't figure out the EGL Cafe. What a monumental effort the Cafes were and still are.

And even before that were the folks who converted me from skeptic to evangelist: Todd Britton who convinced me that EGL wasn't going to forget the i platform; Stef Sergi who (sometimes loudly) made me understand how the future of business development was right before my eyes in this new tool; and Claus Weiss, who showed me that EGL and the RPG could indeed work together. I also remember long rancorous phone calls with Bob Cancilla that helped focus me on the fact that this tool could be the future of the IBM midrange community.

As always, I need to thank Merrikay Lee of MC Press for deigning to work with me on yet another book that was a lot harder to finish than anyone thought it would be.

And last, but certainly not least, is Sue Mitchell, who has been an indispensable asset in ways too numerous to mention (and not just with this particular project). Big tip of the hat to you Sue—this book might well not have seen the light of day without you.

— Joe Pluta
October 2009

Contents

Introduction

The purpose of this book is very simple. I want to show you how to make your IBM i applications look like the one in Figure I.1.

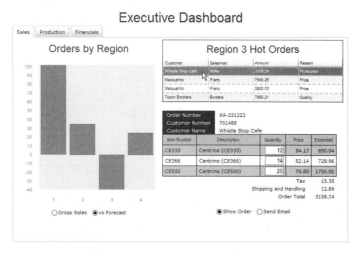

Figure I.1: This rich web application presents multiple related interactive panels.

The application in Figure I.1 highlights the strengths of the rich UI. Multiple panels of related data are shown. Some data is represented graphically, while other data is in a tabular form. Each panel is interactive, and in many cases, a user event in one panel affects the data shown in another. Finally, this is more than just a query; the application can interact with your business logic to execute application functions.

This is definitely not a green-screen application, and that's both a strength and a weakness. It's great to be able to show that the i is capable of this sort of application. However, the danger lies in the fact that the tools exist in other platforms to create the same user interface, and IBM i detractors would argue that is a reason to migrate away from the platform.

This book intends to answer the question, "Why the i?" There are lots of reasons to use the IBM i as your primary server, ranging from security and scalability to an incredibly low cost of ownership. You can stick an i in the corner, and it will run and run. You never need to worry about losing your data. The i rarely needs a reboot, software upgrades are a snap, and it's very good about telling you when something needs to be serviced (such as hot-swapping a disk drive).

The one reason not to use the i, according to its detractors, is that it has no native GUI. Really, though, this is more of a perception issue than a problem. IBM treats the i as a server. Thus, IBM targets its development resources toward making sure the i is the fastest business-logic server on the planet. The integrated DB2 database provides unparalleled flexibility, with a combination of the most standards-compliant SQL engine available. That's not all, though. A unique feature of the i operating system is the blisteringly fast ISAM capabilities of ILE languages, especially free-format RPG (which I like to think of as assembly language for the database). IBM continues to extend and enhance those aspects of the machine, rather than create a native graphical interface. This is entirely logical. The lack of a GUI on the i is really no different than any other server platform, from mainframe to Unix. For example, the primary interface to Unix is a character-based console; you need to use something like X-Windows to get graphical.

In reality, only desktop platforms typically come with built-in graphical interfaces. That makes sense. In fact, I would go so far as to say that you don't *want* graphics on your server. The CPU power required to paint pixels, manage keystrokes, and track mouse movements is better spent on the end-user machine, which typically has lots of extra cycles. Your business-logic server should concentrate on accessing the database and executing business rules as quickly as possible. There is even a reasonable business question as to whether your web application server should run on your server, or on a separate, dedicated machine.

So, if you don't have graphics on your server, how do you create graphical applications? You design a multi-tiered application. Today, that typically means a browser-based application, but even the term "browser-based" is no longer as monolithic as it might have once been. Instead of a browser application being limited to a page-at-a-time interface and a modest graphical repertoire (at least as compared to desktop applications), AJAX and Web 2.0 have introduced the Rich Internet Application (RIA).

A well-designed, easy-to-maintain RIA is the Holy Grail of user interfaces, both for the midrange platform and for the business application industry in general. EGL and its Rich UI component are the tools that let you get there. EGL Rich UI provides a simple path from green to GUI, and even an old green-screen developer like me can create applications like the one above.

What You Will Learn

A significant drawback to any of the browser architectures for IBM i developers is the learning curve, combined with a lack of tooling. In order to build multi-tiered applications, an i developer needs to learn (at the very least) HTML, CSS, XML and/or JSON, Java, and JavaScript, and find suitable tools to develop, debug, and deploy these languages.

RDi-SOA, which combines the EGL development features of Rational Business Developer with the i development capabilities of Rational Developer for the i, reduces that learning curve to the bare minimum. The EGL language is the only additional technology you'll need to learn, and RDi-SOA is the only tool you'll need to use to write, debug, and deploy full-featured, multi-tiered business applications that provide state-of-the-art graphical interfaces. The difference, of course, is that those applications will be powered by the business logic of the IBM i.

This book introduces you to all of the concepts you'll need to create world-class applications. For example, while EGL is not object-oriented, it has reuse features that rival any other language. You'll see how easy it is to separate your code into reusable components, ranging from records to widgets, to library functions, to completely encapsulated shared projects.

EGL is also designed from the ground up to be extensible. You'll learn about the features that allow you to quickly create your own extensions, both in JavaScript and Java.

Debugging is a highly underrated capability, often overlooked in development tools. RDi-SOA is the only tool that lets you debug an application across multiple platforms, using a consistent end-to-end debugging environment. You'll learn how to use RDi-SOA to debug both your EGL and ILE components, from within a single workbench.

You'll also learn how EGL enables full SOA development. To me, EGL's most important feature is simplification: EGL simplifies everything in business application development, from defining data, to inter-platform communication, to user interface design. Because the tool does so much work for you, a well-designed EGL application will *naturally* provide multiple interfaces. A few keystrokes, and you have a web service; a few moments in the WYSIWYG designer, and you have a thin client. The productivity for EGL is far above anything else available. Thus, the return on investment for EGL is much higher. It's even better for IBM i application designers, since the RDi-SOA toolset is only a modest incremental cost for i shops already using RDi. (And if you aren't using RDi, you should be!)

The primary focus of this book, though, is the EGL Rich UI technology. I'll introduce you to the designer for EGL Rich UI, one of the few true WYSIWYG tools for rich web clients, and easily the best. You'll see how the same EGL syntax and architectural techniques used for basic SOA development can be used to quickly build rich Internet applications, without having to learn all the middleware technologies. You'll learn how to use RDi-SOA as a rapid application development tool, allowing you to interact with your users throughout the design process. I'll show you how EGL Rich UI has incorporated the best technologies, from JSON and REST to my personal favorite, the OpenAjax Hub. You'll see how to expose server-side business logic as services, and how to use those services to power your rich web applications. You'll also see how RDi-SOA is the most consistent and productive tool available to test and debug multi-tiered applications.

Finally, you'll get a brief look at the new features that should be available by the time you read this, including the newly announced "EGL Free."

(This is so new that it doesn't even have an official name yet, so don't count on the "EGL Free" moniker sticking.)

The Format of This Book

I like to write technical books for business application developers. I like to make life easier for those who write the applications that help businesses prosper. More specifically, I like to give those developers the information that allows them to most effectively do their job: writing code that makes their users more productive. That means focusing on business logic, not technical minutiae. That's the reason I am so drawn to EGL. It makes complex technology accessible to the programmer, both through simple syntax and through hiding the plumbing. This enables the programmer to focus on the business logic, without having to sacrifice any of the great new advances in technology.

This book is a working introduction to the EGL Rich UI technology and the RDi-SOA tooling, showcasing RDi-SOA's ability to quickly build rich graphical applications for the IBM i platform. This isn't a book on theory. It is entirely grounded in technical reality; the code presented here is fully tested and working. This book is designed to be read from front to back, as a guided tour of developing a real, working, multi-tiered application using nothing but RDi-SOA.

While I don't provide a keystroke-by-keystroke account of every step of the process, I do provide Project Interchange Files (or PIFs), synchronized with each chapter (and in a couple of cases, more than one in a chapter). A *PIF* is the standard technique by which RDi-SOA exchanges projects. You simply import one of my PIFs into a new workspace, and you have a workbench pre-loaded to a specific point in the book. This enables you to follow the progress of the project, and even to make your own modifications at any step of the process.

By the end of the book, I believe you will be convinced that EGL is the best tool available for application design with the IBM i. More importantly, you will be able to be productive as soon as you get your hands on the tool.

The Architecture of Multi-tiered Applications

A multi-tiered application is an application that separates the user interface from the business logic. At its simplest, the application consists of two tiers, as shown in Figure 1.1.

Figure 1.1: The simplest multi-tiered application has two tiers.

There's nothing particularly complex in this design, which has been around since roughly the time the second computer was turned on. More realistically, multiple tiers came into vogue about the same time that end users started demanding access to their data in forms other than printed reports.

The computing world continues to produce ever-more-complex architectures: three-tiered, *n*-tiered, distributed services, grid computing, cloud computing, and so on. The dividing lines between the various tiers provide fodder for endless discussions, and each design has its merits. Some, however, simply aren't applicable to this discussion, which focuses on designing rich graphical applications where the majority of your business logic is in native IBM i languages such as RPG or COBOL.

Although the original midrange applications were of the service-bureau type—enter data, massage it, run reports, print them, and send them back to the client—some of the first online applications were on the lowly System/3. In fact, it was the System/3 Model 15D with CCP that spawned some of the earliest green-screen applications, certainly the first in the line of what would be called IBM midrange computers.

The 3270, the First Multi-tiered Application

Starting the discussion of multi-tiered architectures with a look at the oldest green-screen applications makes a lot of sense, since they are the direct predecessors to a lot of what you'll be looking at in this book. In fact, it's fair to say that the original green-screen display, the 3270, was one of the first multi-tiered applications.

I know you're probably thinking I'm off my rocker, but if you really analyze it, this seemingly simple interface, shown in Figure 1.2, was the definition of the multi-tiered application. Think about it: the program on the host didn't have to actually paint the entire 1,920-character display or the individual pixels on it. Instead, it sent the screen using a series of messages—requests, if you will. These requests were meta-commands and included actions such as setting the buffer address and starting a field. It was entirely up to the 3270 terminal to manage all of those requests and create an interface for the end user.

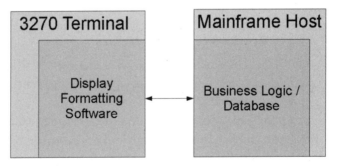

Figure 1.2: The 3270 terminal was the first multi-tiered application.

The 3270 display station actually did quite a bit more. To reduce the traffic back and forth between the display and the host, the 3270 was tasked with keeping track of modified data, allowing access via command keys, and even providing basic editing and keystroke control. It was actually a pretty powerful computer in its own right, especially given the state of the micro-processor at that time. It did exactly what needed to be done: make it easy for users to enter data, while freeing up expensive CPU cycles on the host. Remember that concept; it's going to come up over and over again through this book.

The 5250

Those of us in the midrange marketplace are more familiar with the 3270's younger cousin, the 5250. While similar to the 3270, the 5250 was incompatible with it. That's another thing to keep in mind: the 3270 and the 5250 were both green-screen, block-oriented protocols, but you couldn't attach a 3270 terminal to a host that expected a 5250 device, since the message protocol between the two was quite different.

In the long run, the most important and enduring part of the architecture is the protocol. Think about it: IBM i developers are still writing applications for the 5250 protocol in shops where a physical 5250 device hasn't existed for years, if ever. Emulators such as iSeries Access or TN5250J (the open-source Java 5250 client) act as the client device, something they can do because they are written to respect the 5250 protocol. On the other end of the wire, programs can be written without regard to whether the device is an antique 5250, a modernized version, or an emulator running on Windows, Linux, or even a handheld. The important point, shown in Figure 1.3, is that protocol is king.

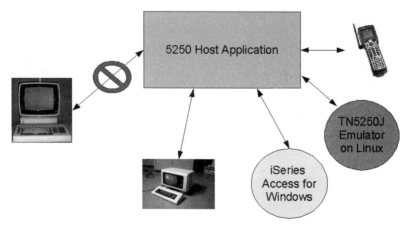

Figure 1.3: The 3270 device cannot communicate, while other devices and even emulation software can.

5250 Emulation

Today, of course, the old 5250 terminal after which the protocol is named is long gone, and even those monitors that emulate the 5250 are few and far between. Except in extreme environments such as factory floors, it's simply easier to have a cheap PC than a 5250 terminal. In most cases, then, we're talking about a PC emulator package, with an architecture something like Figure 1.4.

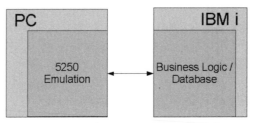

Figure 1.4: This is the environment for which we usually develop: a PC talking to an IBM i.

The environment in Figure 1.4 is the one targeted in this book because, let's face it, if you have nothing but 5250 terminals in your shop, there's little you can do in the way of application modernization. Well, that's not strictly true. Things like standardizing screen layouts, using colors correctly, and re-architecting your applications to use advanced RPG features are available to you, even in the traditional green screen. For the type of UI modernization handled in this book, though, you need to be on a PC.

Screen Scrapers

I have another reason for taking you down this path; it's to address one of the oldest versions of application modernization for the 5250 environment, the screen scraper. As you can see in Figure 1.5, the idea of a screen scraper is relatively simple: put a graphical wrapper around the 5250 protocol.

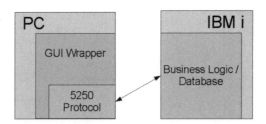

Figure 1.5: This is the essential design underlying all screen scrapers.

Screen scraping can be done in a number of ways, from a simple ad hoc reformatting to a more customized approach that "mashes" screens together and performs the navigation between screens under the cover. In the end, however, you still have the same limitation: the 5250 data stream. As long as your program thinks it is talking to a 5250 device, the application has inherent limitations. You need to break out of that 24-by-80 box to get to the next level of application design.

The Thick Client

Another early attempt at multi-tiered applications was the thick client. I did a lot of work with this particular paradigm back in the 1980s and early 1990s, when the PC was first introduced. Whether the operating system was Windows or OS/2, the idea was the same: create a graphical application that ran on the workstation and communicated with the host, as shown in Figure 1.6.

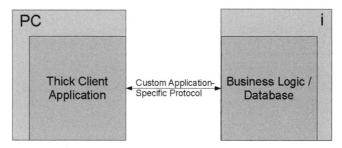

Figure 1.6: This is the classic thick-client application, using a custom protocol to communicate with the host.

Thick-client applications were distinguished by the fact that the code that ran on the PC contained business logic, or at the very least was so tied to the business logic that when that logic changed, the client code changed as well. One reason for this tight binding was that the protocol between the two was very specific to the application. In fact, back in those days, a significant part of the application-development process was simply designing the protocol to be shared between the two tiers. Even a modestly sized application requires dozens, if not hundreds, of specific message formats.

The other aspect of these applications was that the GUI programming was grueling. Developers had to design each window and widget, and often had to use very primitive APIs to build them. A good multi-tiered developer became something of a wizard at the complex, event-driven programming required to handle every keystroke and mouse movement in the brave new graphical world. When even the slightest change to the interface was needed, you had a multiple-phase project: change the business logic on the host or the workstation (depending on where it lay), change the messaging protocol, and finally rework the API.

The straw that broke the camel's back, though, was deployment. Once you made a change on the host, you needed to deploy the corresponding change on the workstation to every PC in your network. Trying to coordinate this in a small shop with a few users was bad enough; trying to implement the same change across multiple sites and time zones was a feat of staggering proportions, and one you wouldn't even attempt in today's anonymous Internet environment. Note that this particular pain point applies to some screen scrapers as well, generally those that have screen-specific custom code that runs on the PC and must be updated whenever a change is made to the underlying green-screen program.

The Thin Client (Browser)

Today, much of the work of creating graphical desktop applications has been removed by tooling, but the architecture is still rendered somewhat less effective by the issues of custom protocol and, more importantly, the redeployment of new code required whenever business rules change. Thick-client code is most effective for power users who need tight integration to desktop software already in place. Day-to-day business-application users, and particularly Internet users, don't need that level of integration, however. That explains the explosive rise of the browser-based thin-client application, shown in Figure 1.7.

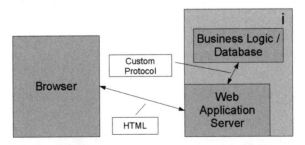

Figure 1.7: The thin-client browser architecture communicates between tiers using HTML.

As you can see in Figure 1.7, the browser-based architecture has two points of communication. The most important one is the communication between the browser and the web application server. This communication is done via HTML. It is the basis for what you could call "Web 1.0," although it was never really called that. Not until the advent of Web 2.0 (also known as "rich Internet applications" or "rich web clients") did it become clear that thin client was a generation unto itself.

I've omitted the rich web client communication from Figure 1.7 because I'll address it separately in a moment. I'm also purposely reducing the complexity of the thin-client landscape. For example, I'm assuming a web application server (something like WebSphere or Tomcat), and I'm including in the web application server's box the HTTP server that goes along with it (typically Apache, although others exist).

Other thin-client architectures exist; for example, scripting languages such as Perl or PHP run as interpreters and are directly invoked by the HTTP server. In fact, dozens of programming possibilities are available, including writing everything in RPG from the ground up. This book focuses specifically on the web application server route via EGL and RPG, all of which is bundled with the IBM i, and all of which can be programmed, debugged, and deployed using RDi-SOA.

JSP 2.0 and MVC

The JavaServer Pages (JSP) thin-client route has matured quite a bit over the 10 years or so that it's been available. JSP 2.0 fully embraced the model-view-controller (MVC) architecture. JSP is also quite friendly with JavaScript, and specifically with AJAX, making thin client a very flexible interface.

While I don't want to spend a lot of time on thin-client interfaces here, I think every green-screen programmer should know that JSP 2.0 is almost exactly equivalent to 5250, as shown in Figure 1.8. The page-oriented nature of the browser makes it a one-for-one replacement for just about any 5250 application, with the addition of fonts, colors, images, and some really nifty additional capabilities that can be applied through simple JavaScript. In fact, I'd say that 80 to 90 percent of traditional green-screen applications could be directly modeled to thin-client applications.

RDi-SOA provides all the tools to build those applications as fast, if not faster, than your old green-screen applications. Why is RDi-SOA faster? Because you have a drag-and-drop WYSIWYG designer. Try that with SDA!

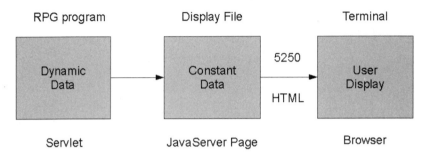

Figure 1.8: The JavaServer Pages architecture is almost exactly equivalent to the 5250 block mode.

Having a drag-and-drop WYSIWYG designer means you don't have to spend a ton of development time on the simple stuff: the file maintenance, data entry, and batch submission tasks that make up the backbone of any enterprise application suite. Let's be honest; no matter what you do, you're going to have to maintain your item master file, and that's not something that needs to have the latest Web 2.0 geegaws. Instead, you want to be able to define your data, drop it onto a screen, and call your business logic. With the thin-client EGL tooling in RDi-SOA, you can do just that.

Rich Client

What about those situations that do require a more graphical interface? That's where the rich client comes into play, shown in Figure 1.9.

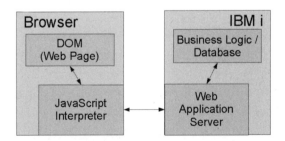

Figure 1.9: The rich-client architecture is more complex than the thin-client architecture.

As you view Figure 1.9, you might notice that I expanded the browser part, and removed the PC from the left side. I did this to make two things clear. First, the PC is no longer a given; browsers are becoming more and more ubiquitous, running in not only traditional PCs but also handheld devices, phones, game consoles, and more. The common denominator is no longer the PC or the operating system. Instead, it is the browser itself.

Rich Web Client Messaging

The second thing I want to make absolutely clear is that rich web clients require an entirely different architecture. In thin-client Web 1.0 applications, HTML pages are the primary communication vehicle. These pages might have snippets of embedded JavaScript, or even make use of an entire JavaScript framework to dynamically alter the page, but for the most part, the interface is still page-oriented. This, I think, is the primary downfall of the portal architecture; at the end of the day, most portal architectures combine chunks of HTML into a single page that is sent to the user. Inevitably, that leads to inefficiencies.

With rich Web 2.0 applications, the focus is entirely different. You don't send HTML to the browser, except perhaps at the very beginning of the application. Instead, you send what is effectively an entire application program, written in JavaScript. That program then runs inside the browser, on whatever client device the end user is using. The JavaScript application first dynamically creates all the widgets required for the application, and then begins communicating with the host using a semi-custom protocol to get dynamic data in response to user events.

I say "semi-custom" because the exchanges between the rich web client and the host typically contain application-specific data wrapped in some sort of standard protocol. In the earliest days of Web 2.0, most of this was done through Simple Object Access Protocol (SOAP) and its rather heavy XML wrappings. This architecture is still relatively well-suited to inter-company transactions such as those envisioned by the original designers of things like the Universal Description Discovery and Integration (UDDI) registry. However, the thinner requirements of multi-tiered applications weigh more toward the lightweight Representational State Transfer (REST) protocol, using JavaScript Object Notation (JSON) as the communication layer.

Without going into a lot of detail, a JSON or REST message contains a lot less metadata to describe the message. This makes sense in a multi-tiered application because the tier that executes in the browser originates on the host anyway, and so the host has complete control over both tiers. This is different from a distributed architecture, where completely independent applications on disparate machines must communicate with one another. In that case, the extra overhead and, perhaps more importantly, the application-independent validation provided by the XML standards can be invaluable in the development stages and in troubleshooting, especially the ability to use a schema to validate messages even before they are sent.

Summary

This first chapter reviewed various levels of application architecture, starting with the simplest two-tier design and working up to the latest Web 2.0 architecture. The most important point to take away from this chapter is that the Web 2.0 architecture is completely different from any of the server-side architectures, despite any superficial similarities. Even JSP Model 2, which affords a very interactive style of thin-client interface, is still modeled on a page-at-a-time request/response cycle, in which any change to the user interface requires a round trip to the host. In contrast, a Web 2.0 application can interact directly with the user without communicating with the host, and can even combine information from multiple host applications. It is this ability that drives the new generation of applications such as "dashboard mashups," applications that can fundamentally change the way users interact with business logic.

Since this book is designed to teach you to use RDi-SOA to develop these applications for the IBM i, the focus is on using EGL Rich UI technology for the user interface, EGL services technology for the middleware, and RPG business logic on the host. Technically, you could call this a three-tiered design. You'll see exactly what that means in the next chapter.

2

Bridging the Tiers with IBM Rational and EGL

Designing a multi-tiered application is a lot more complex than designing a green-screen application. So many design options exist that it's easy to drift into "analysis paralysis," in which you can't even decide on the basic features of your application. As systems grow more complex, I find that perhaps the single most underestimated benefit of the IBM midrange green-screen development paradigm is that so many decisions are made for you.

Think about it. You don't have to choose an operating system; it is part of the platform. You don't need to choose a database; it's already there. Your programming language? RPG or COBOL, with a couple more esoteric languages available for the fringe requirements. User interface? Green, baby. Heck, in the old days, even the reports were on greenbar paper.

With so many decisions made for them, green-screen application developers could focus far more of their time on the actual application code. That is why some of the most essential business applications of the 1980s and 1990s came from the midrange community. Developers were busy solving business problems, not technology issues. Even though the evolving midrange platform provides many more options and much more openness, the purity of design of those simpler times still has a lot of allure.

Technology-centric Design

I don't think I'm too far off the mark when I say that the last decade or so of development has been far more technology-centric than application-centric. From the various new languages to the alphabet soup of technology TLAs ("three-letter acronyms," for the non-TLA literate), a programmer has to be far more of a technician than a business analyst. I think that's what has stalled the application development arena. Whereas in previous decades, some of the best programmers were business analysts who simply had to learn a single language like RPG, in today's modern environment, one needs to be a jack-of-all-trades, essentially a technological plumber, just to design a simple application.

EGL returns to the integrated concept of the original midrange platform by removing much of that "plumbing" requirement. While there are still a few design decisions to be made, they are truly design decisions. In this chapter, you'll learn where those decisions lie. Perhaps more importantly, you'll find out about the more technical decisions that you don't have to make, thanks to the work done by the EGL team.

How Many Tiers?

The first design decision is to actually define the tiers of your application. This exercise helps to define the components you will need for your development process, and in turn, the skills and tools required to build them. In today's technology-centric world, if you start from scratch, you've got a million decisions to make. Let's take a look at just a couple:

- Is the client thick or thin? A thick client entails another language on the PC and its corresponding development and deployment. Choosing Visual Basic or some other .NET language locks you into the Windows platform. Java doesn't, but it still doesn't remove the deployment issues. Besides, Java has consistently proven to be a difficult language to use correctly, especially at the enterprise level.

- Let's say you go thin. You still have a whole host of choices. From the very beginning, you have to decide whether to go with the Java track—servlets and JSP running in an environment such as Tomcat or WebSphere—or the non-Java track, which typically involves a scripting language such as Perl, Python, or PHP. Which language you use depends a lot on which tooling you like. (Interestingly enough, as of May 2009, the various server-side scripting languages were all dropping in popularity, according to the TIOBE programming index. And while the top two programming languages continue to be Java and C, RPG has broken back into the top 20 for the first time in recent memory, coming in at number 15, ahead of even COBOL.)

- Let's talk about tooling. With Java, you have a number of options; NetBeans and MyEclipse are the top two non-Rational choices. PHP also has a wide array of tool choices, including the Zend Studio. I would hazard a guess that this would be the IBM-approved way, since IBM bundles Zend PHP with the box.

And that's just the start. This list doesn't even address the application issues, such as which frameworks to use, or how to access business logic. Another huge issue, often overlooked when selecting simple scripting languages, is that you are pretty much limited to true thin-client applications. PHP, for example, doesn't lend itself particularly well to rich web client development.

EGL Makes It Easy

With EGL, many of the decisions are made for you, including language and tooling. You use EGL for the middleware and a Java-based web application server, such as WebSphere or Tomcat. Your tooling is RDi-SOA. With that, all of your development infrastructure questions are answered.

You're immediately immersed in true application design decisions, such as whether your application is rich or thin, and whether your business logic is SQL, RPG, or a mix of the two. (Whenever I say RPG, you can just as easily insert COBOL, if you are so inclined.) As you'll see, the business-logic issue is really one you can decide on an as-needed basis.

The only real decision to make at the beginning of the application design is whether you want to go rich or thin. The standard thin client is very simple. You have two components: the UI and the business logic.

As you can see in Figure 2.1, the ILE business logic is encapsulated in something called an *EGL library function*. Basically, the EGL library function provides an EGL interface to the ILE program. Calling ILE is not strictly necessary; where appropriate, you can write business logic functions using direct SQL access to DB2, with EGL's intrinsic SQL access syntax.

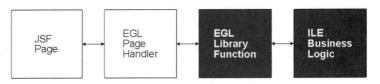

Figure 2.1: This is a standard thin-client EGL/RPG application.

On the UI side, EGL uses an extension of the JSP framework called JavaServer Faces (JSF). JSF pages are essential JSP pages, but with a more standardized MVC syntax. This allows the developer to worry less about the plumbing and concentrate more on the development. In EGL, the JSF page has a backing component (or *part*, in EGL terms) called a *page handler* that is specific to that JSF page. The page handler, in turn, calls the EGL library function.

We can easily segregate the layers this way because EGL functions allow high-level business objects to be easily passed from one layer to another and, as you'll see later, even from one tier to another. This conceptually simple but architecturally powerful feature is one of the things that make EGL a real business programming language, as opposed to a scripting language or a systems language like C or C++.

The power of this high-level procedural aspect of the language becomes even more apparent when you review the rich client architecture, shown in Figure 2.2.

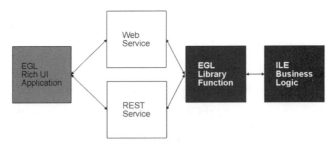

Figure 2.2: Here, the EGL Rich UI application uses EGL services to call the library functions.

Notice in Figure 2.2 how the EGL library function and the associated ILE business logic remain unchanged. Instead, through a very simple service construct (in many cases, no more than a one-line function that calls the original library function), EGL performs all the plumbing of exposing your library function as a service. And in keeping with EGL's idea of leaving the application decisions to the developer, you can use the service as either the traditional SOAP-type web service or the lighter-weight JSON/REST service. A simple checkbox tells EGL to generate either, or both.

So, EGL, and especially the RDi-SOA tooling, provides a development environment that allows a business programmer to create a rich application easily. Let's get to that, shall we?

Assumptions First

First, to avoid that old saw about "assuming," let's get all of my assumptions about your environment out on the table:

1. The IBM i is your application server. You are not designing a platform-independent application. You know where you want your business data and logic to reside: on the most secure, scalable platform available.

2. RPG is your business language of choice. I make this assumption because I believe you should use the best tool for the job: SQL as needed; Java as appropriate; and RPG as your primary language, since nothing beats it for defining business rules. (Again, COBOL programmers should feel free to insert COBOL, where appropriate.)

3. The browser is your *de facto* user interface. That doesn't mean you never use a green screen, just that all business logic will be encapsulated. The rule of thumb is that no single program shall have both a display file and a database file, although like any rule, this one is subject to exception.

4. EGL is your middleware language of choice, and RDi-SOA is your tooling. Since RDi-SOA is the central focus of this book, this should come as no surprise.

5. Finally, the interface will be rich. What does this mean? It means that you will be able to incorporate things like immediate validation on keystroke, changing the interface in response to user events, graphical elements such as charts and images, and third-party tools such as GoogleMaps.

These are relatively simple assumptions. In fact, numbers three and five are nearly platform-agnostic; they could apply to just about anything, from .NET to RPG-CGI. The others simply restate the central theme of this book: you want to design multi-tiered applications for the IBM i using RDi-SOA. So without further ado, let's move forward.

Start with the UI

One of the first questions when designing a multi-tiered application is the design order. Should you design from the UI and work your way back to the business logic, or start with the business logic and work your way forward? There is no "right" answer; each business situation has its own unique set of requirements. In my experience, however, when designing an application for end users, it's almost always best to start with the user interface.

In the "UI first" philosophy, everything is driven from the user interface. Typically, you already have some idea of what you're trying to accomplish, and you might even have one or more specific examples of the type of interface you're trying to create. In fact, the requirement might be to create something seen as "standard." Think of a company trying to add an Internet storefront. Does it make more sense to create something that works like Amazon, or to make something completely unique? Absent any specific requirements to the contrary, familiarity trumps uniqueness, if only to avoid losing new customers due to frustration.

This is an important issue to keep in mind from the very start. Application requirements heavily influence design decisions. For Internet storefronts, frustration is a huge issue, affecting everything from layout to features to performance. The more your site caters to first-time and impulse buyers, the more likely it is that you will need a simple site, where every widget is intuitive. Easy search and selection becomes paramount. On the other hand, if your primary business comes from repeat customers, the idea is to make their experiences as fast as possible. In that case, the focus should be on building orders from historical information and allowing one-click replenishment.

Designing the Interface

How you design the interface depends very much on your tools. When I first started designing GUI screens, I did a lot of mockups with PowerPoint because of the dearth of good WYSIWYG tools. Not only that, but the inherent limitations of HTML, especially in the early days, made it reasonable to lay out screens using primitive representations of widgets, such as tables or forms cut-and-pasted from Excel or Word.

That's no longer the case. Especially in rich web client design, I think it's crucial to lay out at least the basic widget using a WYSIWYG design tool. You might not get colors or fonts exactly right, but you will be able to see the basic shape of your application. You will also get a feel for what is most natural, from a programming standpoint, when laying out a screen. For example, I once had a discussion with someone on GUI designs. That person presented the screen in Figure 2.3 as a design.

The user could click on any of the radio buttons, and the picture in the middle would change in response. While this is certainly a valid design, it's somewhat impractical. Few WYSIWYG design tools are designed to allow multiple radio groups to be treated as one, and the best way to do this would be to have an array of select items, anyway.

◉ Puppy ○ Kitty

○ Bird ○ Fish

Figure 2.3: This is an example of a valid, but impractical, design.

My point here is that not everything you can do in HTML is necessarily easy to translate to Rich UI. So, as long as the tools are available, you should start from day one with a real prototype. This helps to avoid really critical design mistakes that might not come up if you used some sort of pasteboard mockup.

How Widgets Help

While I cover widgets in much more detail in the next chapter, I want to begin to look at them here, since they are such an important part of the entire process. The term *widget* has many meanings. Typically, it means some small mechanical "doohickey," and that meaning has morphed rather well into the world of graphical UI design. If you look at it technically, any graphical component is, in the end, just a set of pixels that might or might not react to mouse and keyboard events. However, it makes much more sense to think of GUI components at a higher level. A label is a set of characters in a specific location. A text field is a label, but with a box around it that supports data entry. A radio button is a label preceded by a small circular icon that changes appearance when clicked. All of these "meta-definitions" make sense from the standpoint of reducing complexity. You don't need to know all the internal mechanics; you just need to know that the widget works.

In EGL, widgets go one level higher. When you create a widget, you can also define its behaviors. You can combine multiple low-level components (labels, fields, and so on) into higher-order widgets. IBM also supplies a number of complex widgets of its own, including a very powerful Grid widget that takes the place of a subfile in business applications. These widgets are reusable, and can be combined with one another very easily to create complex screens.

I think it's time to take a look at the application this book is centered on, to give you an idea of what you're working toward. Figure 2.4 is an order-entry application. It's not intended to be a model of application design, but it does show the basics of any rich Internet application: it prompts for information (the order number), and then displays business information in a grid. The grid itself is interactive; you can change the quantities in the lines, and the entire order will be repriced dynamically. Additionally, it includes a little Web 2.0 highlight: the ship-to address can be mapped using a GoogleMap.

Later in this book, you'll learn the details of how this application is put together. The important point for now is that the application program does not define the order widget. In fact, the application program only defines the prompt field that asks for order number. The order grid widget itself, as

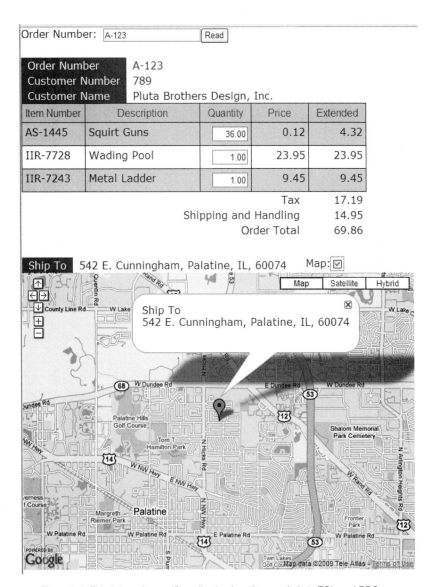

Figure 2.4: This "shopping cart" application is written entirely in EGL and RPG.

well as the associated GoogleMap, is defined separately. This means that any application needing the same sort of order widget can reuse the one shown here. For example, it would be no problem to have another application that showed a list of orders, and then on a click, show the details of that order.

Designing Multi-tiered Applications without EGL

Perhaps the best way to see the value of EGL is to design a multi-tiered application using pre-EGL technologies. The example in Figure 2.5 uses a standard JavaScript and Java environment, although still with the objective of using ILE as the business logic. Please note that this is just an example; there are plenty of other ways to do this, but this is one of the less complicated ways.

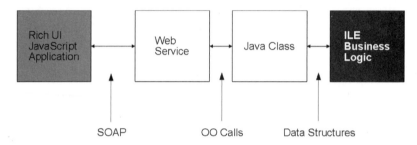

Figure 2.5: Here is a multi-tiered, Rich UI application using non-EGL technology.

As you can see, there are four basic components:

1. A Rich UI application written in JavaScript, running in the browser

2. A web service, which in this case is a servlet written in Java that exposes the Java class

3. A Java class that represents the order object, which is exposed by the web service

4. Finally, the ILE business logic

In order to build this, you'd need a JavaScript framework of some type that supported SOAP processing. While you could also use REST, I picked SOAP for this instance because it's the only one I'm sure has support standardized in the Java EE platform. Then, you'd need to write a web service in Java. Unless you wanted to "roll your own," you'd probably use the JAX-WS protocol, which would take you down into the world of JAXB processing and so on. This isn't anything horrible, but it's a lot of plumbing.

Next, you'd have to define the Java class. Actually, you'd probably need at least three classes: one for the header, one for the detail, and one for the composite order class. The composite class is where you'd insert the getter code, which would in turn invoke the ILE business logic. To do that, you'd use IBM's Java Toolbox, which has classes to identify a server and call a program, and also to convert back and forth between data in Java classes and arrays of EBCDIC bytes that are actually passed to the called program.

You'd need tools. You'd need a development environment to create your JavaScript applications. Next, you'd need an IDE to develop the middleware piece. That could be a Rational product or something like MyEclipse. Finally, you'd need an ILE development environment.

WYSIWYG JavaScript editors are few and far between, and even the ones that claim to be WYSIWYG have limitations. For example, there's an IDE called Visual Ajax Studio that says it is an IDE for Web 2.0 development. However, if you read between the lines, it seems to be pretty specific to using Spring, Hibernate, JAX-WS, and Dojo. That's not necessarily a bad thing, but you are pretty locked in. The middleware IDE is probably the part that is easiest to get done, since it's pretty straightforward: write a Java class and expose it as a web service. Just about any decent Java EE IDE ought to be able to do that for you. ILE development is simple: green screen or Rational. There really aren't a lot of alternatives.

It's very unlikely that you can get any two of these in a single IDE, much less all three. So, picture yourself bouncing back and forth between at least two different development and debugging screens when testing your application.

A Quick Example from the Non-EGL World

As you saw in the previous section, in most other technologies, you would have to define each communication protocol step individually. For example, calling ILE from Java would be a multi-step process:

1. Define a data structure to pass data between the layers.

2. Either handcraft the Java code to invoke the **ProgramCall** object from the IBM Toolbox, defining each field in the data structure, or use a PCML document (an XML document that does the same thing).

3. Write the rest of the plumbing code, including creating a connection and invoking **ProgramCall**, including all of the exception checking.

You'd have to do something similar when creating the XML document. You'd have to name each of the fields and make sure both sides agree on the names, and then your wrapper classes would have to move data from one side to the other, including doing whatever data conversions are necessary from string to numeric, and so on. That's not to mention having to create the Java classes and having appropriate names for each of the member variables (each one representing a field in the data structure and eventually a field in the XML document). You'd also have to create the WSDL, which defines the XML message and will allow other programs to invoke your code. In order to support the Rich UI side, your JavaScript framework would have to be able to use the WSDL to extract the information from the SOAP message. I haven't seen a lot of SOAP frameworks.

You might think it's easier to do this using REST, since JavaScript isn't really built for XML processing. Well, you basically have to repeat the previous paragraph to create a REST interface, substituting JSON for XML/SOAP. Remember, REST will require your web service to format the complex records as strings using the JavaScript Object Notation (JSON). While this is relatively easy to do in JavaScript, you need to use a third-party package to support it in Java.

What it comes down to is that you either do the hard work in Java or JavaScript. Java knows XML pretty well, but not so much JSON, while JavaScript knows JSON, but not so much XML. So, you pay me now, or you pay me later!

Messages the EGL Way: Define Your Records!

All in all, defining messages between the various layers of a traditional multi-tiered application is a tedious and error-prone process. That's because it requires many layers, each of which typically has its own language, which in turn requires its own definitions. With EGL, it's a lot simpler, as shown in Figure 2.6.

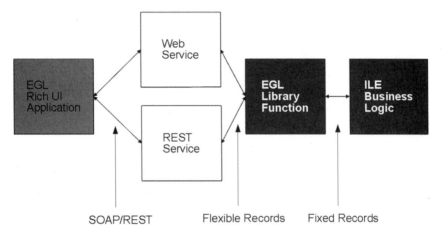

Figure 2.6: Here is the basic EGL/RPG Rich UI architecture.

Figure 2.6 is an enhanced version of Figure 2.3, with the communication mechanisms roughed out. In general terms, it shows how each layer communicates with the next. The EGL Rich UI application will invoke either a web service or a REST service, which will in turn call an EGL library function, which will ultimately call an ILE program containing the business logic.

To do this, you need exactly two definitions:

1. The fixed record, which mirrors the data structure on the IBM i

2. The flexible record, which provides the communication throughout the rest of the EGL application stream

Let's take a look at these two components. First, let's look at the definition of the fixed records, shown in Figure 2.7.

```
record DSOrderHeader{}
   10 OrderNumber string(10);
   10 CustomerNumber decimal(6,0);
   10 CustomerName string(50);
   10 ShippingAddr string(50);
   10 Tax money(9,2);
   10 Freight money(9,2);
   10 Total money(9,2);
end

record DSOrderLine{}
   10 ItemNumber string(15);
   10 Description string(30);
   10 Quantity decimal(9,2);
   10 Price money(9,2);
   10 Extended money(11,2);
end
```

Figure 2.7: These are the fixed records used to communicate with the IBM i.

I won't spend a lot of time here on the syntax of fixed records, but suffice it to say that it corresponds directly with data types on the host. The externally described data structure for say, the order header, would look something like Figure 2.8.

```
A               R DSORDHDR
A                 OHORD        10S 0       TEXT('Order Number')
A                 OHCUST        6S 0       TEXT('Customer Number')
A                 OHNAME       50A         TEXT('Customer Name')
A                 OHADDR       50A         TEXT('Formatted Address')
A                 OHTAX         9S 2       TEXT('Taxes')
A                 OHFRGT        9S 2       TEXT('Freight Charge')
A                 OHTOT         9S 2       TEXT('Order Total')
```

Figure 2.8: This is the data structure on the host that matches the DSOrderHeader record.

A similar data structure would be available for the detail order line. These data structures wouldn't necessarily correspond exactly to physical files on the host. For example, the customer name might come from the customer master file, and the address might be a value formatted from the various individual address fields on the host.

You would have to create the data structure in Figure 2.8 whether or not you chose to use EGL. A data structure is the simplest way to communicate between ILE and other languages. You could probably shoehorn your

requirements into an SQL stored procedure, but that's a completely different subject (one which is supported by EGL, incidentally, but which we're
not using in this example).

Up to this point, you're not exactly saving a ton of work. You have to
define the data structure on the host and, you have to define it to the EGL
library function. However, one thing should be apparent: the definition of
the record in EGL is very similar to the definition of the data structure on
the host. In fact, you could probably generate one from the other without
too much difficulty. It gets really interesting, though, in the next step.

Again, I don't want to get too bogged down in details at this point, but take
a look at Figure 2.9. In it, you see the OrderHeader and OrderLine records,
which are the flexible versions of DSOrderHeader and DSOrderLine from
the previous page. Note that the record names are different, but the field
names are the same. And, except for the character fields, the types are the
same as well.

```
record Order{}
   Header OrderHeader;
   Lines OrderLine[];
end

record OrderHeader{}
   OrderNumber string;
   CustomerNumber decimal(6,0);
   CustomerName string;
   ShippingAddr string;
   Tax money(9,2);
   Freight money(9,2);
   Total money(9,2);
end

record OrderLine{}
   ItemNumber string;
   Description string;
   Quantity decimal(9,2);
   Price money(9,2);
   Extended money(11,2);
end
```

Figure 2.9: This is the flexible version of the record, including the composite.

The character fields are different because currently in the Rich UI world, strings don't have lengths. Without spending a lot of time debating the pros and cons of the situation, just understand that this is really the only difference between defining a fixed record and a flexible record, except of course the "level" indicators (the *10* on every line in Figure 2.7). Just remember that in the fixed record (also known as a "structured" record), you define character data as **char(nn)**, while in flexible records you use **string** without a length. You might be tempted to use the data type **string(nn)**; however, rather than working in both fixed records and in EGL Rich UI applications, it actually works in neither situation.

So, now you have a second definition. I think it's clear that you could rather easily create one from the other. You would simply copy the fixed record to the flexible record, remove the level indicators, and change all instances of **char(nn)** to **string**. Like generating a fixed record from a data structure, you could even write a program to generate a flexible record from a fixed record. More important than the obvious relationship between the two is the fact that you can do this:

```
header OrderHeader;
dsheader DSOrderHeader;
(...)
move dsheader to header byName;
```

The **move byName** capability makes it very easy to deal with the two records of varying attributes. I can call an ILE program with a variable of the fixed record type DSOrderHeader, and then with a single **move** operation, move all the fields from the fixed record variable to a flexible record variable.

Composite Records and Inter-tier Communication

You might have noticed that I defined a record of type Order within the flexible definitions. This is a very powerful feature of EGL. It is very easy to define compound records, including records that contain arrays of other records. With this technique, you can create a record of type Order. You can then easily read a header record and store its data into the header portion of the order with a single move, which might look more like this:

```
move dsheader to order.header byName;
```

You can add lines to the order line array just as easily:

```
move dsline to line byName;
order.lines.appendElement(line);
```

There are no field-by-field moves, just simple, clean code.

You'll see examples later in this book of just how easy it is to write code that interfaces between RPG business logic and its fixed data structures, and the highly flexible (no pun intended) record structures provided by EGL. Why is this so important, then? Because once you've filled the entire order structure, you can pass that order from one tier to another very easily.

Look at this function definition:

```
function getOrder(orderNumber string in, order Order out)
    returns (Error)
```

It's very simple. You pass in an order number and get back an order. The order number parameter is defined as input, and the order is defined as output. It's as simple as that, and the call looks like this:

```
error = getOrder(orderNumber, order);
```

You've no doubt noticed that unlike many "getter" functions in the more traditional OO languages, this getOrder function doesn't return the order. Instead, it returns an error record. Unlike OO languages, there's no implicit try/catch in EGL, so returning errors needs to be part of your application coding technique. EGL has a huge advantage, though, that it shares with RPG: the concept of *bidirectional parameters*.

You can define the order to be returned as a parameter, and the error record is the actual return value of the function; you pass a null value when no error occurs (the normal operation). This allows you to put your return value on the parameter list and even to have more than one, rather than having to have an error parameter somewhere on the parameter list and trying to decide whether to put it at the beginning, after the input values, or at the end. For me, it's simple: input values are followed by output value(s) on the parameter list, with the error code being returned. If the operation completes successfully, a null is returned. This also makes it very easy to have a standard syntax for currently unsupported functions; they just return an error.

While this is entirely an issue of personal programming style, I've found that it really makes programming a lot more consistent. Because of that, it is easier to write and even easier to read when I come back to it later. And don't worry, I'll be covering this particular methodology along with all my other design decisions in detail throughout the book.

A Little Sidetrack Down the Thin-client Trail

Let's take just a moment here to make clear that rich web applications make up only one aspect of this architecture. Yes, EGL Rich UI is the focus of this book, but I want to be crystal clear about the flexibility of this technology. If you chose almost any other technology, you would have to make a decision about whether you wanted to go thin or rich. That's because if you decided to go thin, you would need to make an investment in some tooling. For example, you might choose to go the scripting route. Whether it's RPG-CGI, Perl, or PHP makes no difference; you need to start writing your scripts and focusing your development on how to get the ILE business logic to communicate with your scripting language.

Even if you were to go the route of JavaServer Pages, you'd need to start pushing your development resources in the direction of writing functions or beans that could be used by your JSPs to build actual applications.

With EGL, once you've written the EGL library functions to do things like get an order, your thin-client application development is nearly done. Just create a new JSF page, and EGL automatically creates a backing part for it, which is the page handler mentioned earlier.

In the page handler, you create a variable of type Order. Using the WYSIWYG editor, drop the order header on the page, and then drop the array of lines on the page. The former builds a table; the latter builds a grid. Add a prompt to enter the order number and a button to submit the request. Write a one-line function that calls the getOrder library function with the order number and returns the order, and then go back into the WYSIWYG editor and drag the newly created function onto the button. In five minutes, you're done. You get something like Figure 2.10.

OrderNumber: [A-123   ] [Get Order]

OrderNumber:	A-123
CustomerNumber:	789
CustomerName:	Phta Brothers Design, Inc.
ShippingAddr:	542 E. Cunningham, Palatine, IL, 60074
Tax:	$17.19
Freight:	$14.95
Total:	$69.86

ItemNumber	Description	Quantity	Price	Extended
AS-1445	Squirt Guns	36.00	$0.12	$4.32
IIR-7728	Wading Pool	1.00	$23.95	$23.95
IIR-7243	Metal Ladder	1.00	$9.45	$9.45

Figure 2.10: This is a thin-client version of the application.

Obviously, this isn't going to win any style awards, but for five minutes of work, it's not bad. A whole lot of the basic issues can be taken care of with a Cascading Style Sheet—and just a little bit of love. I won't bore you with the details; just understand that by properly designing the architecture to support rich web applications, the thin client comes along almost for free.

What About Services?

What you've seen so far is pretty cool, what with the ability to easily translate between the strict data structure world of ILE and the sophisticated, multi-layer composite world of EGL. Now, I'm about to rock the house.

Let me show you how to make a web service. Remember the getOrder method? Well, here's the code required to turn it into a web service:

```
service OrderService
  function getOrder(
    orderNumber string in, order Order inOut)
    returns (Error)
      return (OrderLib.getOrder(orderNumber, order));
  end
end
```

Yup, that's it. By defining a service part rather than a library or a program, you're telling EGL that you intend to expose this code either as a SOAP web service or as a REST service.

You do have to do one other thing. You have to click a flag in the deployment descriptor, as shown in Figure 2.11.

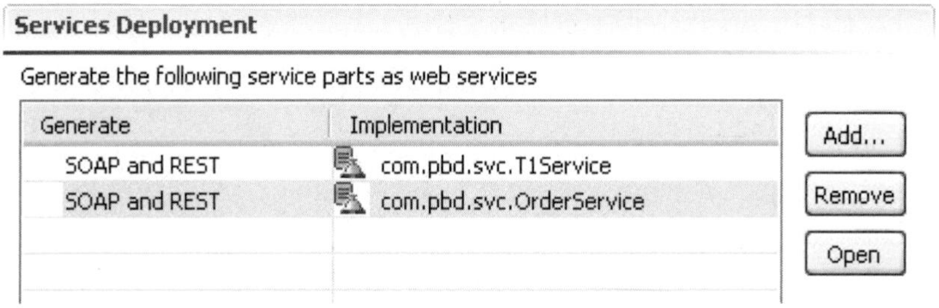

Figure 2.11: You specify the entire service part in the deployment descriptor.

It's quite simple. You just identify the service to be generated as a web service. Here's the fun part: remember all the work we identified in the non-EGL example that we had to do to implement either a web service or a REST service? Well, in the left column of the little list in Figure 2.11, you select SOAP, REST, or "SOAP and REST." Then, you generate the part, and you're done. That's it.

Go back and look at the section on non-EGL implementation. I tried to be as nice as possible, but the reality is that darned few people out there know how to create web services easily, or consume them, and definitely not both. And someone who is an expert on SOAP services is unlikely to have the same success with REST, primarily because they're different skill sets. Nobody has the time to learn all this stuff and make it easy.

Nobody except the IBM EGL developers, that is. In the spirit of EGL's devotion to removing the complexity of technology, the developers have done something unique. The ability to simply flip a switch and completely expose and deploy a function as either a SOAP or a REST web service is simply unparalleled in the industry.

Okay, You've Exposed the Service—Now What?

Recall the amount of work required to enable the web service in a non-EGL technology. Now, you have to do the corresponding work on the client side. While I don't spend a lot of time "rolling my own" web services, I've done enough proof-of-concept work using HTML as a sort of poor man's service to have an idea of how much effort is involved.

Generally, you need to create a listener to capture keystroke or mouse events, and attach the listener to the appropriate widgets in your HTML. In that listener, you create an Ajax request and fire it off. Next, you need to write a callback function that the Ajax request can use. (You can also use a synchronous call, but that tends to make your application unresponsive and/or jittery.) Assuming you've got a callback in place, you next have to add the code to parse the data. If it's a JSON request, it's not terribly difficult, but there's still the issue of everybody agreeing on the format of the request. You basically have to keep the JavaScript code and the host code synchronized, and that's a manual process. I don't even want to think about parsing a pure XML stream.

Finally, once you've gotten the data back to the client, you have to update the appropriate widgets in the user interface. How much work that is depends on the framework. It's the classic tradeoff: the more you rely on third-party code, the easier it is likely to be, but you tend to get locked into that specific infrastructure.

With EGL, the code is simple. Here's the REST version:

```
function getOrder(orderNumber string)
  order Order;
  error Error;
  ios IOrderService { @RESTBinding {baseURI =
    "http://localhost:9080/iEGL/restservices/OrderService"
  }};
  call ios.getOrder(orderNumber, order)
    returning to cbGetOrder
    onException ServiceLib.serviceExceptionHandler;
end
  function cbGetOrder(order Order in, error Error in)
  orderLines.data = order.Lines as any[];
end
```

This is all the code needed to invoke the service. Note that EGL understands the concept of a callback function, and allows you to specify the callback right on the line that invokes the service. So, you can invoke a function in Rich UI (perhaps in response to a button being pressed), and then call this function, passing it the order number the user entered. The call to the function **ios.getOrder** does all the work of formatting a REST request and then invoking the service on the host (that is, the getOrder function of the OrderService service deployed back in Figure 2.11).

You also have to define the service, but that's almost a cut and paste from the original EGL service:

```
interface IOrderService
  function getOrder(orderNumber string in, order Order out)
    returns (Error);
end
```

The trickiest part is defining the URI, which in this example is the somewhat cryptic value for the **baseURI** keyword. (It's the value starting with "http://localhost:9080.") The good news is that it's relatively easy to construct that URI during testing. (I'll show you how to do it in detail in Chapter 7.)

Alternatively, the URI can be retrieved from the deployment descriptor using a slightly different syntax. You use the latter technique when you're ready to deploy in production, and you want to be able to easily configure the REST service information without modifying the EGL source code.

Summary

By this time, you're probably champing at the bit to get started. If you've been following along, it should be clear that once you've designed the user interface, the rest of the process from browser to RPG is a simple, straight line. However, before you can do any serious coding, I need to introduce you to the basic editor and get you comfortable with building in Rich UI. This will be crucial when you actually start developing applications. Once you get comfortable with the editor, you'll find that you can use it as your primary Rapid Application Development tool for working with users.

You'll be able to create the user interface right in front of them, letting them visualize the design interactively, rather than having to go through a tedious iterative process. Then, once you've got the overall layout in place, you can break the interface down into easily programmed (and hopefully reusable) widgets.

So, let's move on!

Chapter 3

Introducing the WYSIWYG Designer

Using EGL Rich UI is very simple, even for us green-screen folks. The WYSIWYG designer in RDi-SOA is a simple, easy way to create applications, so I think it's time to jump in with both feet.

In this chapter, you learn about the EGL Rich UI product and get your first glimpse of rich Internet application development. If you're new to the whole RDi-SOA concept, new to Rich UI and the WYSIWYG designer, or just want to refresh your understanding of the Rational tools, this chapter provides a great high-level introduction. If you've already begun your exploration of EGL Rich UI, are familiar with the RDi-SOA tool, and know how to create Rich UI handlers, you can skip this chapter and move on to Chapter 4.

Installing RDi-SOA

If you haven't already done so, you need to install RDi-SOA. This is a very simple task; IBM has provided not only evaluation software, but also tools to both download and install the software. Information on the latest version of the components, where to get them, and how to install them can be found here:

http://www-949.ibm.com/software/rational/cafe/docs/DOC-3128.

Once you've downloaded the trial packages, you simply run the Installation Manager (IM) to install them. The IM main menu is shown in Figure 3.1.

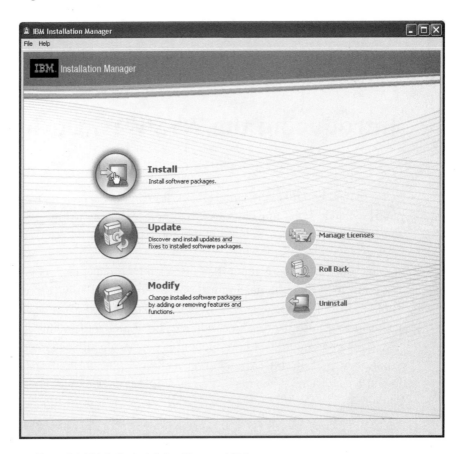

Figure 3.1: This is the Installation Manager initial menu.

IM provides three basic options: Install, Update, and Modify. You use Install for the initial installation. This introduces one of the very cool aspects of the entire Eclipse-based packaging of the Rational products. RDi-SOA is actually an amalgamation of three different products: Rational Business Developer, Rational Developer for the i, and the WebSphere Test Environment. Each of those components is a stand-alone entity, but they can also be installed together into a single product, known as a *package* in

IM terminology. So, you download the three components, point IM at the download locations, and click Install. You'll see a screen like the one in Figure 3.2.

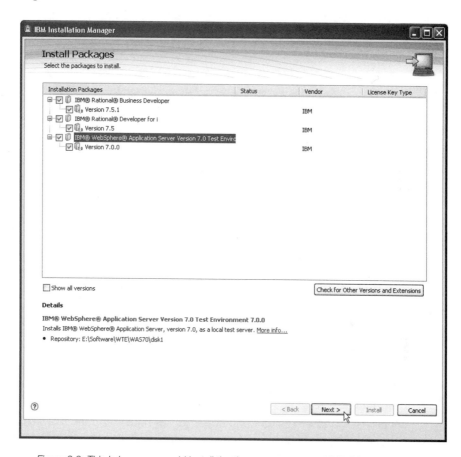

Figure 3.2: This is how you would install the three components of RDi-SOA using IM.

The installation is straightforward. You are prompted for a few pieces of information, such as the location to install. I recommend using a very simple directory structure, starting at C:\IBM. However, you can use any directory structure you want, and IM will adhere to it.

As I mentioned earlier, not only do you install with IM, but you also use it to update or modify your installation. For example, you would use the

Modify function to add a different WebSphere Test Environment or another product, such as the Rational Team Concert for i (RTCi) client. You would use the Update function to install the latest version and/or fixes. IM is very smart about reviewing your current configuration and telling you what is eligible for update. For example, I haven't yet updated my workstation to the latest version of RDi, so I get the display in Figure 3.3.

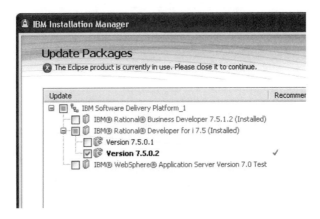

Figure 3.3: This is an example of the Update function in IM.

While this book isn't a reference manual on Installation Manager, I'd like to point out a few of its more interesting features. First, as you can see in Figure 3.3, IM knows all of the components I have, and their versions. Consequently, it knows that my configuration has two up-to-date components (RBD and WTE) and one not-so-up-to-date component (RDi). That being the case, it only shows me an option to update RDi.

The second point is that IM also knows that I'm currently running RDi-SOA, so it won't let me update it. That's a nice feature. (The Rational products generally do a very good job of making sure you don't step on your own toes.) So, there you have it: RDi-SOA installation and management in a nutshell.

Getting Started with EGL Rich UI: Start the Workbench

Now, on to the fun! With the EGL Rich UI technology, you can literally have your first rich client up and running in minutes. If you're not familiar with RDi-SOA or any of the other Rational products, here is a very simple walkthrough of the steps involved:

1. Start the workbench.

2. Create an EGL Rich UI project.

3. Create a Rich UI handler.

That's it! You'll end up in the Rich UI WYSIWYG designer and be ready to go.

So, let's get started. The initial steps are simple. Start by launching the tool. You'll be prompted for a workspace name, as shown in Figure 3.4.

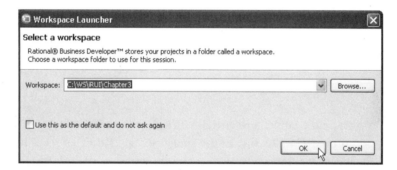

Figure 3.4: First, launch the tool and specify a new workspace.

Earlier, I suggested that you install all your IBM software in an "IBM" folder under the root directory (that is, C:\IBM). I recommend something similar with workspaces. In this case, you can create a folder under the root called "WS" (C:\WS). Under that, you can create either individual workspaces or subfolders containing workspaces. If you do consulting work, you might want one subfolder per client. In my case, I have a subfolder for this book, called "iRUI," and I have individual workspaces for each chapter. This allows me to export the projects at each point in the process, so that you can review them as you need to. In any case, you specify a

workspace name and click OK. This brings up the splash screen shown in
Figure 3.5.

Figure 3.5: This is the RDi-SOA splash screen.

You can now launch either RBD or RDi, and that product will be shown as
the "primary" in the title of the splash screen. (In Figure 3.5, it's Rational
Business Developer.) In either case, the splash screen shows the two major
components, RDi and RBD, in the list of Integrated IBM Products. At
this point, you watch as a progress bar tracks the initialization of the new
workspace.

When the workspace is created, the workbench is displayed with a mostly
empty Web perspective. *Perspective* is the term used by Eclipse, and
consequently by all the Rational tools, to identify a group of related views
organized to perform a specific job function. The term *view* itself has a
specific meaning in Eclipse/Rational: it's a movable pane containing the
controls required to perform a single task, such as managing web servers
or editing source code. Since RBD is all about web development, the initial
perspective is the Web perspective, and the views associated with that
perspective are displayed.

The first thing to do is create a new project. There are a number of ways to do that, including right-clicking to get the context menu within the Project Explorer, as shown in Figure 3.6. Another option is to open the File menu and select New. Yet another option is to click the New tool on the primary toolbar. All of these options do the same thing; RDi-SOA often gives you multiple ways to execute the same function.

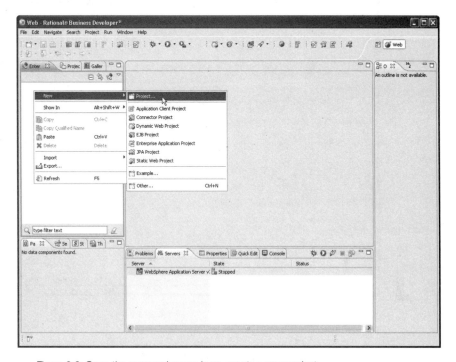

Figure 3.6: Once the new workspace is up, create a new project.

Once you've directed the workbench to create a new project, you will see the New Project wizard, which will walk you through the rest of the steps.

Creating an EGL Rich UI Project

To get started with EGL Rich UI, you create an EGL project. More specifically, you create a new EGL Rich UI project. In keeping with the book's focus on the architecture, I'm not going to provide a keystroke-by-keystroke review of the process; instead, I'll just point out the highlights.

For example, when you select New Project, you get a prompt asking for the type of project to create. After you select EGL as the project type in that initial screen, a panel comes up asking you for the type of EGL project, as shown in Figure 3.7. This is a little different from most other project types, which immediately start asking you for project-specific information.

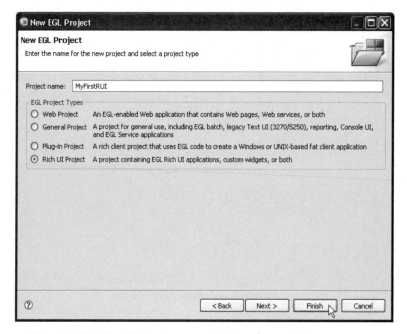

Figure 3.7: The New EGL Project panel asks for the type of EGL project.

With EGL projects, you have to select the EGL project sub-type, in this case "Rich UI Project," which specifically creates a project to be deployed to the client (the browser). Other EGL project types are used for different functions. For example, to create a multi-tier application, you choose "Web Project" for the server-side tier.

Since EGL Rich UI development is best executed in the Rich UI perspective, you are prompted to switch to that perspective, as shown in Figure 3.8. The workbench then performs quite a bit of machination to create a new project and point you to it.

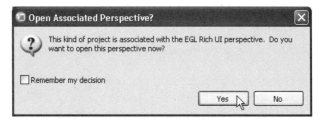

Figure 3.8: You are prompted to switch perspective.

If you remember, I called my project "MyFirstRUI." That new project shows up in the Project Explorer shown in Figure 3.9, along with a special IBM project, com.ibm.egl.rui_1.0.0, which contains the runtime that supports the EGL Rich UI syntax. Think of it as the Rich UI Virtual Machine. You can gain a lot of insight into EGL Rich UI by reviewing the code in that project, as long as you understand that it's not "basic" EGL, any more than the code in the Java runtime libraries is "basic" Java.

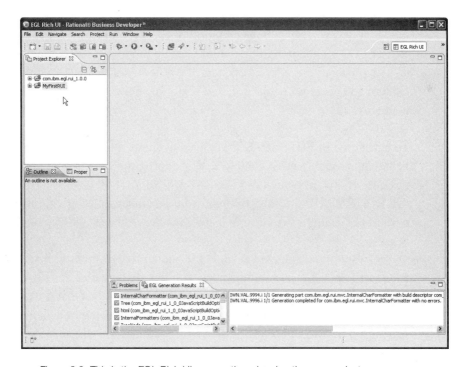

Figure 3.9: This is the EGL Rich UI perspective, showing the new project.

That's it for the "Rational Tools 101" portion of this chapter. If you're already familiar with the Rational products, this might have seemed a bit redundant, but it's good preparation for what comes next.

Creating a Rich UI Application

If you're new to the whole Rich UI concept, it's worth taking the time to create a simple user interface with a few basic features. This gives you an idea of how the tool works, how the WYSIWYG designer works, and also how the syntax is designed. All of these things come in handy when you're developing your real applications later on.

The first thing to do is to get into the WYSIWYG designer. Although you don't have enough information to craft a user interface yet, I want to show you how the tool is designed, to get you right into the development phase.

The WYSIWYG designer, one of only a few Rich UI designers on the market today, is really a powerful tool for Rapid Application Development. RDi-SOA is all about getting you into design mode and getting the UI designed quickly. As you progress, you'll see how you can easily sit down in front of end users with this tool, and prototype the user interface with their interactive input.

To get started in EGL Rich UI, you need to create an application component that is roughly equivalent to a display program in ILE. The term for a program-level component in EGL Rich UI is a *Rich UI handler*. You'll find that EGL Rich UI is a little different from green-screen programming or even the EGL thin-client design using Java Server Faces (JSF) pages.

In green screen, you have a display file and an ILE program (typically RPG or COBOL) that communicates with that display file. In a good modular design, the display program calls other programs that provide the business functions. With EGL, thin-client applications are quite similar in structure. They make use of JSP Model II architecture, which pairs a servlet with a JSP page. In EGL, the JSP page actually uses the more powerful JSF functionality, while the servlet is called a *page handler* and is written in EGL (which, in turn, generates the Java code for the servlet). RBD provides both a powerful WYSIWYG thin-client designer and a completely transparent encapsulation of the complex interaction between the page and the servlet, so the architectures look almost identical, as you can see in Figure 3.10.

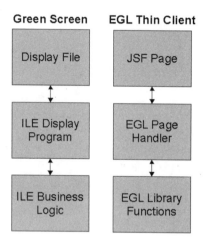

Figure 3.10: The components of modular applications are very similar in green screen and thin client.

As noted, Rich UI is a little different. With Rich UI, the user interface definitions and the handling code are all embedded in the same piece of code, the Rich UI handler. In model-view-controller (MVC) terminology, the handler part is thus both the view and the controller. You can, however, separate the business logic into library functions, as shown in Figure 3.11. This is crucial to the design, in fact, because the idea is to connect those library functions (which will be running in the browser on the client) up to services on the server. So, the design of the Rich UI handler has fewer components.

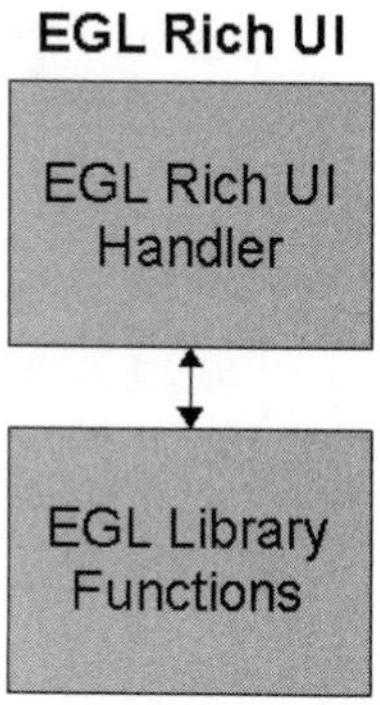

Typically, you have a handler as your highest-level landing page, and then it invokes other handlers as needed. This ability to segment applications into discrete "super-widgets" is one of the keystones of the tool's productivity. I'll review that entire concept in more detail later, when you learn how to design a working business application. For the purposes of this chapter, though, I'm designing a very simple, single-handler application.

Figure 3.11: The EGL Rich UI has fewer basic components.

As you can see in Figure 3.12, there are three folders in a new Rich UI project: the EGLSource folder, the JavaScript folder, and the WebContent folder. The EGLSource folder contains, naturally enough, the EGL source code for the project. The JavaScript folder is the object library, if you will, containing the generated JavaScript code. The WebContent folder is where you place non-EGL components, such as Cascading Style Sheets (another topic that will be covered in more detail later).

EGL uses packages to segregate its parts, in much the same way that Java uses packages to organize classes. For this example, I create a simple package called "test." I only need to do that once, or more precisely once per package. (One of the fundamental architectural decisions in an EGL project is the number and names of the packages in the application. However, since this is entirely a test project, I can skip a lot of that stuff, and just use throwaway values like "test.")

Figure 3.12: This is a partially expanded view of the MyFirstRUI project.

Once I've created my package, the next step is to create the Rich UI handler. To do this, I could either open the File menu and select New, or I could right-click the new package and select New/Rich UI Handler from the context-sensitive menu that appears, as shown in Figure 3.13.

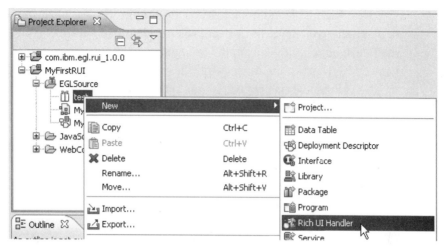

Figure 3.13: Use the context-sensitive (right-click) menu to create a new Rich UI handler.

Either way, the New Rich UI Handler dialog appears, as shown in Figure 3.14. This is where I can create my handler.

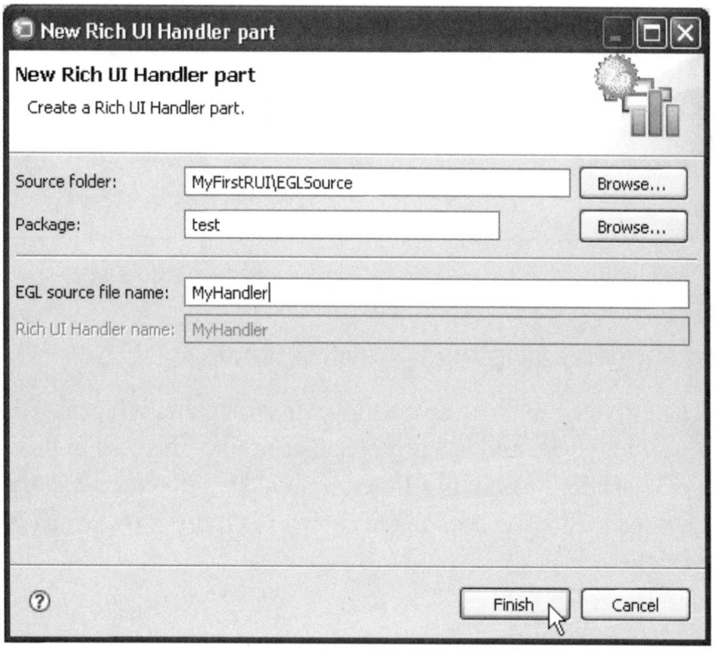

Figure 3.14: This is the dialog to create a new Rich UI handler.

The New Rich UI Handler dialog is quite simple. The only warning is to make sure you have the correct package identified before you click the Finish button. In the example in Figure 3.14, I'm creating a handler named "MyHandler" in the package "test." When I click the Finish button, the Rich UI handler is created. It is automatically opened in RDi-SOA's WYSIWYG Rich UI editor, shown in Figure 3.15.

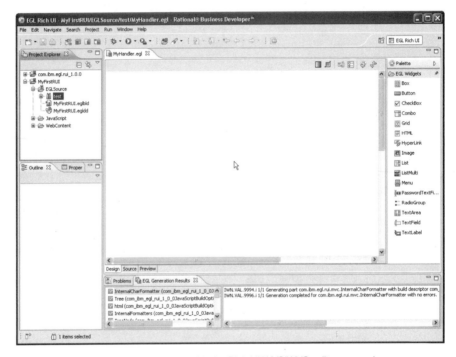

Figure 3.15: This is the workbench with the Rich UI WYSIWYG editor opened.

Adding Widgets Using the WYSIWYG Editor

The next step in creating an application is to add widgets. Typically, the first widget you add is a box. That's certainly the case in this application. Let's just do it, and talk a little bit more about boxes when we're done. To start, take a look at the Palette shown in Figure 3.16, which is a standard view in WYSIWYG editors.

The Palette view shows a nice selection of basic widgets, ranging from familiar ones like "Button" and "Hyperlink" to more unusual ones like "Box" and "Grid." In this case, I'm going to add a box to my new handler. Because this is a WYSIWYG editor, the traditional technique is drag-and-drop: click the Box entry in the Palette using the left mouse button, and while holding the mouse button down, drag the pointer onto the editing panel.

In Figure 3.17, the cursor has changed to indicate that you are dragging a widget onto the editing panel. What's less apparent in this book is that the editing panel has turned green, to indicate that you can drop the box onto the panel by releasing the mouse button.

This color-coding is used to indicate where widgets can be correctly dropped. There is only one place for the first widget of a new handler to be dropped, so the display is quite simple. As you add more widgets, the display gets more complex. All eligible areas are colored yellow. Each one changes to green as you move the cursor over it, indicating the area that would receive the widget if you released it.

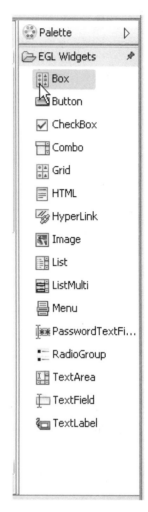

Figure 3.16: This is the basic Palette view of EGL widgets.

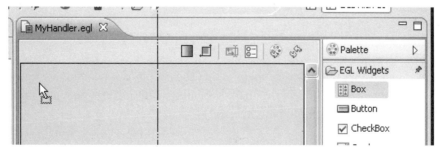

Figure 3.17: When you drag a widget onto the editing panel, the cursor and the background change.

As soon as you drop your widget on an eligible area, you are prompted to name it, as shown in Figure 3.18. While you can turn off this feature, I like to leave it on because I like to give my widgets meaningful names as I add them. This makes it easier for me to remember what they were meant to do. I like to name a top-level box "ui" because it encompasses the entire user interface.

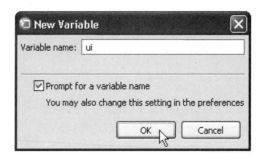

Figure 3.18: When you add a widget, you can rename it.

Two changes occur in the workbench when you finish naming your widget. First, the box is added to the WYSIWYG editor's design panel, as shown in Figure 3.19. It appears as a rectangle of dotted lines, which is a good way to indicate that it's really an invisible container for other widgets, a fact covered in more detail in the next section.

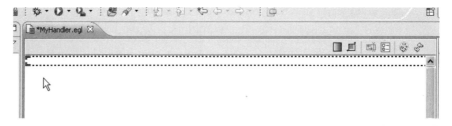

Figure 3.19: The box appears in the editor as a rectangle of dotted lines.

The other thing that happens is that the new box appears in the Outline view. Figure 3.20 shows the new widget, with its type first, and then the name you gave it in parentheses.

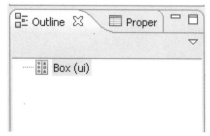

Figure 3.20: The new box also appears in the Outline view, with its name.

What's in a Box?

Now is a good time to introduce the EGL Rich UI concept of a box. A *box* is a very specific concept in EGL Rich UI. Conceptually, it's an invisible container for other widgets. From an HTML standpoint, a box is a table. You can specify a list of children, and they are laid out from left to right within the table. You can also specify a number of columns. If you do not, all the widgets are added to a single row. If you specify a number of columns, the children are placed into the HTML table one at a time. When the number of columns specified is reached, a new row is added to the table, and additional widgets are added to the new row.

Figure 3.21 is a simple example of a box. In this example, the box has two columns specified. Because of this, widgets 1 through 5 get loaded into the table two per row. Since there aren't enough children to completely fill the last row, its second cell is left empty.

Box, columns = 2
children = widget1, widget2, widget3, widget4, widget5

widget1	widget2
widget3	widget4
widget5	(empty)

Figure 3.21: A box gets loaded left to right. Each row is filled in order, from the list of children.

Unfortunately, a simple table isn't really enough. Often, you need an interface broken up into areas that are a little more complex, as shown in Figure 3.22.

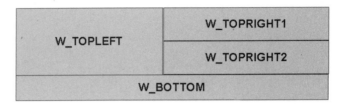

Figure 3.22: This is a more complex UI, with spanned panels.

As you can see, even this simple four-panel display won't fit nicely into a standard table. To do this in HTML today, you need to use row and column spanning. These features aren't currently in the EGL Rich UI product, but they are expected to be added. In the meantime, you can get around the problem if you really need to by nesting boxes, as shown in Figure 3.23.

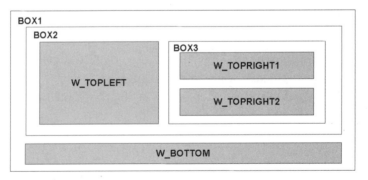

Figure 3.23: To emulate row and column spanning, you need to use nested boxes.

In this example, I have to create three boxes, something like this:

- BOX1: columns = 1, children = BOX2, W_BOTTOM
- BOX2: columns = 2, children = W_TOPLEFT, BOX3
- BOX3: columns = 1, children = W_TOPRIGHT1, W_TOPRIGHT2

Although this can get a little unwieldy, you can use it to create pretty much any sort of layout you need.

Another option is to use absolute positioning. Through careful use of hard-coded size and position values, you can craft a screen as complex as you like, without resorting to boxes. The problem, though, is that the widgets cannot be easily transferred from one page to another unless they happen to be needed in exactly the same position on both pages. This rigidity of structure doesn't lend itself well to the encapsulation and reuse of meta-widgets, an important consideration in the design of larger applications.

Creating Your First Rich UI

Now that you've gotten a general idea of what boxes do and how they are used, it's time to add a few more components, and then an action or two. Let's make a simple edit panel. It will have a title, a couple of entry fields, and a button.

Coming from a DDS mentality, it helps to have some contextual cross-references. For example, a literal constant in a display file is replaced by a TextLabel in Rich UI. A TextLabel is actually more like an output field because it's very easy to change the text at runtime (something you'll see a little later in the chapter). An input field in DDS is replaced by a TextField widget. A TextField is the same as a TextLabel, except that it can handle input.

The only other required widget is the button. A button is the replacement for a command key in a green screen. The user sees the button on the display and clicks it with the mouse pointer.

In this example, I'm editing two rows of data. The data is contact information: a phone number and an email address. The title includes the person's name. Since the editing rows have two widgets, I need to put them in their own box, and then include that box in the larger box that defines the overall user interface. (I already added that one, and called it "ui.")

Figure 3.24 shows the intended layout. I've already boxed the components. Since the editable data requires two cells, and the title and button are only one cell wide, I need to use nested boxes, as shown.

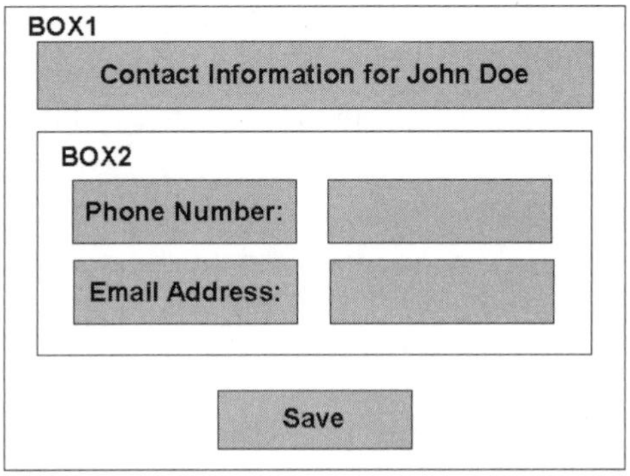

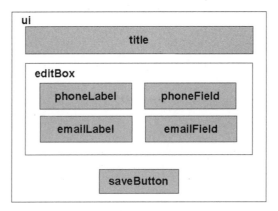

Figure 3.24: This is the layout of the new user interface.

Figure 3.25 shows the same layout, with widget names assigned. As mentioned earlier, the top-level box is named "ui." The rest of the names are pretty self-explanatory.

Figure 3.25: This is the same layout, but with widget names assigned.

Now I need to add all of these widgets to the user interface. This part takes just a few minutes. I'll show you the highlights of the process.

Changing the Box Properties

The very first thing to do is to change the number of columns in the top-level box. From top to bottom, I want a title, a box of fields, and a button. Since that's a vertical layout, I need to change the number of columns to one. Like just about every widget property in the WYSIWYG designer, this is changed using the Properties view, which appears in the menu when you right-click a widget, as shown in Figure 3.26.

Figure 3.26: To view the properties for a widget, right-click it and select Properties.

This causes the Properties view to appear, as shown in Figure 3.27. In this figure, the entire Properties view isn't visible. With more real estate for your workbench (that is, a higher resolution), you could see the entire view. Alternatively, you could take advantage of basic Eclipse behavior and double-click the blue tab marked "Properties" at the top of the view. This would expand the view to the size of the workbench. (Double-clicking the tab again restores the view to normal size.)

Figure 3.27: Here is the Properties view in the default 1024x768 workbench.

The expanded Properties view is shown in Figure 3.28. Actually, this is sort of a "semi-expanded" view. While it is wide enough to display all the values, at the bottom of the view, you can see a number of expandable subsections, such as Border and Spacing. These subsections are currently closed, as you can see by the arrow pointing to the right. I'll expand one of those sections later. For now, all I want to do is change the columns. So, I type a 1 into the boxed marked "columns," as shown in Figure 3.29, and click back on the designer.

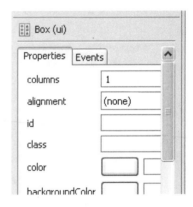

Figure 3.29: Just type a 1 in the columns field and go back to the designer view.

Note that there is no "Save" or "Update" button on the Properties view. Property changes take effect as soon as you exit the field you've changed. For example, if I entered a 1 into the columns field, and then pressed the Tab key, my cursor would go to the alignment field, and the WYSIWYG designer would immediate show the change to the columns. If, like me, you are used to pressing a command key or clicking a button to actually execute an update, this can take a little getting used to.

Figure 3.28: Here is the expanded Properties view.

Adding More Widgets

Now that the box is set up, I can add the widgets. Remember, I want to add three basic components: a title, a table of data-entry fields, and a button.

Since the entry fields will be in their own nested box, I add them as a box, and then fill that box in later.

In the discussion of Figure 3.17, I mentioned that, as you drag a widget onto the design panel, the screen changes color to indicate both the valid drop zones and the "active" drop zone. I also noted that the color change wasn't particularly apparent in a black and white book, so I was thrilled to learn about a setting in RDi-SOA that makes the designer even easier to use. This particular setting makes the active drop zone appear crosshatched, so that you can more easily distinguish it from other possible drop zones.

To set this preference, use the Preferences dialog by opening the Window menu and selecting Preferences. You'll see a dialog similar to the one in Figure 3.30. The left side is an Explorer-type control that allows you

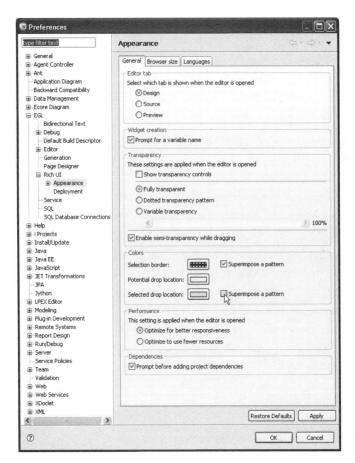

Figure 3.30: This is the Preferences dialog.

to navigate to one of the dozens of categories of preferences. (Literally hundreds of different preferences are available.) In this case, you'll want to drill into EGL, and then into Rich UI to find the Appearance dialog. Inside that dialog is a section called "Colors," and within is "Selected drop location." Here, along with setting the color for the active drop zone, you can click the "Superimpose a pattern" checkbox. If selected, this box will add a crosshatch pattern to the selected drop zone.

Since I wanted that crosshatching, I selected that checkbox and then clicked OK, as shown in Figure 3.31. Now I'm ready to start adding widgets.

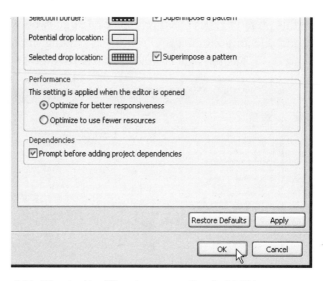

Figure 3.31: After checking "Superimpose a pattern," click OK.

The first widget to add is a nice TextLabel. Remember, this is a drag-and-drop operation. Note that when you first start dragging the widget, you get the universal "no" symbol (a circle with a line through it), as shown in Figure 3.32. This tells you that you are not in an appropriate place to drop the widget. Until you drag the widget to a proper place on the design screen, the cursor will remain this way.

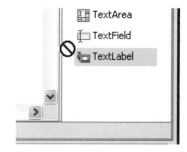

Figure 3.32: Clicking and dragging the TextLabel widget looks like this.

Once you drag the widget onto the designer, the cursor changes to a drag symbol (the arrow with the little box under it), as shown in Figure 3.33. However, just because you see a drag symbol, doesn't mean you can drop your widget. Again, it's difficult to see in this picture, but all of the available drop zones on the editor are displayed in yellow. If you move the cursor over one of those drop zones, two things happen: the zone turns green and cross-hatched, and a popup appears that depicts the location of the new element within the current UI hierarchy.

In Figure 3.33, the popup shows that I will be adding the new widget to the existing ui box. You have to look closely at the hierarchy lines to be sure you're adding the widget correctly.

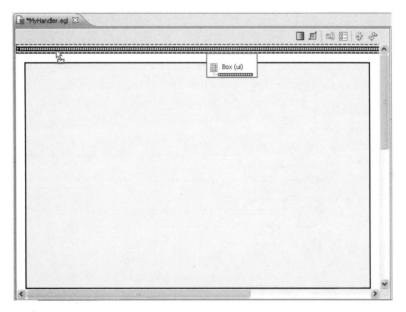

Figure 3.33: In this high-level view of the designer, the cursor has changed to a drag symbol.

Figure 3.34 shows a closer look. I'm adding a box for the edit fields, and I want to add it under the TextLabel widget. I drag the new box to the

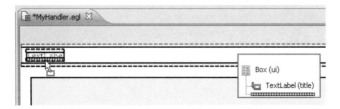

Figure 3.34: Here's a closer look when adding a new box.

designer, and position it under the TextLabel I added last time. There are several drop zones (yellow areas) on the screen at this point, but I want to use the one directly under the existing TextLabel.

The hierarchy popup is helpful here, especially as the UI gets more complex. When the popup appears, you see the entire user interface as it currently exists (in this example, a box and a TextLabel inside the box), with a green bar denoting the place where the new widget will be added. When I position the cursor on the drop zone immediately beneath the TextLabel widget, the popup shows that the new widget will be added inside of the box, but under TextLabel, which is exactly what I want. (Note, by the way, that I named that TextLabel "title" when I dropped it.)

The last thing for this pass is to add the button, as shown in Figure 3.35. Be careful here; you can easily add the button to the editBox box, rather than adding it to the ui box, *below* editBox. It requires a bit of dexterity to get this part correct. Again, the hierarchy popup is very helpful.

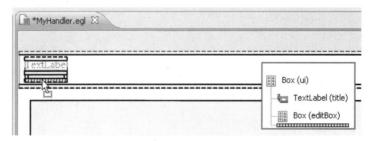

Figure 3.35: The hierarchy popup is helpful when adding the button.

As you can see in Figure 3.36, I've created a complete user interface. It's not a very good interface, with generic text for the title and the button (not to mention that the box in the middle that's supposed to hold the fields is currently empty), but it's an interface nonetheless.

The next thing is to assign literal text as necessary. In this case, I can add the text to the title and the button very easily, using the Properties view. The Properties dialog is, like

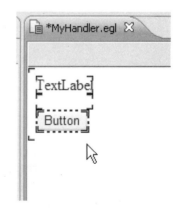

Figure 3.36: This is a complete, albeit generic, Rich UI!

all things in Eclipse, context-sensitive. Therefore, it's a little different for each widget. For both the TextLabel and Button widgets (and some others), the Properties dialog has a property named "text." As you might guess, this property allows you to update the text.

Changing Some More Properties

First, I'll change the text for the label and the button. Figure 3.37 shows the workbench after I've changed the text for the title, and right as I'm

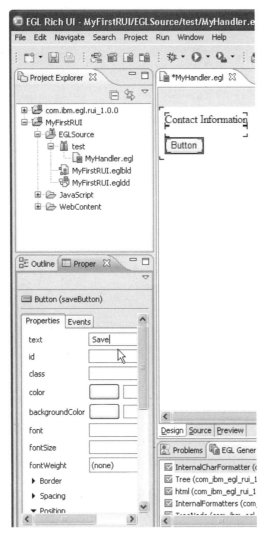

Figure 3.37: Use the Properties dialog to change text on labels and buttons.

about to change the text for the button. Note that I've already changed the text in the Properties dialog. The change will take effect as soon as I exit the field or leave the dialog in any way.

Now it's time to add the editable fields. In this example, the editable fields are laid out essentially the same as you would for a green-screen interface: two columns, with prompts on the left and data fields on the right. To accomplish this in the Rich UI, I need to set the number of columns to two in the box named "editBox," as shown in Figure 3.38.

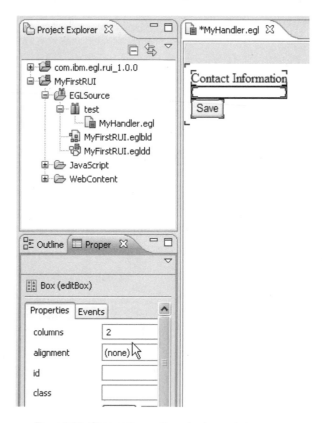

Figure 3.38: Change the number of columns to two.

Adding the Rest of the Widgets

The next step is to add the field-editing widgets to the nested box. That's all I'm doing in this example, but if I had multiple nesting levels, I'd simply repeat this process as many times as necessary.

Basically, there are two fields to be edited, for the phone number and email address. Each field has two widgets, a TextLabel for the prompt, and a TextField for the actual enterable field. I won't go over the New Variable dialog again for each; assume that it popped up and I gave each widget the correct name from Figure 3.25. However, I do want to carefully review how the designer acts, both as to how the drop zones are displayed and how the hierarchy popup works.

In Figure 3.39, I am adding the first field. You can (sort of) tell from the drop zones that I'm adding a new widget inside a box, although it's not crystal clear. The hierarchy popup, however, makes it absolutely clear that the new widget will be added inside the box named "editBox." Perfect!

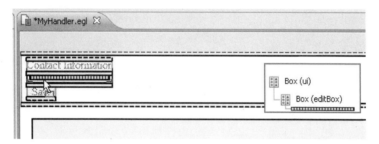

Figure 3.39: The first field-editing widget is added to the nested box.

The hierarchy popup in Figure 3.40 is even more interesting. Using it, you can tell for sure that the widget is being added to the box underneath (after) the TextLabel named "phoneLabel." (Remember, I'm not showing you the dialog where I named it, but rest assured that it came up after I dropped the widget in Figure 3.39.) Even more important than the popup, though, is the designer. It shows the new widget being added to the right of the new TextLabel. Think about it: the designer examines the code to determine

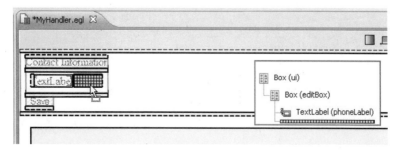

Figure 3.40: The designer adds a second widget to the right of the first widget.

that the box has two columns, and then changes the visible characteristics of the drop zones accordingly. That's a whole lot of work, and it's really a great concept.

At this point, I've added the prompt and enterable field that make up the first line. Now I just have to do the same for the next line. Note that, at this time, I could go into the source code and make changes there. However, this chapter is all about WYSIWYG design, so I'll finish the interface using the designer.

The first row is filled, so the drop zone appears to the right of the row, as shown in Figure 3.41. I could also drop the new widget before the first cell (the label) or between the two cells. Dropping the new widget at the end causes it to be added as the first cell in a new row.

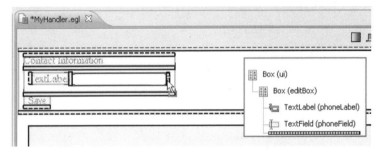

Figure 3.41: I add another TextLabel for the email address prompt.

As you can see in Figure 3.42, the drop zone for the second row shows up as a cell right underneath the TextField for the first row. That's perfect.

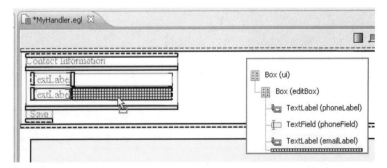

Figure 3.42: Finally, I add the editable TextField widget for the email address.

Just a Few More Properties, and I'm Done

I have to go in and change the text for the two labels. (Remember, that's done using the Properties dialog.) Figure 3.43 shows what the screen looks like as I'm changing them.

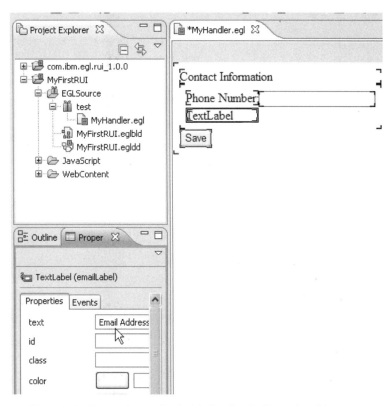

Figure 3.43: Change the text for the labels using the Properties dialog.

Here, I've changed the text for one of the prompts and am about to change the text for the other. Once I've done that, I can admire my results. In this case, I decided that having everything left-justified gives the dialog a sort of jumbled look, so I want to center everything. Luckily, that's easy to do.

As you can see in Figure 3.44, I just need to change the alignment property of the outermost box (the one named "ui") to **CENTER**. That will center it and everything inside it.

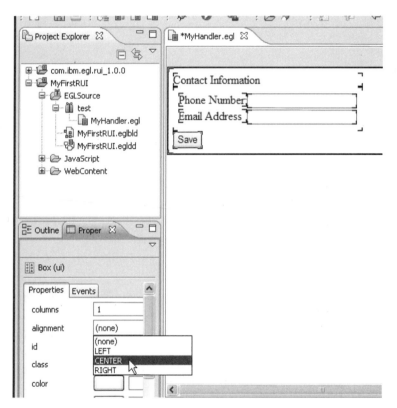

Figure 3.44: Centering the entire dialog is just a change in a property.

Unfortunately, it seems that the default width of the ui box is way too wide, as shown in Figure 3.45. I can fix that, though, by simply

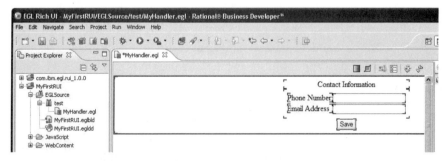

Figure 3.45: When centered, the default pane is too wide.

changing the width of the box. As you probably guessed, that's done via a property.

There's one little trick to changing the width: you have to find it. The width property happens to be under one of the subsections, in this case the Position subsection. I expand the Position subsection by clicking the arrow. I can then see all the properties, including the width. In Figure 3.46, I have changed it to 400. The number to choose will depend on your corporate UI standards. I used 400 in this case to make it display nicely within the limited real estate of the book, but your number will be larger or smaller depending on whether this is supposed to be an entire page, or just a pane in a larger interface.

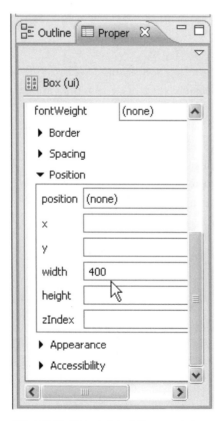

Figure 3.46: Change the width property in the Position subsection.

Anyway, I make the change, and there you have it! A nicely slimmed-down dialog, as shown in Figure 3.47.

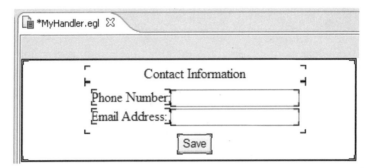

Figure 3.47: This is the newly slimmed-down dialog.

Action!

The only thing left is to add some action. This is another area where the WYSIWYG designer really excels. It's very easy to add an event to a widget.

First, click the widget in question. In Figure 3.48, that's the Save button. If the Properties view is visible, the dialog will automatically present the properties for the widget selected. If the Properties dialog is not currently visible, you need to right-click the widget and select it from the context menu.

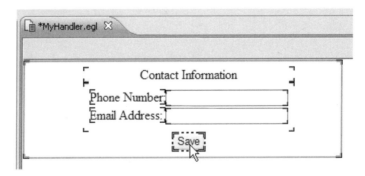

Figure 3.48: Click the Save button.

Once the Properties dialog is visible, I need to go to the Events tab. However, this tab is too large to process in my 1024x768 workbench. I suggest temporarily maximizing the dialog using the standard Eclipse technique of double-clicking the tab, as shown in Figure 3.49. This will result in the full dialog, as shown in Figure 3.50.

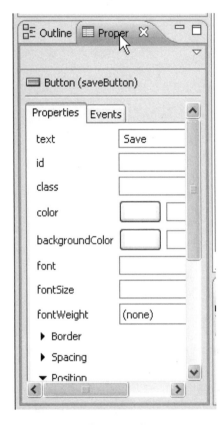

Figure 3.49: The Properties dialog is particularly cramped for event processing.

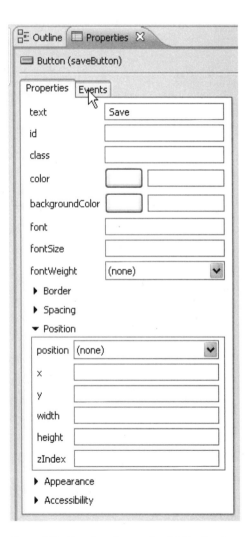

Figure 3.50: Now there is room to click the Events tab.

Now that I have enough room to show the whole dialog, I can click the Events tab, resulting in the screen shot in Figure 3.51.

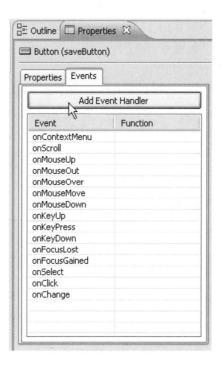

Figure 3.51: The Events tab even has a button to add a new event handler.

This is how much they've thought things through over at Rational. I could manually write my own event-handler function and then add it, but typically, the sequence is to create a widget and then write the backing code for it. So, it makes sense to have a button right on the Events tab to add an (empty) event-handling routine. I click the Add Event Handler button, and the dialog in Figure 3.52 pops up.

Figure 3.52: This is the New Event Handler dialog.

In this dialog, I can enter the name of the new event handler, and an empty function will be automatically added to my RUI handler. Here's a really cool point: this is the first time we've discussed the source code. I've done all this work creating the UI, and I haven't had to code a single line of EGL yet!

Figure 3.53 shows the last visual step: picking an event for an action. EGL has a robust event-handling core, so pretty much any event you can imagine is available, including things like **onFocusLost** and **onMouseOver**. I'm going to be very vanilla, and simply enable the button to be clicked. I select the **onClick** event, and then select the new **doSave** function from the dropdown list. Note that if I had other event-handling functions in my RUI handler, they would also show up in the list.

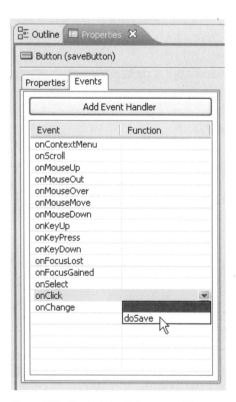

Figure 3.53: The last step is to connect the new function to an event.

Okay, that's it for a quick run-through of the visual designer. The very last step is to actually write a line or two of code to show how it works.

Adding EGL Rich UI Code

Adding the code is easy. Now, what I'm about to do isn't exactly fancy. In fact, it isn't even the kind of thing I'd normally recommend, primarily because it involves hardcoding some HTML attributes. However, it serves the purpose of this example.

One of the most typical activities for an event handler is to perform basic validation. In this example, I want to validate that the email field is not blank. If it is, I'm going to turn its background red. Of course, hardcoding the color red isn't exactly robust; in reality, I would simply change the class of the field and use a Cascading Style Sheet to determine the actual representation of it. The code for changing the color, however, illustrates the simplicity of event-handling with EGL Rich UI. Later in the book, you'll learn more about the right way to handle validation.

Figure 3.54 shows the code created by the designer. This is definitely not the time for a code review; instead, just focus on the bottom of the source, which shows the empty function **doSave**. This is the event handler I added in the previous section.

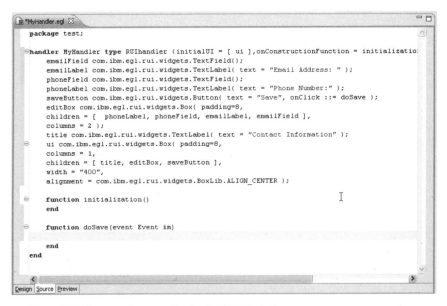

Figure 3.54: This code is created by the WYSIWYG designer.

EGL has a very simple syntax. In Figure 3.55, I fill in the details of the **doSave** function by comparing the text of the emailField widget to blanks. If the field is indeed blank, I change the widget's style to a red background. (The string "**background-color:red**" is standard HTML style syntax. It's a little too hardcoded for my taste, but it's completely functional, as you'll see in a moment.)

```
function doSave(event Event in)
    if (emailField.text == "")
        emailField.style = "background-color:red";
    end
end
```

Figure 3.55: With just a few lines of code, I provide some basic editing.

To test, I click the Preview tab at the bottom of the designer. The application starts running, presenting the dialog in Figure 3.56.

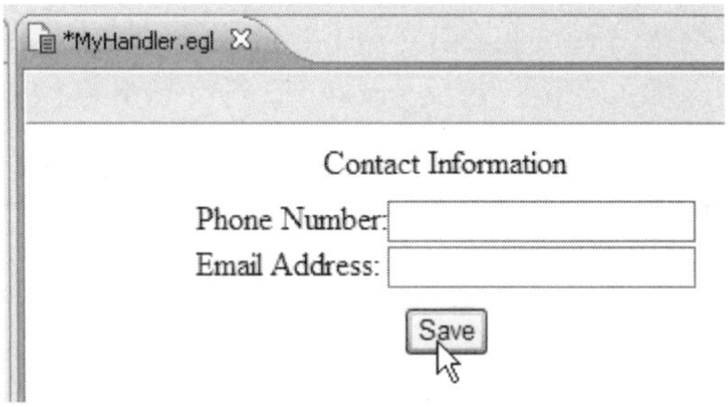

Figure 3.56: Leave the fields blank and click Save to test the event handler.

The result of the validation test is shown in Figure 3.57. Leaving the fields blank and clicking Save forces the **doSave** function to see an error. Thus,

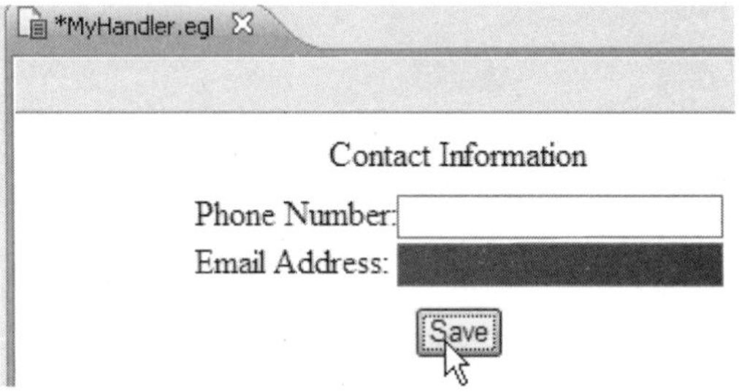

Figure 3.57: The results of the test are exactly as expected: the field turns red.

the email field is set to a red background. It's a clean, elegant syntax that rivals any other language. Obviously, this little bit of test code is hardly enterprise ready; a lot more would be added in a real application. Still, this should be enough to give you an idea of the productivity of the tool.

Summary

So far, I've introduced you to four different widgets. You are probably already familiar with three of them, since TextLabel, TextField, and Button are all pretty standard. In a later chapter, you will learn about one of the most important widgets, Grid. For us green-screen folks, a grid is sort of a subfile in the EGL Rich UI world.

EGL Rich UI has a lot more to offer. Many other widgets exist, and you should take time to get comfortable with them all. This book is a guide to multi-tiered architecture, not an in-depth reference for widgets. As always, however, IBM provides a lot of help text and tutorials. In particular, you should be able to find some good resources on the EGL Cafe website.

I hope you've enjoyed this little excursion into the EGL Rich UI WYSI-WYG designer. However, it was just that, an excursion. Now, let's get back to the real work at hand. Hold on tight; the ride is just getting started!

Chapter

4

Establishing the Framework

A multi-tiered application needs a solid framework. Since you're working at many different levels, it's crucial that you have a common framework that crosses the tiers. Such a framework is hard to develop when you have multiple languages in the mix, but EGL provides a very simple solution: the record.

Defining the Tiers

Earlier chapters introduced the concept of application tiers. Now it's time to define them very concretely. Figure 4.1 shows the tiers in an EGL Rich UI environment. (You might remember these tiers from Chapter 2.)

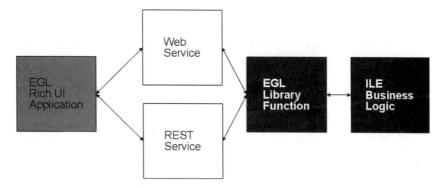

Figure 4.1: These are the components of an EGL Rich UI application.

While this is not a particularly complex design, it does need a little more detail. This is shown in Figure 4.2.

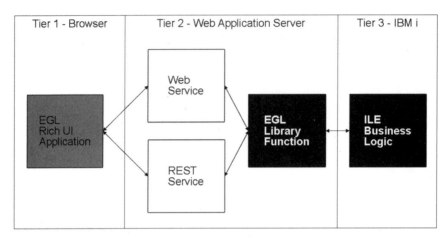

Figure 4.2: Here are the same components, segregated by tier.

As you can see, the EGL Rich UI component runs in Tier 1, which in turn runs in the browser, while the ILE runs in Tier 3 on the IBM i. Tier 2 acts as the bridge between those two very different worlds. This tier is really the anchor for the entire application.

First Steps

When I design an application like the one in Figure 4.2, I follow some very simple procedures. First, I try to get an idea of what I want to see in the user interface. Obviously, I need to get the users involved at some point, but I usually have enough information from the basic definition of the problem to make a first pass at the interface.

For example, consider a project to create a simple order-entry front end, something along the lines of an Internet storefront. I might have a design document that tells me the fields I need, or maybe just the request to "make it look like such-and-such.com." Whatever the input, I sketch out a list of fields needed.

You might remember the records described in Chapter 2. They are from the mental list of fields in Table 4.1.

Table 4.1: Two Records, Each with a List of Fields	
Order Header Fields	**Order Detail Fields**
Order Number	Item Number
Customer Number	Description
Customer Name	Quantity
Shipping Address	Price
Tax	Extended
Freight	
Total	

Is this an exhaustive list? Certainly not, but it's more than enough to get me started. You might have noticed that some of the fields could be calculated, such as "Total" in the order header. That's not important in the first phase of the design. The goal here is to get something visible, as quickly as possible. It's not hard to add or change fields later in the process.

You might also have noticed that I don't include the order number in the order detail. That's because the order lines will be part of the larger order structure, which will also include an order header, which will in turn have an order number. Although you might feel more comfortable including the order number on every line, keep in mind that it introduces unwanted redundancy. I suppose the most persuasive argument against redundant data is that the goal is to minimize the data traffic, since these messages are used to communicate between tiers, potentially over relatively slow connection speeds.

Adding a New Project for Tier 2

The next thing to do is to create a project for Tier 2 of Figure 4.2. Eventually, I'll also create a project for Tier 1, the Rich UI browser component. I don't need an EGL project for Tier 3 because that is ILE code on the IBM i. I will be able to edit, compile, and test that code using the IBM i tools integrated into RDi-SOA. For now, let's concentrate on the Tier 2 code.

In Chapter 3, you saw how to create a simple EGL Rich UI project. Figure 4.3 uses the same menu option to create an EGL web project. (This is the New/Project option from the Project Explorer's context menu, or from the

File menu in the main menu bar.) In this example, though, Web Project is selected from the radio buttons to create a web project named "iEGL."

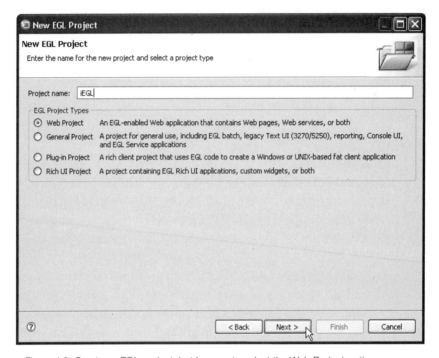

Figure 4.3: Create an EGL project, but be sure to select the Web Project option.

The only thing to worry about in a typical setup is which WebSphere runtime to use. Figure 4.4 shows the configuration for a WAS 7.0 project. It's important to select the runtime you'll be deploying to when you create an EGL project (or any web-based project). Otherwise, you won't be able to run your project in production.

Once the Finish button is clicked in Figure 4.4, RDi-SOA will create the iEGL web project. By default, it will also create an EAR (Enterprise Archive) project named "iEGLEAR." You can change the name of the EAR project, along with some other attributes, in the Advanced tab. However, I rarely find that necessary.

Packaging the Application

Now it's time to actually describe the data. Before doing that, however, I have to make some decisions about how to package the application. That

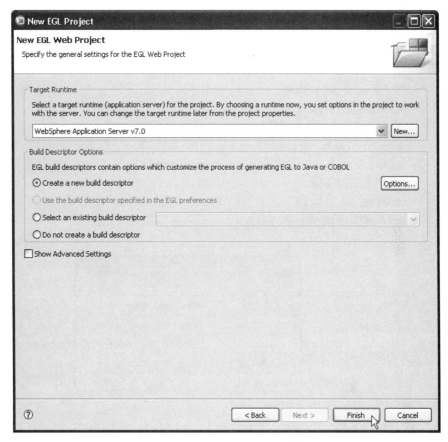

Figure 4.4: Target Runtime is the important option on the second panel.

is, how will I define the packages in my EGL source code? The IBM i side is relatively simple; I create a library and store my programs there. I might have several libraries for different applications, and I probably have a source library separate from my program library, but that's all second nature for an ILE developer. The package concept is a little more off the beaten path, so let me take a moment to tell you how I like to do things.

First, I need to create the overall package name. EGL uses the same dot-notation for naming that Java uses, so it makes sense to use Java-style conventions. In Java, you always use "reverse domain" naming for your packages. That is, if your corporate domain is xyzcorp.com, you start any of your custom packages with "com.xyzcorp." The trick, though, is to come up with a good convention for the parts after the reverse domain name. If you've already got good standards for Java code, you might be able to extend them. If you're coming straight from the green-screen world, though, you're unlikely to have such a naming system in place. Then what do you do?

Well, a lot depends on your expected application design. Let's go through the naming logic I use for the packages in this particular book.

I use the basic packages listed in Table 4.2. There are two things to keep in mind: first, the com.pbd.app package is typically only used in Tier 1, the EGL Rich UI browser component. The com.pbd.data and com.pbd.bl packages reside only in Tier 2, the EGL service portion. The two other packages live in both packages, though for slightly different reasons.

Table 4.2: Package Names	
Package	**Contents**
com.pbd.bl	Business Logic
com.pbd.data	Data Definitions
com.pbd.svc	Exposed Services
com.pbd.util	Utility Functions
com.pbd.app	Application Programs

The com.pbd.util package is simple enough. It contains utility functions, some of which are specific to the tier, and some of which are shared. For example, it's a good place to put extensions to the EGL language, but extensions to Tier 1 are made in JavaScript, while extensions to Tier 2 use Java. Tier 1 extensions don't make sense in Tier 2, and vice versa.

The com.pbd.svc package is a little more specific to my own programming style. In Tier 2, I use com.pbd.svc to expose EGL business logic from the com.pbd.bl package. In Tier 1, however, I use the com.pbd.svc package to hold the proxy libraries that use the services in Tier 2's com.pbd.svc to communicate with the libraries in Tier 2's com.pbd.bl. The proxy libraries have the same name as the business logic libraries in Tier 2, but they use services in Tier 2 to call the library functions. As an example, OrderLib in Tier 1's com.pbd.svc calls OrderService in Tier 2's com.pbd.svc, which in turn calls **OrderLib** in Tier 2.

This means that if you need to get an order, you call getOrder, regardless of your tier. In Tier 2 (e.g., the thin client), you call getOrder from Order-Lib in com.pbd.bl. In Tier 1, you call getOrder from OrderLib in com.pbd. svc, which in turn calls getOrder in OrderService in com.pbd.svc in Tier 2, which finally calls getOrder from Orderlib in com.pbd.bl. All very simple, right?

Certainly, this is not the only way to do things, but for me, it ties the components together nicely. I suppose an equally valid option might be to name the package "com.pbd.ifc" in Tier 1, but I like it the way it is. You'll see the whole hierarchy in use when the tiers are tied together.

Creating Placeholders in Tier 2

The first thing to do to tie the tiers together is create placeholders in Tier 2. To do this, I create data definitions in com.pbd.data and a simple "get" function in com.pbd.bl that will return hardcoded information. In minutes, I can have a complete test environment up and running. (It really takes me longer to describe it than to do it!) The code for this chapter contains four simple source files, one each in three of the standard packages, and a fourth one in a special test package, which you'll learn about a little later.

Let's take a look at the new parts in the three standard packages. First, a member called Order is added to the package com.pbd.data. Typically, I'll add one part (one source file) for each set of related records. Sometimes this will only be a single record, such as a customer record. It's unlikely that a customer will have a very complex structure, so it's probably represented by a single database record. An order, on the other hand, is almost always made up of multiple records. At the very least, you'll have an order header and order detail.

Let's take a look the parts for an order. Here is the part Order.egl in the package com.pbd.data:

```
package com.pbd.data;
record Order{}
  Header OrderHeader;
  Lines OrderLine[]
end
```

```
record OrderHeader{}
  OrderNumber string;
  CustomerNumber decimal(6,0);
  CustomerName string;
  ShippingAddr string;
  Tax money(9,2);
  Freight money(9,2);
  Total money(9,2);
end
record OrderLine{}
  ItemNumber string;
  Description string;
  Quantity decimal(9,2);
  Price money(9,2);
  Extended money(11,2);
end
```

You can see how easy it is to represent complex data types in EGL. After the **package** statement, you immediately see the definitions of the data, starting with the definition of the complex Order structure. Order is made up of an OrderHeader record and an array of OrderLine records. One nice thing about EGL is that arrays are self-sizing; you don't have to muck around with determining an optimum maximum value for an array.

You might notice that the code uses **String** for all character fields. That's because EGL, especially in the Rich UI component, isn't really built on fixed-length data. The whole idea of a fixed-length string has positive and negative connotations. It's obviously easier to define data when you don't have to worry about the length, but it's harder to set up your user interface when you don't know the width of a given field. Tradeoffs exist, as always.

The next thing is to create what I call the "placeholder" function. This is a simple data-access function, designed to support the actions that will eventually be required by the application. Typically, the first thing you need is a fetch function (or a "getter," if you prefer object-oriented terms). In this example, I will create a part that has a function to get an order.

While I put the data definitions in my data package, the placeholders go into the business logic package. (If you remember, that's the one named com.pbd.bl.) The part that has the functions directly related to a given record has a name derived from that record; in this case, the part for Order functions is OrderLib. OrderLib looks like this:

```
package com.pbd.bl;
import com.pbd.data.*;
import com.pbd.util.*;
library OrderLib type BasicLibrary {}
   // Get an order
   function getOrder(orderNumber string in, order Order inOut)
     returns (Error)
     order = new Order { Header = new OrderHeader {
       OrderNumber = orderNumber,
       CustomerNumber = 789,
       CustomerName = "Pluta Brothers Design, Inc.",
       ShippingAddr = "542 E. Cunningham, Palatine, IL, 60074",
       Tax = 17.19,
       Freight = 14.95,
       Total = (17.19 + 14.95 + 4.32 + 23.95 + 9.45)
     }, Lines = [
       new OrderLine {
          ItemNumber = "AS-1445", Description = "Squirt Guns",
          Quantity = 36, Price = .12, Extended = 4.32 },
       new OrderLine {
          ItemNumber = "IIR-7728", Description = "Wading Pool",
          Quantity = 1, Price = 23.95, Extended = 23.95 },
        new OrderLine {
          ItemNumber = "IIR-7243", Description = "Metal Ladder",
          Quantity = 1, Price = 9.45, Extended = 9.45 }
     ]};
     return (null);
   end
 end
```

The function is very simple, although it shows off a number of very interesting features of EGL. For example, EGL supports bidirectional parameters, and even allows you to control the directionality of those parameters. In this case, the getOrder function has two parameters: the key, orderNumber, is an input-only string, and the order itself is a bidirectional parameter of type Order. Many of these capabilities become even more important in the world of SOA, because they allow you very fine-grained control over the amount of data sent back and forth.

Initializing Data in EGL

This function also shows how easy it is to create and fully initialize complex data structures with EGL. Although it might take you a few moments to work your way through the syntax, you'll find that the entire function is made up of only two statements. The first statement creates the order and encompasses the first 19 lines of the function. The second line returns a null value (something I'll get back to momentarily). For now, focus on the first line, if you will.

Even though the Order record is complex, with both a nested record *and* a nested array of records, it is still relatively easy to create a fully initialized order. That's because of EGL's simple, keyword-based approach to initialization. For example, if I already had a record of type OrderHeader named orderHeader, and an array of lines named orderLines, I could have done this:

```
order = new Order { Header = orderHeader, lines = orderLines };
```

That's all it would take. Note that the field names defined in the record (in the Order.egl listing earlier in this chapter) can be used as keywords to assign values when creating a new variable of that record type. By using curly braces, { }, after the **new Order** syntax, you can now specify one or more fields using their names as keywords. This is quite spectacular, actually; the EGL editor is smart enough to make use of the code in other EGL source to edit the current source. You can also use *auto-completion*. If you press Ctrl-Space within the braces, you will get a list of the fields that (still) need to be initialized, as shown in Figure 4.5.

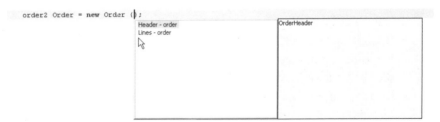

Figure 4.5: Auto-complete works very nicely when initializing complex structures.

What really makes your job easier is that, for complex structures, the initialization code can be nested. An example of that is shown in the code for the OrderLib.egl part. First, the Order record is initialized using an instance of new Order, with the two keywords **Header** and **Lines** (similar to the one-line snippet in the previous paragraph). Then, each of those fields is initialized by further use of the new keyword. **Header** is initialized by creating a new OrderHeader record and then setting each of the fields in the OrderHeader (OrderNumber, CustomerNumber, and so on). Even more fascinating is that you can initialize the array by simply using square brackets and then defining a list of OrderDetail records (each using new and then setting the values for its own inner fields). What might have taken a whole bunch of initialization lines and a number of work variables can all be done quickly and easily using this syntax.

Suppose you tried to do the same thing for Java records. You'd have to create a class for each component, and each class would need a constructor that takes all of the variables. When initializing each level, you'd have to remember the order of the constructor's parameters and specify every one (or at least null). The keyword syntax in EGL lets you easily change the order of initialization and leave out fields you don't need to initialize. To do the same thing in Java, you'd have to have multiple constructors.

The point is that with EGL, it's very, very easy to create dummy data. That's crucial to testing. It's easy to set up even the most complex data, including data that tests boundary conditions or bad data, and use that to rigorously test your code.

Handling Errors

I glossed over the issue of bad data earlier, simply because this topic needed its own section. One of the only things I'm not thrilled about with EGL is the lack of good, custom error-handling. I'd like to have the try/ catch capabilities of Java, but since they're not available, I had to come up with my own technique.

I've created a standard error record, named "Error." This record is the return value for every function that can fail, or at least whose failure I need to be able to recognize, handle, or at least report cleanly. The Error record is contained in com.pbd.util, in the Error part. It looks like this:

```
package com.pbd.util;
record Error
  severity int;
  message string;
end
```

Right now, there's almost no support; it's just a bare-bones record with a couple of fields, the severity and the message. However, neither one of these is really defined to any degree. My primary purpose for creating this part is to define my functions. The Error record will get more capabilities and support later in the project.

So, now I can go on creating functions. As you can see in Table 4.3, all are variations on the same basic structure.

Table 4.3: Functions		
Function	Input Parameters	Output Parameters
Get (single)	Unique key	Instance of record
Get (multiple)	Selection criteria	Array of record
Put/Update	Record to write	n/a
Delete	Unique key	n/a

You can see that the getOrder function follows this structure. It has an input parameter of the orderNumber and a bidirectional Order record to return the result, and it returns an Error record to indicate the outcome of the operation.

Note that none of these routines has a completion code or status parameter. They are all assumed to complete successfully. Instead, they all return an Error record. If a function returns a null value, then the function completed successfully. Otherwise, the error information is in the Error record.

It can get a little more complex for editing; instead of a simple error message, you might have to return more information. That's not a problem, however; you can easily extend the Error record if needed. For the purposes of this exercise, though, a single error string will suffice.

Testing

Now that I have defined the basic framework for my functions, I can return to the task at hand, which in this case is testing the function. It's really easy. I can test using a simple EGL program:

```
package test;
import com.pbd.bl.*;
import com.pbd.util.*;
import com.pbd.data.*;
program Test1 type BasicProgram {}

  function main()
    order Order;
    error Error = OrderLib.getOrder("ABC654", order);
    writeStdout(
      "Order: " :: order.Header.OrderNumber ::
      ", lines: " :: order.Lines.getSize());
  end

end
```

I usually create test programs in a separate package that isn't part of the standard reverse-domain hierarchy. The test programs are internal components that should never escape the lab, so they can be defined using a different, simple package name; such as "test." That's what I've done here.

The program itself is very simple, which makes sense given how little actual logic I've actually written thus far. This code creates an empty order, and then invokes the getOrder function from OrderLib. Upon completion, it writes out the order number from the newly retrieved order. This sort of test program takes almost no time to create and is really easy to run using the context menu. The **writeStdout** command sends data straight to the console.

If you're new to EGL, you might be wondering about the syntax of the **writeStdout** command. Basically, **writeStdout** will output any sort of data. You use the double-colon operator, ::, to concatenate values. (This is similar to the two vertical bars, ||, in CL or SQL.)

The context menu for an EGL program part (one that has the type **BasicProgram**) has the Debug EGL Program option enabled, as shown in

Figure 4.6. Select it, and the workbench will run your program, sending any output to the console.

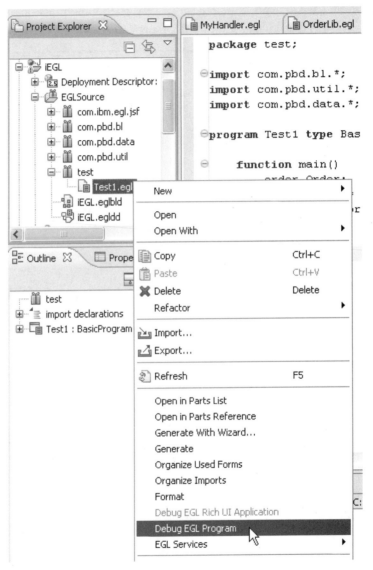

Figure 4.6: Right-clicking the test program gives you the option to debug an EGL program.

As you can see in Figure 4.7, the output shows the order number and the number of lines.

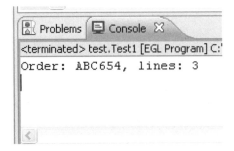

Figure 4.7: The output of the program is shown here.

The order number is actually the one passed into the program. If you review the code for the getOrder function, you'll see that I initialize the order number from the input parameter:

```
function getOrder(orderNumber string in, order Order inOut)
   returns (Error)    order = new Order { Header = new OrderHeader {
      OrderNumber = orderNumber,
```

The last line sets the OrderNumber field in the OrderHeader record from the orderNumber parameter on the function.

The number of lines is calculated by getting the size of the Lines array.

Summary

That's all there is to it. Just like that, your program is running, and your library function is tested. What I want you to take away from this chapter is that you don't need a user interface to create your business logic. While at first this seems almost counterintuitive, it's actually the underlying premise of this entire book: your user interface and your business logic should be fundamentally independent of one another.

Achieving complete independence is of course, impossible; your tiers must have some knowledge of one another. But you can strive for it with the only binding between the layers being your messages. In EGL, those messages are Records which are passed between the tiers. By writing your tiers to those Records, they can remain as independent as possible. And as I'll demonstrate throughout the rest of the book, that also means that you can build and evolve your user interface as needed without having to rewrite your business logic, and that's the very definition of leveraging your legacy assets.

Now you've got a test environment that provides a foundation for your business logic and that you can test without having to commit to any particular user interface strategy. Of course, a hardcoded test program that dumps to the console isn't always the best or even the easiest way to test a routine. The next chapter shows you another option.

The Thin Client Comes Along for the Ride

As mentioned in Chapter 4, the thin client can be a very useful debugging tool because it's so easy to create, and yet so functional. By using the thin client for debugging and testing, you avoid two complete categories of debugging issues: SOA communications and JavaScript debugging.

I could build all of my test programs the same way I did at the end of Chapter 4, using the **BasicProgram** part type and the **writeStdout** opcode. However, the amount of code required becomes prohibitive when you need to emulate a user interface. Instead, it's much easier to use a real interface. The beauty of EGL and the RDi-SOA tooling is that it is incredibly easy to create a thin-client interface to use for testing.

A Quick Review of Thin-Client Design

Most of this book is *not* intended to be a step-by-step guide. However, the point of this particular chapter is to show you just how easy it is to build a thin-client user interface. To do that, I'm going show you all of the steps necessary to test the new getOrder function in a thin-client interface.

Remember, the getOrder function returns a complex record (Order) consisting of a single instance of the OrderHeader record and an array of OrderLine records. Although I could dump all of that data using **writeStdout**, it would get very tedious, very quickly. Instead, I'm going to use the tool to do all the work for me. I'll start out by creating a web page. Before I do even that, however, I want to create a folder to segregate my test pages. I'll name that folder "Thin" because it's my thin-client test folder.

Organization through Folders

An EGL Web project is like any other web project in Rational. It follows the J2EE conventions and stores its browser pages in the WebContent, shown in Figure 5.1. This folder ends up containing all the web artifacts, including JSP pages and Cascading Style Sheets. The servlet code is compiled Java, which is in turn generated from the EGL. The EGL code is in the EGL Source folder, and the generated Java code is in the Java Resources folder.

To create a new folder called "Thin," I first use the context menu for the WebContent folder to create a new subfolder, as shown in Figure 5.2. In Figure 5.3, I name the folder. And while this step isn't absolutely necessary, I like to organize my pages. You don't want to go overboard because, by default, additional folder levels show up in your URL, but organizing by folders is still a great concept.

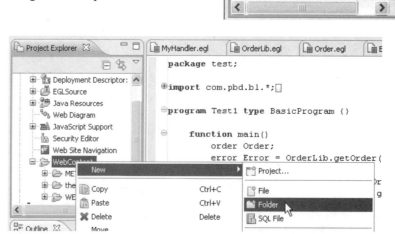

Figure 5.2: Create a new folder.

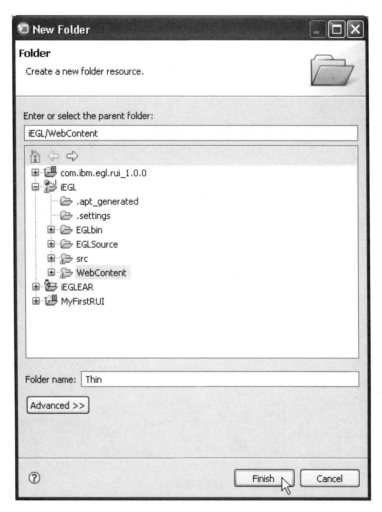

Figure 5.3: Name the new folder "Thin."

Creating the Web Page

Next, I need to create a new web page. This is simple. I just right-click the new folder, select New from the context menu, and then select Web Page from the submenu, as shown in Figure 5.4.

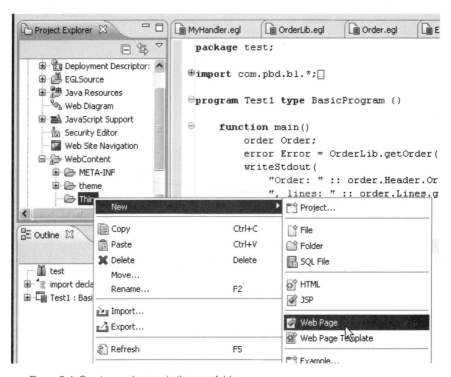

Figure 5.4: Create a web page in the new folder.

Even though I'm creating a new EGL page, this is the standard New Web Page wizard. You can create vanilla JSP pages, HTML pages or fragments, use the supplied templates for more complex paging, or even use your own templates. All of that is way beyond what I'm trying to accomplish here, though, so I just make sure the basic JSP template is selected, as shown in Figure 5.5. Then, I click the Finish button.

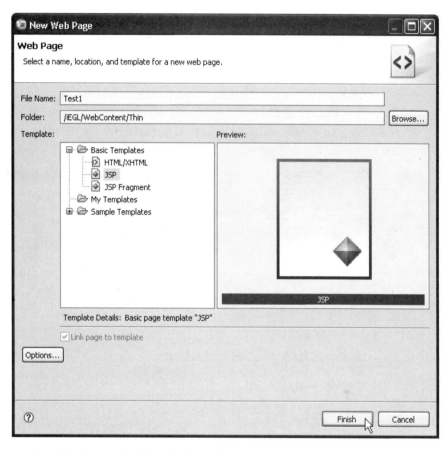

Figure 5.5: The standard New Web Page dialog appears.

When you create a new web page, RDi-SOA automatically takes you to the WYSIWYG designer. There's one little point that can be confusing: while the wizard said that I was creating a JSP page, I really created a JSF (JavaServer Faces) page. JSF is a superset of JSP, with a bunch of tags designed to reduce the plumbing requirements. Those tags are further extended by a set of additional JSF tags from IBM. It doesn't matter; the WYSIWYG designer can handle them all.

The designer has several modes, one of which is the default split-screen mode shown in Figure 5.6. In split mode, the editing pane is split in two, with one side showing the source and the other showing the resulting page. I don't have the real estate for this here, and I really don't have the need for it right now, either. I do use split-screen mode when I'm designing pages, but I also use a monitor set at 1920x1200 resolution, which I highly recommend. (I prefer to split the screen horizontally, by the way, because I see more lines of code that way.)

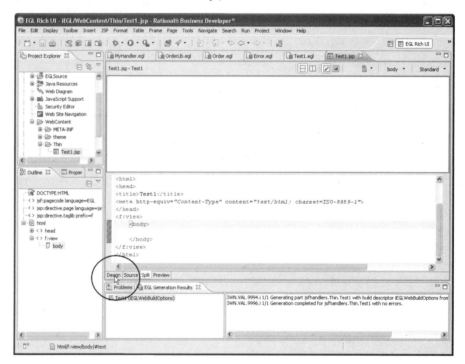

Figure 5.6: By default, the WYSIWYG editor for JSF pages comes up in split mode.

At the 1024x768 used for this example, I'm very tight on room, so I'll want to switch out of this split mode. Figure 5.7 shows how to switch into pure Design mode.

Figure 5.7: Click the Design tab to get into Design (non-split-screen) mode.

In Design mode, you have more room (by default, twice as much) for designing your page, as shown in Figure 5.8. That can come in very handy.

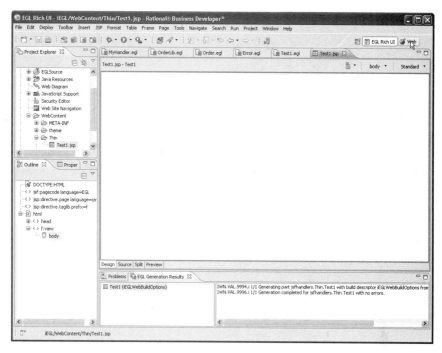

Figure 5.8: Design mode provides more room for WYSIWYG work.

Adding a Variable

At this point, I've created a page. Now I need to use it to debug my new function. The function returns a record of type Order, and I want to display that result. So, let's start by adding an Order to the page.

The easiest way to do that in the designer is to use the Page Data view. However, for reasons that aren't entirely clear to me, the sequence of events described up to now leaves me in the EGL Rich UI perspective, and that perspective does not contain the Page Data view. The remedy is to switch to the Web perspective. You can do this using the tools in the upper-right corner of the workbench.

Once you've switched to the Web perspective, you should see the Page Data view in the lower-left pane, as shown in Figure 5.9. There will be a folder named "JSF Handler," which contains all the pertinent components (variables and actions) from the EGL page handler for this JSF page. (Actions are functions that can be attached to widgets and assigned to events.)

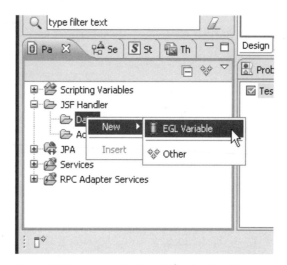

Figure 5.9: You can use the Page Data view to add a new variable.

I don't want to spend a lot of time on this, but it's important to understand the basic tenet of thin-client design in EGL: each JSF page has a specific "backing part" called a page handler. The page handler is the source code used to generate the servlet, which in turn handles requests from the JSF page. This is standard JSP Model II stuff, except that the tools are highly integrated, with the WYSIWYG designer being able to access all the variables and functions within the page handler. I'm going to take advantage of this tight integration to quickly create a test page for my getOrder function.

First, I expand the JSF Handler folder. Next, I right-click the Data folder to bring up the context menu. I then select New/EGL Variable to create the variable. (I could also have gone directly into the page handler's source, but I'm saving that until later.)

The New EGL Data Variable wizard lets you add a new variable. I could add a primitive variable or a DataItem. (A *DataItem* is a field with metadata, which you can then use to build records. It's very much like a field in a field reference file.) I want to add a variable of type **record**, so I'll click the Record radio button, as shown in Figure 5.10.

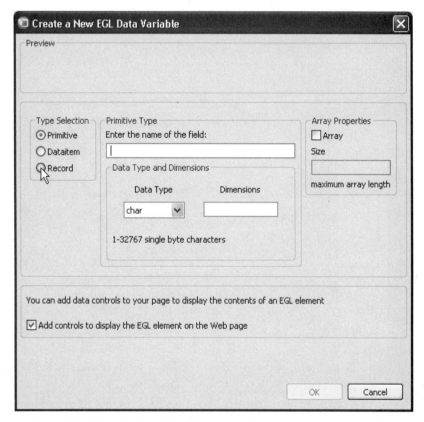

Figure 5.10: This is the New EGL Data Variable wizard.

When I click the Record radio button, a list of all the available records appears in the center pane. I click the Order record, and the name of the field is automatically entered (as "order," in all-lowercase), as shown in

Figure 5.11. The checkbox "Add controls to display the EGL element on the Web page" is checked by default. I leave that checked, and click the OK button.

Figure 5.11: Be careful not to add the controls for this record!

The next page of the wizard, shown in Figure 5.12, is a list of all the fields. This particular pane is pretty amazing. It shows all the fields of the **Header** record, but it also shows the array of lines. I can select and deselect fields to display, change their input/output characteristics, move them around, and more. I can also drill into the **Lines** array, and do the same for its fields.

More important, though, is the fact that I want to display the lines after the header fields. This isn't a big deal; I just click the **Lines** field and use the down-arrow button on the right side of the pane to move the field down a line, as shown in Figure 5.13.

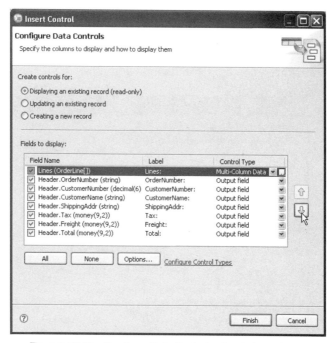

Figure 5.12: The Configure Data Controls wizard shows the contents of the Order record.

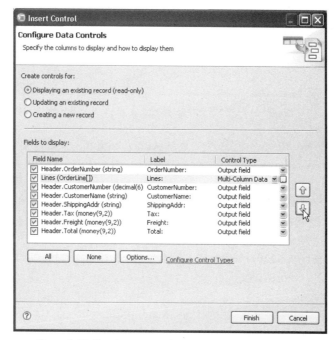

Figure 5.13: The down-arrow button moves the field down, one line at a time.

I can continue to press the down-arrow button until the **Lines** array is positioned at the end of the list, as shown in Figure 5.14. Since this is just a testing page, I really don't have to do this, but I'm accustomed to seeing header information on the top. I also thought you'd like to see how easy this is.

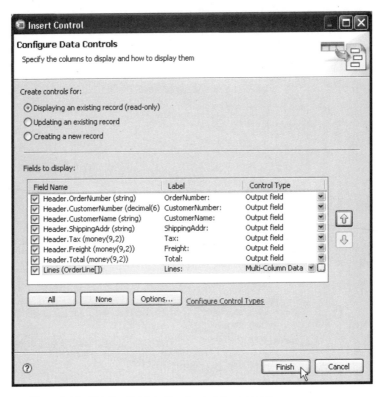

Figure 5.14: Click the Finish button to start the process.

Once my fields are in the correct order with the correct attributes (I can even change the labels), I just click the Finish button, as shown in Figure 5.14. Then, magic occurs. I don't use that phrase lightly. Think about it: not only is a variable added to the page handler, but all of the controls are also added to the JSF, along with the appropriate plumbing information to move the data from the page handler to the JSF page. It's a prodigious effort if done manually; the fact that everything is handled by the tool is hugely impressive.

As you might expect, even in Design mode without the spit screen, the order record has a little more information than can comfortably fit. (The default size for the editing panel at 1024x768 resolution is only

600x400.) I can, however, resort to the old Eclipse standby of temporarily maximizing the size of the panel by double-clicking the tab, as shown in Figure 5.15.

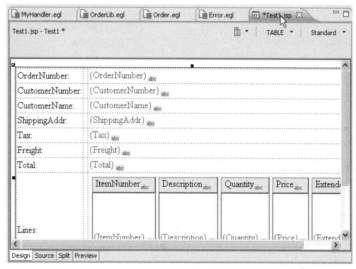

Figure 5.15: The widgets don't quite fit at 1024x768.

Now, even at 1024x768, the whole page is visible, as shown in Figure 5.16. And really, if your page is too big to fit in the maximized display, you

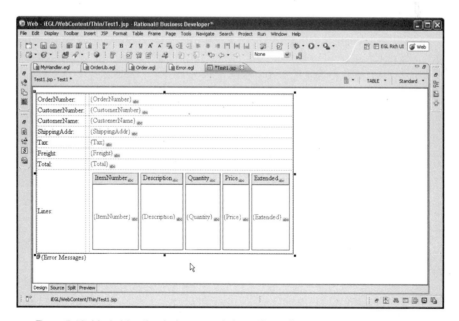

Figure 5.16: Maximizing the designer panel shows the entire page.

might need to revisit your design. In any case, that's how easy it is to add the page controls. Point, click, and you're done! Next, you'll see how easy it is to write the code to test your logic.

Initializing the Data

Earlier, you learned that behind every JSP/JSF page created in EGL is a page handler. RDi-SOA creates these automatically, and even pre-populates them with some skeleton code. When I added the variable **order** to my page using the Page Data view, that variable was added to the page handler. Now, I have to add the code to initialize that variable.

To start, I have to open the page handler. I could do that by digging into the EGLSource folder; the tool creates a "magic" folder called "jsfhandlers." Within that, you'll see a hierarchy of folders matching the hierarchy (if any) you created under WebContent. For example, since I created a folder called "Thin" and a web page named "Test1" in that folder, I'd find my page handler in EGLSource\jsfhandlers\Thin\Test1.egl.

There's an easier way, though. Just right-click in the WYSIWYG designer, and select Edit Page Code from the context menu, as shown in Figure 5.17. You'll be brought right to the page code.

The code shown in Figure 5.18 was entirely created by the tool. The only thing *not* created by the tool is the line with the red circle. That's an error indicator for the line I'm adding.

By default, RDi-SOA populates the handler with two functions: onConstruction and onPrerender. The onConstruction function is called when the page is invoked for the very first time. The onPrerender function is called every time the page is displayed. In this case, there's really no reason to put my initialization code in one function versus the other, so I put it in the onPrerender function.

I know that my function is in a library called "OrderLib," so I can type **Ord** and then press Ctrl-Space. This brings up the content-assist box, from which I can select OrderLib. After that, I can type a period, and I'll get a list of functions (in this case, only one, getOrder). The tool will fill the line in for me.

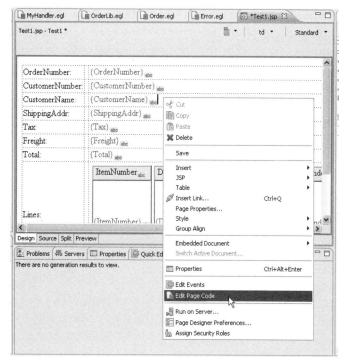

Figure 5.17: Right-clicking the designer provides a shortcut to the page-handler code.

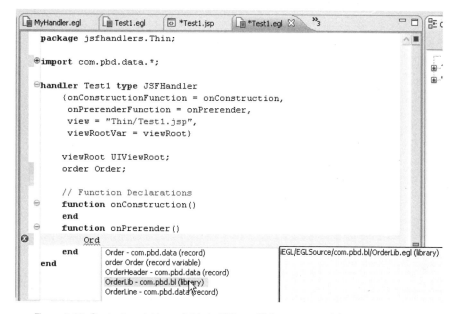

Figure 5.18: Content-assist is available in EGL, and it is very powerful.

The code, shown in Figure 5.19, is almost trivial. Since I got the skeleton of the function call by using the content-assist feature, I just have to modify the code to make it specific to my test example. I set the first parameter to a hardcoded order number, and then make sure that it's going to fill the **order** variable.

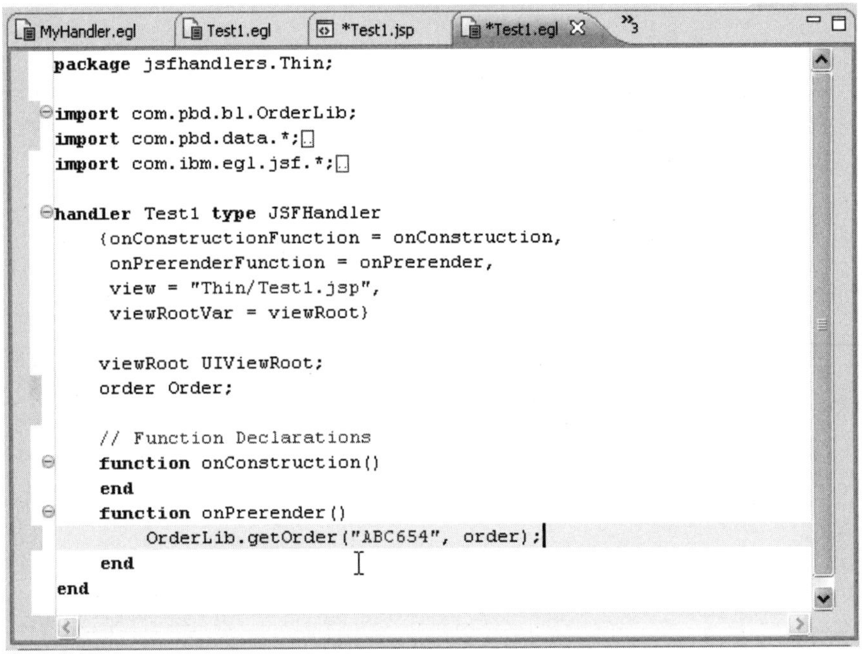

```
MyHandler.egl    Test1.egl    *Test1.jsp    *Test1.egl

    package jsfhandlers.Thin;

    import com.pbd.bl.OrderLib;
    import com.pbd.data.*;
    import com.ibm.egl.jsf.*;

    handler Test1 type JSFHandler
        {onConstructionFunction = onConstruction,
         onPrerenderFunction = onPrerender,
         view = "Thin/Test1.jsp",
         viewRootVar = viewRoot}

        viewRoot UIViewRoot;
        order Order;

        // Function Declarations
        function onConstruction()
        end
        function onPrerender()
            OrderLib.getOrder("ABC654", order);
        end
    end
```

Figure 5.19: Adding a function call is very easy.

One thing to note: when you add a function call using content-assist, the function is added with the variable names defined in the function itself. Because I used "order" for the parameter in my function definition *and* for my variable name in the calling routine, I don't have to retype the name. Thus, consistency in naming can really help you be more productive.

Note also that I'm ignoring the error record that is returned. I can do that in a test program. Obviously, I'd be a little more careful in a real application, but this is all I need to do for now.

Running the Test Page

Testing is very easy, as well. After saving all the code, I simply need
to right-click the new page, select Run As on the context menu, and
then select Run on Server from the submenu, as shown in Figure 5.20.
This will attempt to launch the page on one of the servers I've defined in
the tool.

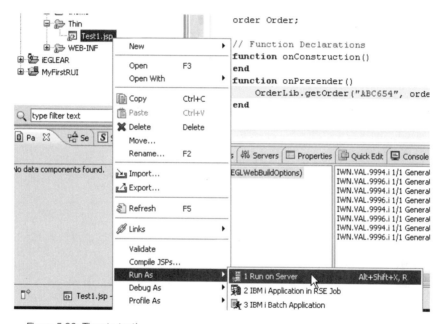

Figure 5.20: Time to test!

The list of servers in the dialog in Figure 5.21 depends on a whole host
of things, including what you've installed and what you've run to this
point. It's outside the scope of this book to go through all of the possibilities. In my case, I installed only the WAS 7.0 runtime, so that's what I have
available to test with.

In Figure 5.21, note the checkbox labeled "Always use this server when running this project." If you're sure you will only be using one server, you can check this box, and you will not see this dialog again. I usually don't do this, but it's up to you.

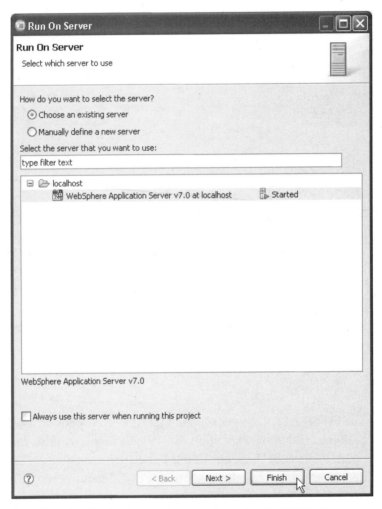

Figure 5.21: The Run On Server dialog prompts you for the server to use.

The results of the test are shown in Figure 5.22. All of the data is displayed nicely in the panel. You might not like the exact layout, but considering the amount of manual work (almost zero), I think it's a really powerful way to be able to test things.

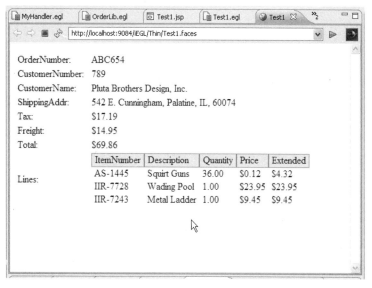

Figure 5.22: This is the result!

Summary

There are some very important points in this chapter. First, the thin client is perhaps the fastest and easiest way to test EGL library functions. In fact, the example in this chapter took me a lot longer to explain than to actually create and run. Once you're comfortable with the tool, creating and running a page like this takes less than a minute.

Second, it's very easy to make these pages bidirectional, although I didn't show it here. When you add the controls to the page, a simple click will make one (or all!) of the fields input-capable. So, while this example is great for testing an output-only function like getOrder, the same basic technique can be used to create pages to test input functions.

Finally, although the focus of this book is on Rich UI technology, it's important to remember that there are places where simple thin-client design is perfectly acceptable, and even preferred. And, unlike nearly any other technology or framework, with EGL, you can reuse most of your code and share it between rich and thin interfaces. That level of reuse really lives up to the promise of reusable, SOA design. The next chapter provides another example of that promise being fulfilled.

Chapter

6

Enabling the "S" in "SOA"

In Chapter 5, you saw that one of the side benefits of the multi-tiered architectural framework was that you got thin client for almost nothing. While
that's true, even that ease of use is no match for what you'll learn in this
chapter: how to get SOAP services simply by clicking a checkbox.

A Quick Review

Back in Chapter 2, you learned that communication between the EGL Rich
UI application and the EGL library functions occurs via either SOAP or
REST web services, as shown in Figure 6.1.

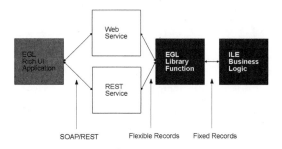

*Figure 6.1: EGL library functions can be exposed as
either SOAP or REST services.*

Either SOAP or REST is technically adequate. However, for a multi-tiered
architecture like this one, where you have complete control over both sides
of the conversation, it makes sense to use the most efficient communication mechanism. With services, I find REST to be leaner, since it uses little
more than a simple JavaScript Object Notation (JSON) representation of

the data. SOAP, on the other hand, uses rather verbose XML, contained inside a bulky message envelope.

There are, however, times when traditional SOAP services provide the best solution. Typically, these situations involve dealing with external consumers, whether truly external (such as a trading partner), or simply "intercorporate" external (such as another business unit using a different technology). The point is that with EGL, you're not locked into either approach. In fact, you can use both, with just the click of a checkbox.

First Things First

Before creating a service, I need one crucial piece of information: the port that my test server is listening on. It's a one-time process that gets as close to the edge of WebSphere knowledge as many RPG programmers dare to go. Really, though, it's pretty easy.

I go to the Servers view (usually located in the stack of views on the bottom of the workbench), and then right-click the server I'll be testing with. It's a lot easier if, as in Figure 6.2, you only have one server. In that case, just right-click it, select Administration from the context menu, and then select Run administrative console from the submenu.

Figure 6.2: Run the administration console for your server.

When the console comes up (you might have to log in), you can find the port. Basically, I drill into Servers, then WebSphere application servers, then my server instance (usually server1), then Ports, and finally click WC_defaulthost to get the port that the server is listening to for regular requests. In the example in Figure 6.3, it's listening to port 9084.

It's important to do this because the tooling defaults to port 9080. This is great if this is your only WebSphere instance, since 9080 is also the default port for this particular function. If, however, you've managed to install or configure multiple instances of WAS over the life of your workstation, you are likely to see a different port number, as is the case here.

Figure 6.3: Drill into the ports for the server to find the "default host" port.

Before I create my first service, I have to create the package for it. In keeping with the naming conventions laid out for the architectural framework back in Chapter 2, this package will be named "com.pbd.svc." As I did for other packages, I just right-click the EGLSource folder, select New from the context menu, and then select Package from the submenu. This will create the new package, as shown in Figure 6.4. Now I've done all of my setup work, and I'm ready to create a service.

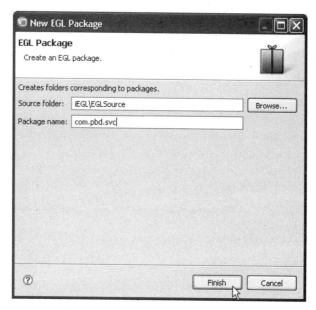

Figure 6.4: The New EGL Package wizard lets me create the com. pbd.svc package.

Creating a Service

The next step is to create my service part. First, I right-click the new com.
pbd.svc package, select New from the context menu, and then select Service from the submenu, as shown in Figure 6.5.

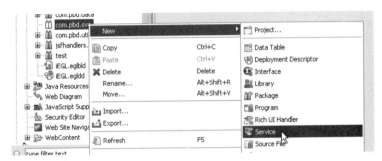

Figure 6.5: Select the New/Service option from the new package's context menu.

As long as I click the correct spot, the New EGL Service Part wizard,
shown in Figure 6.6, is a breeze. First, I enter the name of the new service.
Notice the two checkboxes in the middle of the wizard, labeled "Create as
Web (SOAP) service" and "Create as Web (REST) service." Depending on
your needs, you can check one or both of these. In this example, I'm going
to use the service both as a SOAP service (for external SOA access) and as
a REST service (for multi-tiered messaging). Therefore, I check both boxes
before clicking the Finish button.

This is what I mean by creating a SOAP service with just a checkbox. I
have to create the REST service, but by simply checking an additional
checkbox, I also create the SOAP service. How cool is that?

What I get is a typical EGL template, shown in Figure 6.7. In this case, it's
geared specifically toward writing services.

I need very little from this. Instead, I type the following source:

```
package com.pbd.svc;
service OrderService

    function getOrder(orderNumber string in, order Order inOut)
        returns (Error)
        return (OrderLib.getOrder(orderNumber, order));
    end
end
```

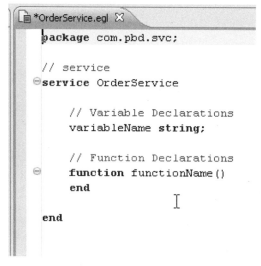

Figure 6.6: Enter the name of the new service part.

```
package com.pbd.svc;

// service
service OrderService

    // Variable Declarations
    variableName string;

    // Function Declarations
    function functionName()
    end

end
```

Figure 6.7: Here is the default service part template.

I do this to add a getOrder function to the service. If you look carefully, you'll see that the signature (the parameters and return value) of the new getOrder function is identical to the original getOrder function. That's intentional; I want the service to act as little more than a proxy for the library function. This is my personal technique for all services: write the library function, and then expose it directly through a service. What's nice about this is that I can just copy the function definition from the OrderLib library directly into the OrderService service part. Then, I just add the middle line that passes the parameters through, and I'm done:

```
return (OrderLib.getOrder(orderNumber, order));
```

However, if I do this, I get lots of errors, as shown in Figure 6.8. Since the function uses records such as Order and Error, and those definitions are in

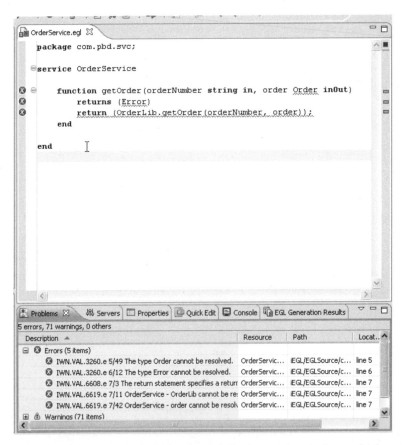

Figure 6.8: Just copying in the function definition leaves a bunch of unresolved references.

other packages, I have problems. That's not to mention the problem that I'm having because I'm trying to call a function in another library.

Remember, though, that EGL is all about productivity. One way it reaches that goal is by fixing problems. With one simple move, EGL will resolve all my external references (provided they're correct, with no typos). I just right-click in the editing pane, and select Organize Imports (or just press Ctrl-Shift-O), as shown in Figure 6.9.

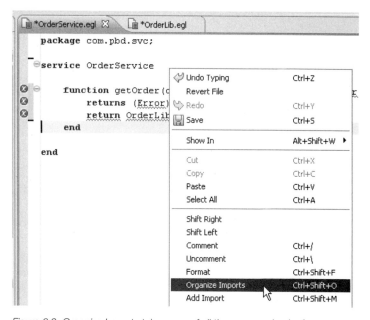

Figure 6.9: Organize Imports takes care of all those unresolved references.

EGL will find all my unresolved references and insert the appropriate import statements, like so:

```
package com.pbd.svc;
import com.pbd.bl.OrderLib;
import com.pbd.data.Order;
import com.pbd.util.Error;
service OrderService
    function getOrder(orderNumber string in, order Order inOut)
        returns (Error)
        return (OrderLib.getOrder(orderNumber, order));
    end
end
```

That's what I call productive!

I want to add one more line of code, and then we can move on. This is the reason I like to use service parts as proxies for the library functions; the function in the service part can add any features that might be required to better support the communication medium.

In this case, the order parameter is an **inOut** parameter, which means you must send a value in as well as receive a value back. The Order type is fairly complex, but in EGL, it's easy to create a dummy parameter (**order Order = new Order**). Therefore, the library function never needs to worry about the parameter being null.

In the case of web services, however, it's easier and more efficient just to send a null value. Since the library function is not coded to handle a null value in the order parameter, I need logic in the service part to handle the null value. Therefore, the final version of the getOrder function in Order-Service looks like this:

```
package com.pbd.svc;
import com.pbd.bl.OrderLib;
import com.pbd.data.Order;
import com.pbd.util.Error;
service OrderService
    function getOrder(orderNumber string in, order Order inOut)
        returns (Error)
        if (order == null) order = new Order; end
        return (OrderLib.getOrder(orderNumber, order));
    end
end
```

The new line adds a test to see if the parameter passed in is null. If so, it initializes the parameter to a new Order. This example is simple enough, but you can add a lot of front-end processing here, including things like authorization and pre-validation.

Okay, my service is done! I then generate it, which will make it available to the web application server. At this point, I have both a REST service and a SOAP service that will talk to my library function. Now I can test the service. The truth is that the best service-testing tool is the

Web Services Explorer, so generating the SOAP service has an added benefit.

Sharing the Service—Going SOA!

The next part of the process is simple: if I really want to play in the SOA world, I have to share the service with others. Typically, that's done through something called a *Web Services Definition Language* (*WSDL*) file. A WSDL file is an XML document that details the structure of the call. It can be relatively simple when the parameters are simple. However, with a structure like mine, containing nested arrays of structures, the document becomes very complex.

Luckily, I don't have to write it myself. Instead, there's a simple menu option, shown in Figure 6.10, that does it for me. Once done, I can give this WSDL document to anybody, and that person can access my service! More important, perhaps, is the fact that I can also use the WSDL with the Web Services Explorer to test my newly created service.

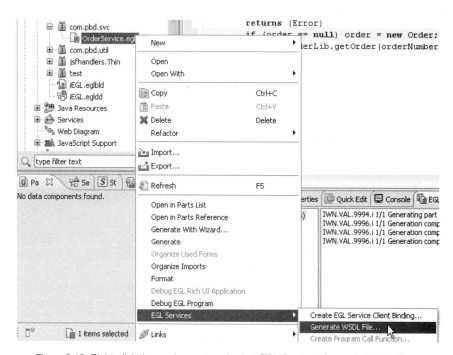

Figure 6.10: Right-click the service part, and select EGL Services/Generate WSDL File.

The menu option shown in Figure 6.10 will bring up the Create WSDL File wizard, shown in Figure 6.11.

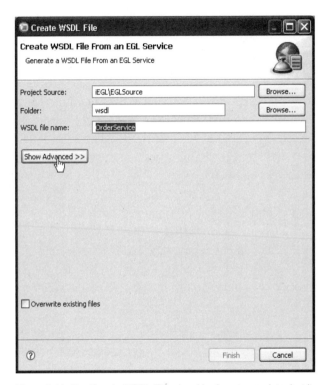

Figure 6.11: The Create WSDL File wizard is almost complete, but it needs one extra setting.

Remember earlier in this chapter, where I determined that my server port is 9084? This is where I need that port number. If it had been 9080 (the default port number), I wouldn't have to do this next step. However, since it is indeed different, I have to use the Advanced tab of the Create WSDL File wizard, shown in Figure 6.12.

Although the Advanced tab of the wizard is quite tall, I only need to change a single field in it: the Port field, which defaults to 9080. As you can see in Figure 6.12, I change it to 9084 to match the WC_defaulthost port number that I identified earlier.

When I click the Finish button, the WSDL is created. The first time you do this, a new folder called "wsdl" is created. Then, the new WSDL is created

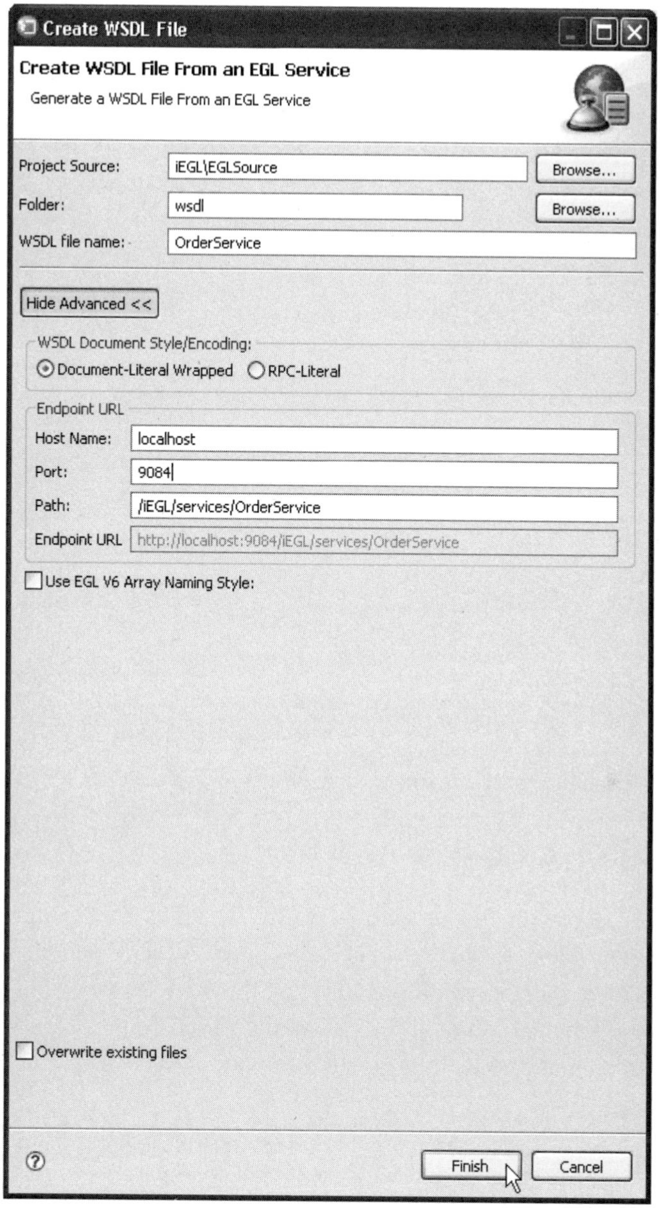

Figure 6.12: The Create WSDL File Advanced tab is one of the taller dialogs.

in that folder. Finally, the workbench brings the new WSDL file up in its WSDL editor mode, as shown in Figure 6.13.

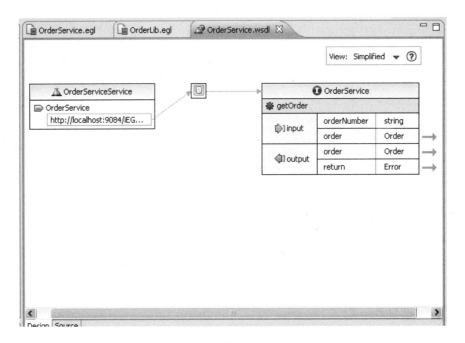

Figure 6.13: The WSDL editor shows the WSDL file graphically.

Testing the New Service

The last part of this process is testing. The previous paragraph mentions a new folder named "wsdl." Opening that folder, I see the new WSDL file, OrderService.wsdl. I right-click this file, select Web Services from its context menu, and then select Test with Web Services Explorer from the submenu, as shown in Figure 6.14.

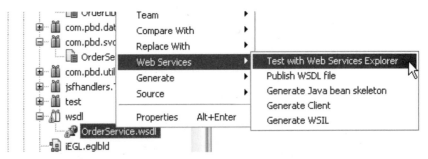

Figure 6.14: Right-click the WSDL file, and select Web Services/Test with Web Services Explorer.

This will bring up the Web Services Explorer. In the Web Services Explorer, I just click the getOrder function, shown in Figure 6.15.

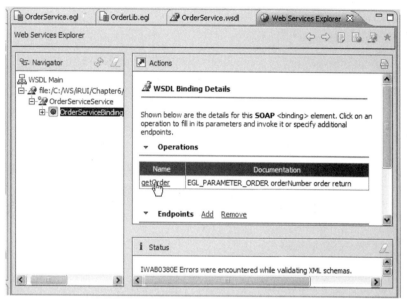

Figure 6.15: The Web Service Explorer is a very polished interface.

At 1024x768, the resulting pane is too cramped, so I maximize it by double-clicking the Web Service Explorer tab. That done, I can enter the appropriate information, as shown in Figure 6.16.

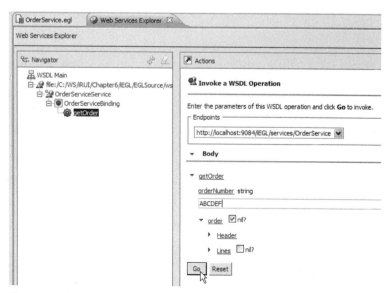

Figure 6.16: Enter an order number, set the order to "nil," and click the Go button.

This is the amazing part. Despite the complexity of the interface, I just set the key value (the order number) to test it. I can leave the order parameter set to "nil." (That's why I added the line of code that checks for a null value in the order.) As soon as I click the Go button, I'm done.

(It's time to make a confession. I wasn't able to find an easy way to make the order number null-capable, or *nillable* in WSDL terms. I had to go in and manually change a line in the WSDL. Still, that's a minor point. You can see the result in the project files; I'll leave finding the modified line as an exercise for you.)

When the result comes back, I still can't read it because it's the third pane in a multi-pane display. One more double-click gets to the result, shown in Figure 6.17.

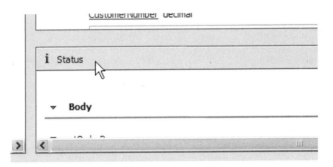

Figure 6.17: Double-click the Status box to maximize it.

Once I've maximized the view, I can see the data returned from the web service, shown in Figure 6.18.

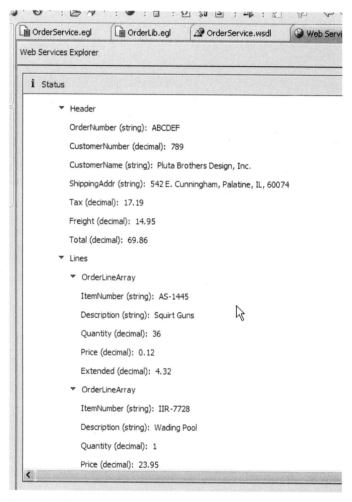

Figure 6.18: The final result is worth it!

Summary

At first glance, it might not seem like much, but what you've seen to this point in this book is pretty impressive:

- I created a complex data definition, made up of multiple records.

- I wrote a small function to return a hardcoded version of that structure, and then tested that library function using a simple EGL program.

- I created a thin-client JSF page that used the same library function and displayed the returned data.

- In this chapter, I created both SOAP and REST interfaces to that same library function, and tested them with an industry-standard web service tool.

Having run all of these pieces, you can see that the data returned from the web service is exactly the same as the data shown in the simple EGL program from Chapter 4, and in the thin client from Chapter 5. That's to be expected, of course, since they all call the same library function. That's really the point of all of this: the same library function can be reused for every possible interface requirement.

That's not bad for a few dozen lines of code and some pointing and clicking, I must say!

7

Building an EGL Rich UI Application

Up to this point, this book has focused on the technical details of writing EGL code: defining data, packaging functions, creating user interfaces, and enabling services. All of these are important components of application design, but they need to be coordinated within a larger architectural vision. This chapter begins to provide that vision. This is the longest chapter in the book, coming close to a step-by-step approach.

The Foundation of a Rich User Interface

Green screens are simple. In the final analysis, even subfiles are little more than 24x80 arrays of characters. (Okay, 27x132 in extreme cases, and frankly, I've never been a fan. But I digress.) You have output data, input fields, and a command key to indicate the next action to perform. While some criticize the green screen as primitive, this simplicity makes it relatively easy to design a green-screen interface. Even after throwing in the complexities of the subfile, a good screen design is usually a straight-forward proposition.

Contrast that with Rich UI. With Rich UI, you need to design small, modular components that may be combined in various ways. Each of those components might need to respond to events as subtle as a mouse-over. More importantly, those events may cause changes in other components, as may external events.

In fact, in a multi-tiered architecture such as that provided by a browser-based rich client, the user interface no longer calls the business logic synchronously. Instead, it sends requests to a server, and then acts on the results only when notified. It is this asynchronous nature that makes designing rich applications difficult.

In this chapter, you'll see how to move from a standard, synchronous design ("call a function, show the data") to an asynchronous design ("send a message, act on the response"). The good news is that in EGL Rich UI, IBM has integrated the OpenAjaxHub technology to handle all the messages flying around. EGL's implementation, the Infobus, makes application coordination a lot easier, but you need to understand how it works and how to take advantage of it. To do that, you need to go through three stages: from synchronous, to delegated, to asynchronous.

Going Asynchronous

Synchronous processing is the simplest stage, as shown in Figure 7.1. It's what we procedural programmers do every day.

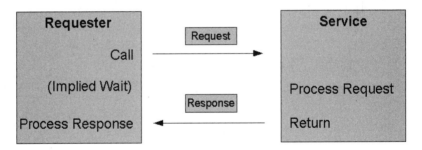

Figure 7.1: Synchronous request processing is simple.

Whether it's calling a subroutine, a procedure, or another program, the steps in synchronous processing are the same:

1. You call the service, passing a request (usually parameters).

2. The call implicitly waits for the service to process that request.

3. The service returns a response.

This is the easiest solution when the requester and the service are both running in the same process. The compiler requester executes a call opcode, which transfers execution of the job to the service. The service processes the request and executes a return opcode, which returns control back to the caller. It's simple and requires no architectural or syntactical complexity.

Unfortunately, synchronous processing doesn't work very well in the world of multiple tiers. Whether you're dealing with two jobs on the same machine or on machines halfway around the world, the problem is that there's no easy way for the requesting job to block on (wait for) the response from the other side. Waiting can be done using artificial constructs such as queues and semaphores, but it gets complex quickly. It also introduces the "wait forever" concept.

If you write the code as if it were synchronous, and the other side doesn't respond, or responds slowly, then your user interface stops responding. We've all seen this: the browser hangs, or a never-ending wait occurs. It's a bad approach, especially for user interaction. Instead, you need a design in which events can be processed asynchronously.

In asynchronous processing, the request is sent to the server, and then the user interface goes on to other things. When the request completes, the logic to handle the response is automatically invoked, and the user interface is updated. This concept has had a lot of names over the years, but my favorite has always been "event-driven processing" because it clearly indicates that processing (logic) is invoked in response to an event. The simplest way to implement event-driven processing is through the concept of a delegate, or listener, shown in Figure 7.2.

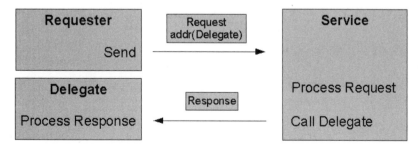

Figure 7.2: The requester sends the address of a delegate (the listener) to process the response.

Listeners are relatively uncomplicated, a baby step toward a full event-handling infrastructure. In an asynchronous environment, the requester simply sends the request, and then rather than wait for the response, it moves on to process other user events. How, then, is the response from such a request handled? As you can see in Figure 7.2, one element of the request is the address of the routine to call when the request completes. This routine is executed when the response comes back from the service.

The idea of passing the address of one routine to another routine isn't limited to asynchronous processing. The generic name for this programming construct is a *callback routine*, and such routines can be used synchronously. For example, callbacks are used in sorting and in XML processing. Callbacks often have language-specific names; in EGL, a callback is called a *delegate*. The name is also dependent upon the routine's use. When a callback or delegate is invoked asynchronously to process an event, it is called a *listener*. The listener is said to be *notified* that the event has occurred.

Listeners require some sort of queuing mechanism. More importantly, they also require a second task to actually send the request and wait for the response. When the service is finished, the second task calls the delegate (the listener) to process the response. This might seem pretty simple, but there's still a lot of magic occurring under the covers, since the two tasks have to be able to share data without stepping on each other. It works, though, and EGL supports this sort of delegation quite well. However, as your user interface becomes more complicated, lots and lots of events will need this sort of support. Eventually, management of all the delegates will get really difficult. This is nothing unique to EGL. In fact, this very problem has led to a concept called *publish-and-subscribe*, shown in Figure 7.3.

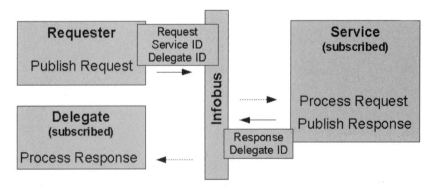

Figure 7.3: Publish-and-subscribe can be an alternate notification technique.

In EGL Rich UI, publish-and-subscribe uses a construct called the Infobus, which is an implementation of the OpenAjaxHub technology. The idea is very simple, and my explanation will be simpler still, because I'm not going to go into all the details. For the purposes of this discussion, here's how it works: the Infobus allows different pieces of the code to subscribe to events by name. The name is called the *ID*, and can be just about any string value you want. I typically use a dotted naming approach, similar to package naming, to help keep the event names straight. (You'll see that in detail later in the chapter.) Whenever someone publishes a message with a matching ID, the subscriber is automatically notified.

So, to replace the delegation of Figure 7.2 with publish-and-subscribe, my service and my listener/delegate both subscribe to different events. Then, my requester publishes a request to the service ID.

My little twist on the whole thing is that the request also contains the event ID for the delegate. That way, when the service processes the request, it publishes the response to the listener's event ID, which in turn invokes the listener. This is very simple and very flexible.

Another technique I've implemented is a generic status listener that any part of the application can use. It's a great way to provide feedback to the user, and can also be used to implement debugging consoles.

This application, although interesting, barely exercises the capabilities of the Infobus. For example, multiple listeners can listen to the same event ID. Think of a user interface with two views of the same data: a graph and a table. If the model changes, both views can be notified with a single event. The process that modifies the model doesn't even know how many views exist. It's really pretty amazing. Even more amazing is how tightly integrated and easy to use IBM made the EGL implementation. It's a brilliant example of the philosophy of EGL: hide the plumbing, and let the developer focus on business requirements.

Step 1: Synchronous Processing

To being the journey, let's first set up the UI using synchronous processing. However, I want to be very clear that you cannot create a multi-tier EGL application using synchronous processing. The EGL mechanism for invoking a service requires the use of a callback, and that in turn means that you will be using either a listener or the Infobus. This chapter walks you through both concepts because I think it's a logical progression.

You *can* create a synchronous process if you use a placeholder function. In Chapter 3, I created the placeholder function getOrder in the library Order-Lib, in the package com.pbd.bl. Eventually, that function will be expanded to invoke business logic on the host, because that's the responsibility of the middle tier.

In the browser tier, I need the same placeholder. It can't be in the com. pbd.bl package, though, because the user-interface tier never directly calls that package. Instead, I'll create a placeholder in the com.pbd.svc package. Even though it won't be in the same package, I can use the exact same code. EGL will translate the code to the correct target environment; in Tier 1, that's JavaScript rather than Java. This is another reason why I named things the way I did; it makes the move through the various steps from rapid prototyping to actual production very easy.

The first step, of course, is to create a new Rich UI project. You can refer to Chapter 3 to review the details, but it's pretty simple. I right-click in the Project Explorer view, and select New/Project from the context menu. I pick EGL, and click Next to display the New EGL Project Wizard.

I have to enter the project name. I use "iRUI" to identify this as the RUI tier and distinguish it from the middle tier, iEGL. Then, I make sure the Rich UI Project is selected. Once I do that, the Finish button is enabled, as shown in Figure 7.4. I click it to create the new project.

The workbench suggests switching to the RUI perspective, as shown in Figure 7.5. That's fine with me.

Now, I have to create a few packages. (Again, refer to Chapter 3, if necessary, for details on how to create packages.) For this example, I create two packages: com.pbd.app.widget, which I'll explain in a moment, and com. pbd.svc, which I'll use immediately.

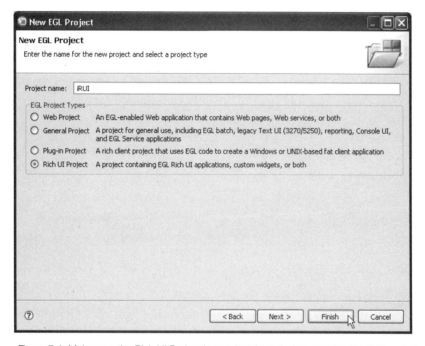

Figure 7.4: Make sure the Rich UI Project button is selected when creating the iRUI project.

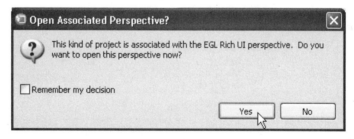

Figure 7.5: I'll let the workbench switch me to the RUI perspective.

Earlier, I said I could use the same code in both tiers. I wasn't kidding! I am going to directly copy the placeholder library, OrderLib, from Tier 2 (iEGL) to Tier 1 (iRUI). Also, for the remainder of the book, I will refer to iEGL and iRUI rather than Tier 2 and Tier 1. iEGL is Tier 2, the middle tier, which is running in the web application server. iRUI is Tier 1, the browser tier.

Technically I don't even have to copy the library. (I'll show you how that works shortly.) In this case, however, I want to copy it because once I start connecting the two tiers, the version of OrderLib in Tier 2 will be different than the one in Tier 1. It's really easy to do the copy. First, I right-click the

OrderLib.egl source file in the com.pbd.bl package in the iEGL project.
Then, I select Copy, as shown in Figure 7.6.

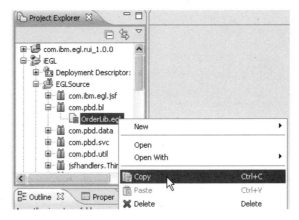

Figure 7.6: The OrderLib placeholder library can be copied
from one tier to another.

Next, I move down into the iRUI project. I right-click the com.pbd.svc
package, and select Paste, as shown in Figure 7.7. That's it!

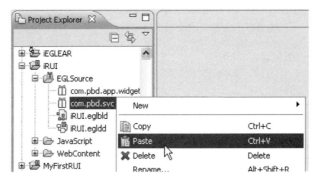

Figure 7.7: First I copy from Tier 2, and then I paste into Tier 1.

Immediately, errors appear in the new version of OrderLib. I double-click
the new source file to see the errors, as shown in Figure 7.8.

You'll notice that all of my records are showing up as not found. Indeed,
even my import statements are flagged as errors. That's because, even
though my little placeholder doesn't have a lot of code in it, it still requires
the data definitions from com.pbd.data. I *could* copy that entire package
from iEGL to iRUI, but as it turns out, it's even easier than that. I just have
to add a reference to the iEGL project in my iRUI project. I do that through

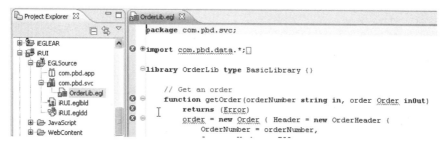

Figure 7.8: The newly copied member has lots of errors.

the Properties dialog. The easiest way to get there is to right-click the iRUI project and select Properties.

In the navigation panel on the left, I click the EGL Build Path option, which causes the EGL Build Path dialog to appear, as shown in Figure 7.9. At this point, there are three other projects in the workspace: iEGL and MyFirstRUI, the projects I created, and the IBM project com.ibm.egl. rui_1.0.0, which you might recall was added automatically when I created MyFirstRUI.

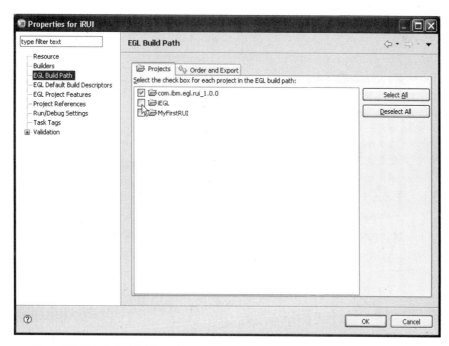

Figure 7.9: This is the EGL Build Path dialog for my EGL Rich UI project.

As you can see in Figure 7.9, the comi.ibm.egl.rui_1.0.0 project is already selected; that's what lets me import the base RUI components. To use the definitions in iEGL, I also need to have iEGL as part of my build path, so I simply have to check the iEGL checkbox, as shown in Figure 7.10, and then click the OK button.

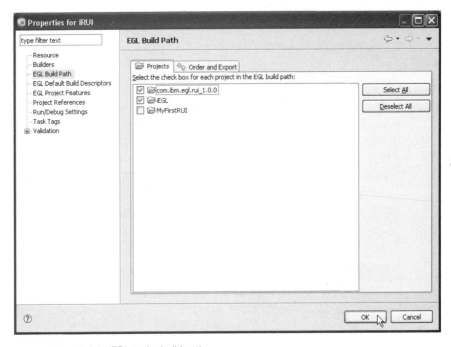

Figure 7.10: Add iEGL to the build path.

The workbench senses that I've changed the build path, and so it re-validates the code. All of the errors go away, as shown in Figure 7.11.

Now, I have to test. Remember when I said I could copy a package as easily as a source member? Yep, I wasn't kidding there, either! I'll copy the test package from iEGL to iRUI, so I can run a quick non-browser test of the new OrderLib proxy.

You copy a package the same way you perform any copy-and-paste maneuver in RDi-SOA. Start by right-clicking on the test package and selecting Copy, as shown in Figure 7.12.

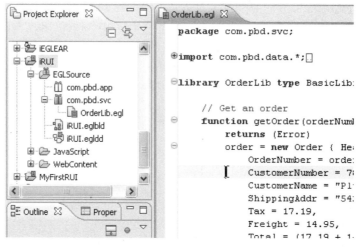

Figure 7.11: All the errors magically disappear!

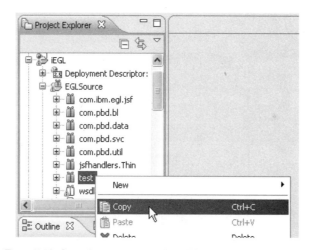

Figure 7.12: Copy the test package from iEGL.

Then just right-click the destination (in this case, the EGLSource folder in iRUI), and select Paste. as shown in Figure 7.13.

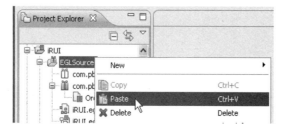

Figure 7.13: Paste the test package into iRUI.

Next, I change the import statement to use com.pbd.svc, as shown in Figure 7.14. This ensures I'm calling the correct function. Then, I run the code, as shown in Figure 7.15.

```
Test1.egl

    package test;

import com.pbd.svc.*;
import com.pbd.util.*;
import com.pbd.data.*;

program Test1 type BasicProgram ()

    function main()
        order Order;
        error Error = OrderLib.getOrder("ABC654", order);
        writeStdout(
            "Order: " :: order.Header.OrderNumber ::
            ", lines: " :: order.Lines.getSize());
    end

end
```

Figure 7.14: Change the import of com.pbd.bl to com.pbd.svc.

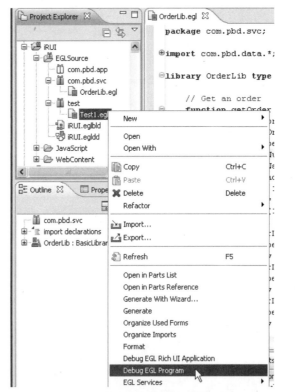

Figure 7.15: Use the Debug EGL Program from the context menu to run the test program.

After the code runs, I see output in the console, as shown in Figure 7.16.

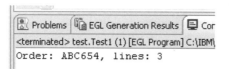

Figure 7.16: The test program has run successfully.

Note that this will only work as long as I'm calling a placeholder function that doesn't actually try to invoke a service. That's all I need; now that I have a function that will return an order, I can concentrate on the user interface.

Step 2: Putting the "R" in "Rapid Application Design"

While it took a lot of pages to document this process, it's really only a few minutes of work to go from project creation to prototyping, which is our next step. I've now got a placeholder function that will return a fully initialized order, and I'll use the WYSIWYG designer to quickly put together a panel for the user to review. Once the user signs off on the basics, I can return to the architectural portion of the process.

When I say I'll put together a panel quickly, I don't mean quite as quickly as the WYSIWYG JSF design tool you saw in Chapter 5. Rich clients take a little more finesse, but I'm sure that as the Rich UI designer evolves, it will start to gain some of those same automatic-generation capabilities. Even without them, the basic widgets provided by the tool make it very easy to do the same thing, using a little manual effort.

The result I'm trying to achieve is shown in Figure 7.17. It might seem like cheating to show you the finished result first, but in the Rich UI world, the prototype really is the end result.

Figure 7.17: This is the expected result of the order-entry screen.

As you can see, there are a couple of distinct areas: the order grid at the top, and a nifty little GoogleMap widget at the bottom. I'm going to create my own "super-widget," which I'll call an "OrderGrid." This super-widget will be designed to display the order. In fact, in its initial incarnation, the widget will not have input-capable quantity fields. It will, however, be a self-contained widget designed to be used inside of a larger application.

In a more robust application design, I might separate the order-display widget and the map widget, and then combine them into an "OrderMap" widget. I might have options to display more header data or sort the lines. The variations are limited only by your imagination.

Back in Chapter 3, I explained that in EGL Rich UI, the user interface definition and the backing code are written in the same component, the RUI handler part. (Remember, "part" is just EGL's term for pretty much any program component.) For a green-screen programmer, it's a little like having your display file DDS and the RPG that handles it in the same source member, except that in EGL, it's all the same basic EGL syntax. Personally, I find it helps me to think of the two sections of the handler as distinct pieces.

Let's break down the RUI handler, piece by piece. This is the standard preface for any RUI handler:

```
package com.pbd.app.widget;
import com.pbd.svc.*;
import com.pbd.data.*;
import com.ibm.egl.rui.widgets.*;
Handler OrderGrid Type RUIHandler {
  initialUI = [orderBox],
  onConstructionFunction = onConstruction,
  cssFile = "css/iRUI.css"
  }
```

This preface identifies the packages, imports pieces from other packages, and then identifies two other components of the handler: the UI and the code. The UI is specified by the **initialUI** parameter. In this case, I do *not* call it "ui." Since it's a super-widget, meant to be included in another handler, I try to use a meaningful name. In this case, I call it "orderBox." The code is identified by the onConstruction function. This is the logic that is initiated when the handler is first created. I would dearly like to be able to pass parameters on the construction, but that doesn't work. One last thing defined is the CSS (Cascading Style Sheet) file. Ignore that for now; I'll cover it in the next section.

Okay, on to the user interface:

```
// Display selected order
orderBox Box { columns = 1
  children = [header, lines, totals, shipping, mapBox] };
```

As mentioned earlier, the name of the overall user interface for this super-widget is "orderBox," and this statement identifies it. The line says that orderBox is a box with a single column, with five components: a header, lines, totals, shipping, and a mapBox.

The header is one of my standard patterns, a two-column table of prompts and values:

```
header Box = new Box { columns = 2,
 children = [
  hblOrderNumber, hbfOrderNumber,
  hblCustomerNumber, hbfCustomerNumber,
  hblCustomerName, hbfCustomerName
 ]};

hblOrderNumber TextLabel { text = "Order Number" };
hbfOrderNumber TextLabel { };
hblCustomerNumber TextLabel { text = "Customer Number" };
hbfCustomerNumber TextLabel { };
hblCustomerName TextLabel { text = "Customer Name" };
hbfCustomerName TextLabel { };
```

We use this pattern all the time in the green screen, with literals on the left for the field prompts, and data values on the right. Since this example uses TextLabel widgets for everything, it's actually more like output fields because I can change the values of the "literals" (the left column) just as easily as the right.

My naming convention might seem a little strange here. I use a prefix that defines the box the field is in and whether it's a label or a field. The labels are the descriptions in the left column, and the fields are the actual data values in the right column. So, "hblOrderNumber" is the label for the order number in the header box. (The "hbl" stands for "header box, label.") Similarly, "hbfOrderNumber" is the data field that will contain the actual value of the order number. (The "hbf" stands for "header box, field.") If possible, the rest of the widget name is the field name that the data will be coming from. This first field comes from the order header, specifically Order.Header.OrderNumber, so I use the name "OrderNumber."

Obviously, naming conventions are a very personal thing. It's up to you what to use, but I highly recommend two simple rules: be consistent, and if you're working with others, come up with a shared naming convention.

Also, this box can be created very easily using the WYSIWYG designer. Just remember to name each field as you drop it, and the designer will do the heavy lifting for you. There's one caveat: the designer tends to add new fields at the *top* of the list, so you might see the fields in the opposite order from which you added them. There's no functional difference; I'm just an old green-screen guy, and I like my fields listed from top to bottom, left to right, so I will go into the code and rearrange them.

The next portion of the UI displays the order lines, using the EGL Rich UI's Grid widget:

```
lines Box = new Box { children = [ orderLines ]};
orderLines Grid {
 columns = [
  new GridColumn{name = "ItemNumber",
   displayName = "Item Number"},
  new GridColumn{name = "Description" },
  new GridColumn{name = "Quantity" },
  new GridColumn{name = "Price" },
  new GridColumn{name = "Extended" }
 ],
 data = (new any[])
};
```

You'll learn about the Grid widget in detail later in this chapter. It is perhaps the most important widget for any business application. In its simplest form, it's a set of column definitions and an array of data. However, there's a lot more to it than that. For now, just take a look at this simple grid, in which I define the column names and widths. The names, in particular, are important, as you'll see later.

Next, I need another box, this time showing the totals. It's functionally equivalent to the header box:

```
totals Box = new Box { columns = 2,
 children = [
  tblTax, tbfTax,
  tblFreight, tbfFreight,
  tblTotal, tbfTotal
 ]};

tblTax TextLabel { text = "Tax" };
tbfTax TextLabel { };
tblFreight TextLabel { text = "Shipping and Handling" };
tbfFreight TextLabel { };
tblTotal TextLabel { text = "Order Total" };
tbfTotal TextLabel { };
```

This is the map control box:

```
shipping Box = new Box { columns = 4, paddingTop = 30,
  children = [
    new TextLabel { text = "Ship To" },
    new TextLabel { },
    new TextLabel { text = "Map:" },
    mapCB
  ]
};
mapCB CheckBox { };
```

The map control box has four columns: the label "Ship To," the actual ship-to value, the label "Map:," and a checkbox. The checkbox has a name, "mapCB," and is defined right under the box. Right now, that checkbox doesn't do anything. Later, I'll connect it to a function to display or hide the actual map.

I did this box just a little differently. I created each of the widgets anonymously, *except* for the checkbox. If you do this, the only issue is that you can only access the anonymous widgets through the children array of the parent box, using the absolute index of the field. It's an option, especially for labels that don't change, but as you'll see, it's a bit messy for fields that need to be modified. I went out of my way to give a name to the checkbox, though. You'll learn why as I expand the logic section.

The code stub that supports the map is shown here:

```
mapBox Box { visibility = "hidden", children = [ map ] };
map TextLabel { text = "YOUR MAP HERE" };
```

This is a very simple box, with one child component. Eventually, this will be a GoogleMap, but there's another step involved for that. For now, it's just a dummy field.

There's something special about this particular box. Its visibility is set to "hidden" at construction time, meaning it doesn't display. I'll have to do something to make it appear. (Think checkbox!)

That's enough to give you a good introduction to the user interface. Now, it's time to review the logic. The initial construction function just calls the function that shows the data:

```
function onConstruction()
  showOrder("ABC123");
end
```

In a production super-widget, you really shouldn't have any code in the construction function, since the super-widget needs to be told by its parent what to display. So, before I go into production, I have to disable this line of code. That's why I would really like parameters to be passed during the construction, or at least be able to identify whether I'm running in production or design mode.

The code to show an order is pretty straightforward:

```
function showOrder(orderNumber string)
  order Order;
  OrderLib.getOrder(orderNumber, order);
```

I get the order using the library function getOrder. (Remember, this is currently a placeholder.) Once I've gotten the order, I stuff the values into the widgets:

```
hbfOrderNumber.text = order.Header.OrderNumber;
hbfCustomerNumber.text = order.Header.CustomerNumber;
hbfCustomerName.text = order.Header.CustomerName;
```

The named widgets are very easy. Simple widgets are basically treated as text, so I just set the **text** property of the widget to change the displayed value.

The code to fill the grid, though, is pretty amazing. This single line of code updates the entire grid from the Lines array in the Order record:

```
orderLines.data = order.Lines as any[];
```

It does this by field name. The Lines array is an array of OrderLine records, and the names in the OrderLine record must match the names of the GridColumns. For example, the item number field is identified in the grid with the first GridColumn definition. (Go back to the UI definition, if you want to see the grid definition.) The name, ItemNumber, is the name that must be found in the OrderLine record.

Note that the columns don't have to be in the same order as the fields in the record, and the column heading doesn't have to match the field name. If they don't match (as happens to be the case in the column), you override the column heading using the **displayName** keyword in the GridColumn definition.

Updating the totals table is the same as updating the header table:

```
tbfTax.text = order.Header.Tax;
tbfFreight.text = order.Header.Freight;
tbfTotal.text = order.Header.Total;
```

This is the last bit, the anonymous widget in the shipping table:

```
(shipping.children[2] as TextLabel).text = order.Header.ShippingAddr;
end
```

As noted earlier, you can update a widget by accessing it directly through the children array of the parent box. However, it's a little more involved, and not entirely intuitive. Entries in the array aren't necessarily widgets, so I have to cast the entry as a widget. Of course, I also have to know the specific index of the widget I want to update; if that changes, I have to change this code. I could use a named constant for the index, but if I'm going that far, why not just name the widget, and be done with it? I'd say my position is that anonymity is probably best for widgets whose values never change or need to be accessed, which pretty much leaves boxes and TextLabels.

One very important note: I've done absolutely nothing regarding formatting. All I've done is add the widgets to the user interface and then fill them from the placeholder function. Before presenting this to the end user, I need to add at least some basic formatting. Before I do that, let's take a look at the barebones interface.

First, Figure 7.18 shows the panel in design mode. As you might recall from Chapter 3, design mode presents the widgets within a grid that displays their extents, with rectangles delineating the various components.

Next, Figure 7.19 shows the preview mode for the same widget. Since the preview mode is actually the output resulting from running the code in a

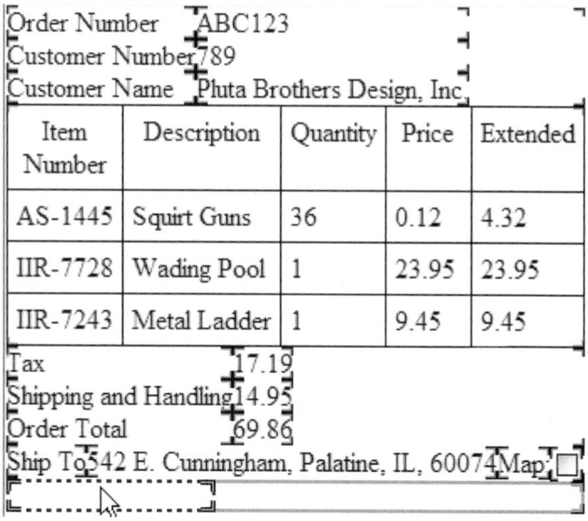

Order Number	ABC123			
Customer Number	789			
Customer Name	Pluta Brothers Design, Inc.			

Item Number	Description	Quantity	Price	Extended
AS-1445	Squirt Guns	36	0.12	4.32
IIR-7728	Wading Pool	1	23.95	23.95
IIR-7243	Metal Ladder	1	9.45	9.45

Tax 17.19
Shipping and Handling 14.95
Order Total 69.86
Ship To 542 E. Cunningham, Palatine, IL, 60074 Map:

Figure 7.18: This is what the UI looks like in the WYSIWYG designer.

sort of interpreted sandbox, you see what the widget would look like in real time, without any grid marks or bounding rectangles. This is a much cleaner view, better suited to judging the visual characteristics of the panel.

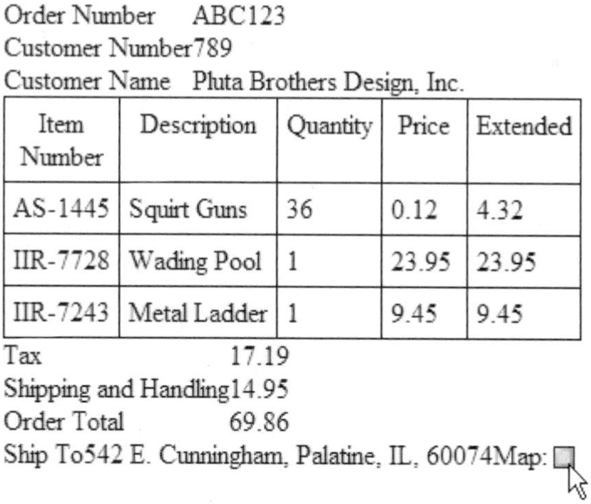

Order Number	ABC123			
Customer Number	789			
Customer Name	Pluta Brothers Design, Inc.			

Item Number	Description	Quantity	Price	Extended
AS-1445	Squirt Guns	36	0.12	4.32
IIR-7728	Wading Pool	1	23.95	23.95
IIR-7243	Metal Ladder	1	9.45	9.45

Tax 17.19
Shipping and Handling 14.95
Order Total 69.86
Ship To 542 E. Cunningham, Palatine, IL, 60074 Map:

Figure 7.19: This is the preview of a completely unadorned user interface.

Whether you look at the design view or the preview mode, you see that the basic interface is just that: basic. Everything is tightly compressed, with no real formatting. Now, I want to add some flair.

Step 3: Adding a Little Style

HTML formatting has evolved quite a bit over the years, but probably the single most important enhancement has been the introduction of style sheets, or more precisely the *Cascading Style Sheet* (CSS) concept. While CSS had a bit of a rocky road at first, it is now universally accepted as the primary method to provide formatting to HTML.

EGL Rich UI is well positioned to take advantage of the features that CSS provides. For one thing, the CSS editor inside of the Rational tools is probably the best one available. More importantly, the EGL Rich UI syntax is built to support CSS classes.

Right off the bat, when you create a new EGL Rich UI project, you get a CSS file with the same name. Since it's not an EGL file, it's located in the WebContent folder. More specifically, it's in the WebContent\css folder. In the example we're discussing, the project is named "iRUI," so the CSS file is named "iRUI.css." You can expand the WebContent folder to see it, as shown in Figure 7.20

Eventually, I'll go back and add some styles to that file. First, though, I have to get the UI ready to handle it. I'll start with something simple: formatting the non-grid boxes so that the labels are differentiated from the fields. I'd do something similar on a green screen, usually by using color. Let's do that here. The beauty of CSS is that I don't have to select the colors yet; I'm just going to add a class to each of the boxes, and then add another class to the labels and fields. Once that's done, I can edit the iRUI.css file to apply my styles.

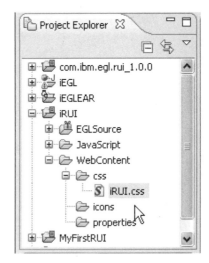

Figure 7.20: The project's CSS file (iRUI. css) is located in the css folder under WebContent.

If you remember the original intent, you can see that I've got two basic box styles: headings and totals. In one, the labels are dark blue and left-justified, while in the other, the labels normal (black) and right-justified. (There's no particular reason for these design choices; that's just the way I want to do it.)

It's quite simple to do this, really. I just have to assign an overall class to each of the boxes I want to style, and then I have to assign a different class to each of the widgets, to identify the labels. Here's an example of the kind of changes I need to make:

```
header Box = new Box { columns = 2, class = "heading",

hblOrderNumber TextLabel {
  text = "Order Number", class = "label" };
```

I change the style of the header box to "heading," and I change the style of the hblOrderNumber TextLabel to "label." Then, I edit iRUI.css and add a couple of lines:

```
body { font-family: "Verdana"; }
.heading .label { text-align: left;
  background-color: blue; color: white; }
```

The first line changes the font to Verdana, which is one of the nicer sans-serif fonts and is pretty universally supported. (I don't like serif fonts, so I usually use a sans-serif one for my panels.) Note that the labels are now blue-on-white and left-justified. These decisions about colors and fonts are ultimately in the hands of the folks who make the screens pretty. It's my job to just get the classes assigned to the widgets, and EGL makes that really easy.

Figure 7.21 shows what I get after this simple change. It's not even close, but the point is that it's easy to finish the job.

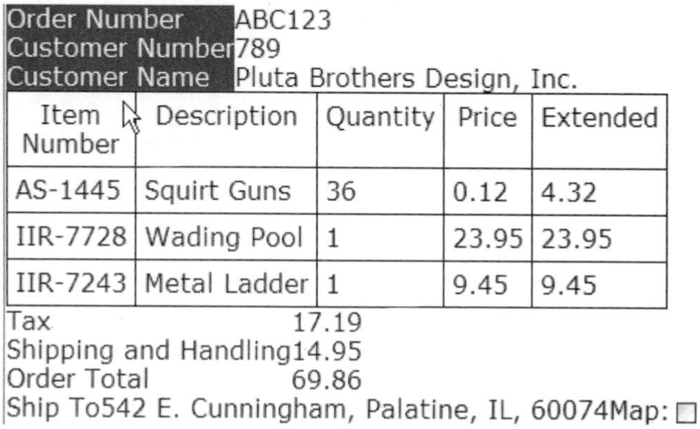

Order Number	ABC123			
Customer Number	789			
Customer Name	Pluta Brothers Design, Inc.			

Item Number	Description	Quantity	Price	Extended
AS-1445	Squirt Guns	36	0.12	4.32
IIR-7728	Wading Pool	1	23.95	23.95
IIR-7243	Metal Ladder	1	9.45	9.45

Tax 17.19
Shipping and Handling 14.95
Order Total 69.86
Ship To 542 E. Cunningham, Palatine, IL, 60074 Map: ☐

Figure 7.21: The first style changes make a difference right away.

I'm going to add a few more tweaks, and then I'll assign the **heading** class to the header and shipping boxes, and the **totals** class to the totals box. I'll also assign the **label** class to every label, and **field** to every field.

Now, back to the CSS to right-justify the totals, add a little padding between the fields, and add a gap between the bottom of the totals and the top of the shipping section:

```
.totals .label, .totals .field { text-align: right }
.label, .field { padding: 3px 10px 2px 10px }
.totals { padding-bottom: 20px }
```

As you can see in Figure 7.22, the results are not too shabby, especially since none of the actual formatting is done in the program. Unfortunately, things don't always work that way. I haven't yet established an easy way to assign classes to grid columns, and because of that, I can't easily assign formatting. The most important piece of that is the width. For now, I have to do that manually.

Order Number	ABC123			
Customer Number	789			
Customer Name	Pluta Brothers Design, Inc.			

Item Number	Description	Quantity	Price	Extended
AS-1445	Squirt Guns	36	0.12	4.32
IIR-7728	Wading Pool	1	23.95	23.95
IIR-7243	Metal Ladder	1	9.45	9.45

Tax	17.19
Shipping and Handling	14.95
Order Total	69.86

| Ship To | 542 E. Cunningham, Palatine, IL, 60074 | Map: | □ |

Figure 7.22: Add a little padding and right-justify the totals, and things start looking very good.

The good news is that the only thing that usually requires width adjustment is the grid, so let's get that done. I basically assign a width in pixels to each column, like this:

```
new GridColumn{name = "ItemNumber", width = 90,
```

I end up with the result in Figure 7.23. Still, the grid is pretty bland. The problem is that it's not particularly easy to assign classes at the individual cell level, or even at the row and column level. Even if you could, you would still run into issues if the formatting of a cell in one row needed to be different than the formatting of the same cell in a different row.

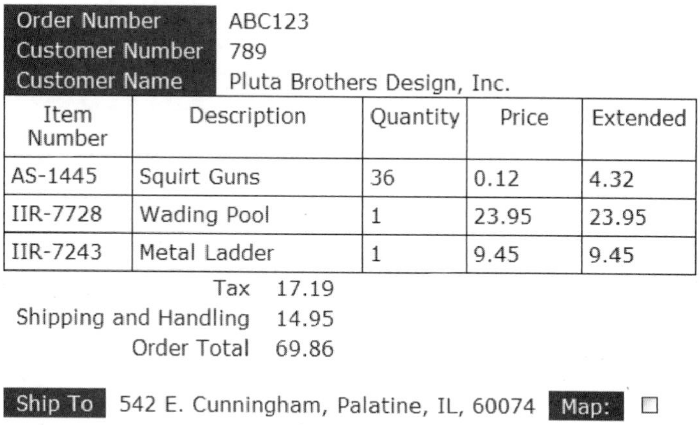

Order Number	ABC123
Customer Number	789
Customer Name	Pluta Brothers Design, Inc.

Item Number	Description	Quantity	Price	Extended
AS-1445	Squirt Guns	36	0.12	4.32
IIR-7728	Wading Pool	1	23.95	23.95
IIR-7243	Metal Ladder	1	9.45	9.45

Tax 17.19
Shipping and Handling 14.95
Order Total 69.86

Ship To 542 E. Cunningham, Palatine, IL, 60074 Map: ☐

Figure 7.23: Here is the table with widths assigned.

To address this, the EGL Rich UI designers came up with an extremely flexible mechanism called a *behavior*. A behavior is a callback function that is invoked as each cell is rendered. It's like an exit point that allows you to get in and change things manually. A number of predefined behaviors have been supplied with the tool. I'm going to use two of them to show you how they work. (These behaviors actually are assigned by default when you add a table; I removed them for this example, so that I could show what happens when I add them back in.)

I'll revisit behaviors again shortly, but for now, watch what happens. By simply adding the **behaviors** and **headerBehaviors** keywords and the names of the appropriate behaviors, I assign two predefined formatting styles. One alternates the colors on the rows, while the other distinguishes the header cells from the data cells:

```
orderLines Grid {
  behaviors  = [ GridBehaviors.alternatingColor ],
  headerBehaviors = [ GridBehaviors.grayCells ],
  columns = [
```

The result is shown in Figure 7.24. The last thing I need to do, then, is to line up the totals. I do that by right-justifying the columns in the grid, and then manually adjusting the width of the totals fields until I get a pleasing match.

Order Number	ABC123			
Customer Number	789			
Customer Name	Pluta Brothers Design, Inc.			

Item Number	Description	Quantity	Price	Extended
AS-1445	Squirt Guns	36	0.12	4.32
IIR-7728	Wading Pool	1	23.95	23.95
IIR-7243	Metal Ladder	1	9.45	9.45

Tax	17.19
Shipping and Handling	14.95
Order Total	69.86

Ship To   542 E. Cunningham, Palatine, IL, 60074   Map: ☐

Figure 7.24: Here is the basic table with a few predefined EGL behaviors added.

Unfortunately, space does not permit a complete tutorial on all of the Rich UI widgets, and the Grid widget in particular, here. Much like the ability to create the best green screens depends on expertise with subfile programming, your ability to develop really powerful Rich UI business applications depends on your knowledge of and ability to manipulate the Grid widget. In this example, right-justifying columns in a grid requires adding a style, and adding a style in a grid requires at least a brief introduction to behaviors.

A lot more information on behaviors exists in the EGL Café (IBM's online EGL community). In fact, the particular technique I'm going to use here came from something Chris Laffra posted back in December, 2008. Again, this isn't a tutorial on EGL Rich UI programming, but I'll try to explain the basics. Whenever a grid is rendered, EGL Rich UI creates an HTML table based on the GridColumns defined for the table. EGL Rich UI then iterates through the rows and columns of the data table (the one assigned to the keyword **data** on the grid definition), and starts formatting the rows and cells.

Each time a cell is created, EGL Rich UI checks one of two keywords, depending on whether this is a column heading or a data cell. For column headings, EGL Rich UI checks the **headerBehaviors** keyword, and for data cells, it check the **behaviors** keyword, to see if any functions have been defined. If one or more functions are listed, those functions are called in sequence, to allow the programmer to modify the cell in whatever way he or she thinks is needed. As a first example of this, let's right-justify the data columns for quantity, price, and extended quantity.

Remember, I previously added **GridBehavior.alternatingColor** to the grid. The **alternatingColor** behavior is a predefined behavior. You can find it in the GridBehaviors source file of the com.ibm.egl.rui_1.0.0 project, shown in Figure 7.25.

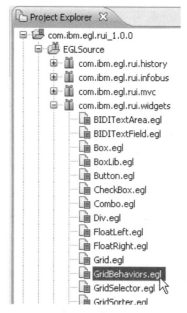

Figure 7.25: Expand the com.ibm.egl. rui_1.0.0 to find the predefined behavior GridBehaviors.

The code for that particular behavior is here:

```
function alternatingColor(
  grid Grid in, td Widget in, row any in,
  rowNumber int in, column GridColumn in)
  if (rowNumber % 2 == 1)
   td.backgroundColor = "lightblue";
  end
end
```

All behaviors have the same structure. They receive five parameters:

- The objects that represent the entire grid
- The GridColumn for the current column
- The formatted cell
- The data row where the data came from
- The row number

This gives the programmer everything necessary to modify the cell as needed. In the case of **alternatingColor**, the logic checks the row number. If it's an odd number, it changes the background to light blue. This illustrates the concept very well, although I prefer using CSS over a hardcoded formatting value, and that's how my behavior will work.

The modifications are very simple. First, I add another behavior to the grid, called **formatCells**:

```
behaviors = [
 GridBehaviors.alternatingColor,
 formatCells ],
```

I don't qualify the function name because it is local. Now, I just have to write the formatCells function. That's easy:

```
function formatCells(
 grid Grid in, cell Widget in, row any in,
 rowNumber int in, column GridColumn in)
 // On all rows, set values
 if (column.name == "Quantity"
  or column.name == "Price"
  or column.name == "Extended")
  cell.class += " right";
 end
end
```

Note that this code uses the same parameter list as the alternatingColor function.

After that, the code is almost trivial: check the column name to see if it's one of the three columns I want to right justify. It is, so append "right" to the cell's class value. Note that I am appending, not replacing, by using the "+=" operator instead of just an equal sign. If I were to replace the class, I would lose any previous classes, including the predefined value **EglRuiGridCell**, which is added by the EGL Rich UI runtime and provides some specific formatting. When I lose that particular class, I do get right-justified data, but I lose some other formatting, and the cell doesn't match other columns in the table.

You might be thinking, "What is this 'right' class?" I did gloss over that; I had to add that particular class to the CSS file with one little line:

```
.right { text-align: right }
```

Now, any cell with a class of **right** will be right-justified. The result is shown in Figure 7.26.

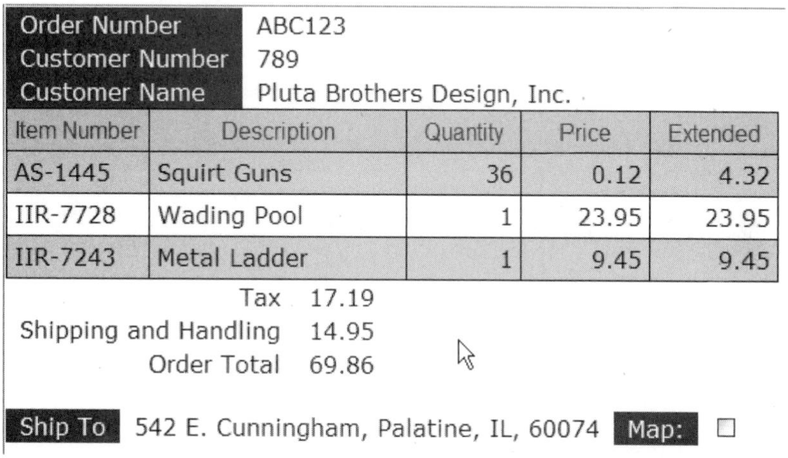

Order Number	ABC123			
Customer Number	789			
Customer Name	Pluta Brothers Design, Inc.			

Item Number	Description	Quantity	Price	Extended
AS-1445	Squirt Guns	36	0.12	4.32
IIR-7728	Wading Pool	1	23.95	23.95
IIR-7243	Metal Ladder	1	9.45	9.45

	Tax	17.19
Shipping and Handling	14.95
Order Total	69.86

Ship To 542 E. Cunningham, Palatine, IL, 60074 Map: ☐

Figure 7.26: The new formatCells behavior right-justifies my columns nicely.

Now that the appropriate columns in the grid are right-justified, I can turn my focus to the last part of the user interface, lining up the totals. It's pretty simple; I just have to widen the label and field cells in the totals box. I can do that either in the CSS or in the EGL code itself.

Since I have to specify the widths for the grid columns in the code, it's reasonable to do the same for the totals box. All it takes is adding the width to the first instance of **label** and **field** in the totals table. While the exact widths take a little trial and error, I start by adding the widths of the first four columns to get the width of the label and then use the width of the fifth column for the field. After a little tweaking for cell padding and column separators, I end up with the following:

```
tblTax TextLabel { text="Tax", class="label", width=430 };
tbfTax TextLabel { class="field", width=80 };
```

This, in turn, produces the interface shown in Figure 7.27. I can sit in front of users with this, and get their feedback. At this point, changing columns around, adding and removing fields, modifying prompts, and even changing fronts and colors is very easy to do with the WYSIWYG designer. More importantly, it can be done interactively, with the user.

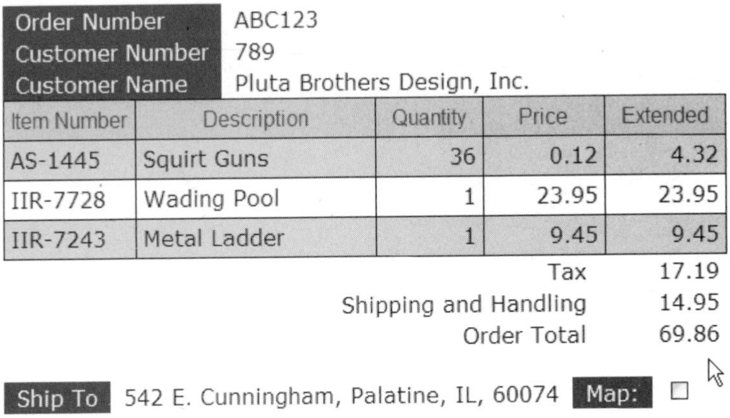

Order Number	ABC123			
Customer Number	789			
Customer Name	Pluta Brothers Design, Inc.			
Item Number	Description	Quantity	Price	Extended
AS-1445	Squirt Guns	36	0.12	4.32
IIR-7728	Wading Pool	1	23.95	23.95
IIR-7243	Metal Ladder	1	9.45	9.45
			Tax	17.19
		Shipping and Handling		14.95
		Order Total		69.86

Ship To 542 E. Cunningham, Palatine, IL, 60074 Map: ☐

Figure 7.27: A little "class" goes a long way to making a nice interface!

Step 4: Integrating Additional Technologies

The focus of this chapter is supposed to be the multi-tiered applications. Instead, I've gone a little off track, focusing on style and such. Let me digress just a tiny bit further, and then I'll get right back to the meat of the discussion. I promise that you'll appreciate this particular side trip.

The purpose of this excursion is to introduce the concept of extending EGL to integrate other technologies. EGL, both the basic syntax and the Rich

UI, have intrinsic capabilities for extending the language through the use of **ExternalType**. As an example, at one point, the IBM team provided a *very* basic integration to the GoogleMaps API. To get more information, go to *http://code.google.com/apis/maps*.

In short, GoogleMaps is a service of Google than can be accessed freely using some relatively simple JavaScript. What IBM did was wrap that API within **ExternalType** in EGL Rich UI. I'm going to show you how to incorporate that particular API into your interface. You would use a similar procedure for any other external technology, whether you wrote the interface yourself or got it from a third party.

You usually need two pieces of code to add an external type: the native code for the component (in Java or JavaScript), and the EGL definition that extends the language to call that native code. The EGL code goes into your EGL source folder, while for EGL Rich UI, the native code goes into the WebContent folder. Where exactly this code goes depends on the code itself, but I like that the GoogleMap extensions go into the same folder, google.map, in both locations.

So, I have to create a package called "google.map," and also a folder in WebContent called "google.map." Creating a package in EGL is easy enough; you've seen it several times in this book already. Creating a folder in WebContent, however, is new. Right-click the WebContent folder in the iRUI project, select New from the context menu, and then select Folder from the submenu, as shown in Figure 7.28.

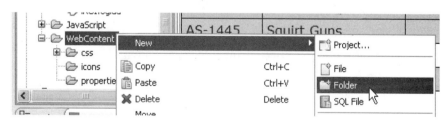

Figure 7.28: Adding a new folder is a simple operation.

Figure 7.29 show the google.map folder being added to the WebContent section of the project. Once I've done that, I just have to copy in the two pieces I mentioned earlier.

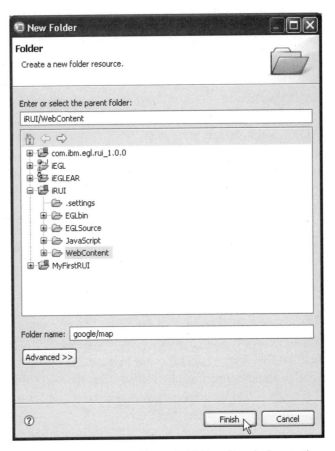

Figure 7.29: You can even add a nested folder with a single operation.

When I'm done, the iRUI project looks like Figure 7.30.

The GoogleMap.egl source file gets pasted right into the google.map folder, as shown in Figure 7.31.

The corresponding native code file, GoogleMap.js, goes into the google/map folder under WebContent, as shown in Figure 7.32. I would do the same thing (with different names) for any third-party external type.

Figure 7.30: Note the package "google. map" and the folders "google" and "google/map."

Figure 7.31: Paste the GoogleMap.egl file into the google.map package.

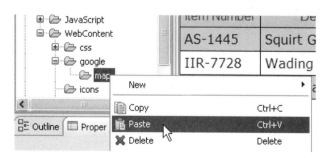

Figure 7.32: Paste the GoogleMap.js file into the google/map folder.

That does it. Now, the iRUI package has all the components needed to take advantage of the GoogleMap external type. Figure 7.33 shows the project and its two new files.

Figure 7.33: Here is the iRUI project, with its two new components in place.

This would be a good time to take a look at the GoogleMap.egl file, which defines the external type:

```
/*
 * Licensed Materials - Property of IBM
 *
 * Copyright IBM Corporation 2008. All Rights Reserved.
 *
 * U.S. Government Users Restricted Rights - Use, duplication or
 * disclosure restricted by GSA DP Schedule Contract with IBM Corp.
 */
package google.map;

ExternalType GoogleMap extends Widget type JavaScriptObject {
  relativePath = "google/map",
  javaScriptName = "GoogleMap"
}
  function showAddresses(address String[] in, labels string[] in);
end
```

Since this is the entire file, I've kept the IBM copyright intact. You'll see a snippet of the corresponding JavaScript file a little later; remember that it, too, is governed by the same copyright.

External types are beyond the scope of this book. However, I think they're a key to the long-term success of the language, both on the server side (in Java) and on the client (in JavaScript). The recent introduction of external types to access Dojo widgets is a perfect example of their power: EGL can be quickly extended to make use of the latest technology, without having to wait for fundamental changes to the language. And these external types can be developed by anyone, not just IBM. This opens up the possibility of a rich set of components created by the third-party community.

Therefore, despite the very technical nature of external types, I want to briefly discuss their basic structure. The EGL part is actually relatively simple, as the previous listing shows. You basically define the new type, make sure it has a name, and then identify the location of the backing native code. In this case, the external type is in package google.map. It is of type **JavaScriptObject** (server-side objects are of type **JavaObject**), with native code in the file GoogleMap (the .js extension is implied), in the folder google/map. This neatly ties together the two files I just added.

The only other bit of code is defining the functions. That's done using standard EGL syntax, as if you were defining a local function. The only difference is that, instead of the body and an **end** opcode, the function definition for an external type's function is just a semicolon. (This is the same syntax used in interface objects, something you'll see in the next section, when I tie the tiers together.)

The function needs to match a corresponding definition in the native JavaScript file. In this case, the function is showAddresses. It is defined to take two parameters: an array of strings for addresses, and another array of strings for descriptions. The JavaScript code looks like this:

```
"showAddresses" : function(
 /*String[]*/ addresses,
 /*String[]*/ descriptions ) {
 if (this.key) {
  this.addresses = addresses;
  this.descriptions = descriptions;
  var googleMap = this;
  egl.keepTrying(
   function() { return (googleMap.geocoder); },
   function() { googleMap.refresh(); },
   100);
 }
},
```

Although I don't have the space to go into this code in detail, it does show the way that the EGL external type can encapsulate JavaScript of any arbitrary complexity. It comes down to the person who writes the external type, but done correctly, this is a hugely powerful concept.

Let me show you what I mean. In just a few lines of code, I can enable a checkbox-enabled GoogleMap. First, add an event handler to the mapCB checkbox:

```
mapCB CheckBox { class = "field", onClick ::= doMapCB };
```

This says whenever someone clicks the checkbox, call the doMapCB function. You'll get an error because the function hasn't been defined yet, but that's okay.

Next, change the map widget from a dummy TextLabel to a GoogleMap:

```
map GoogleMap { };
```

This, by the way, requires importing the GoogleMap widget. You can use content-assist to find the GoogleMap widget, which will automatically add the import. Alternatively, if you know the name of the widget, you can simply add the line above. When you see the error "GoogleMap cannot be resolved," just put your cursor on the line, and press Ctrl-Shift-M to add the import.

The last piece of code is the actual function that updates the map:

```
function doMapCB(e event in)
  if (mapCB.selected)
   address string =
    (shipping.children[2] as TextLabel).text;
   map.showAddresses([address], ["Ship To"]);
   mapBox.visibility = "visible";
  else
   mapBox.visibility = "hidden";
  end
end
```

If someone can show me something easier, I'll be impressed. The signature is common to all event handlers: you get a single parameter with the event that caused the function to be called. This is especially important when you have a common event handler to handle lots of events; the event parameter will tell you which widget caused the call. In this case, however, I've got what amounts to a dedicated event handler, so I know what widget was selected and what happened—the checkbox was clicked. The only thing I don't know yet is whether it was clicked on or off, and that's really easy to check.

The code first checks the state of the checkbox (the selected variable). If it's true, I invoke the GoogleMap to show the address. However, some of my bad habits are coming back to haunt me: since I didn't give the address field a name, I have to go get the data from the address field using the **shipping.children[2]** technique, which as you can see is a bit of a pain. Had I given the widget a name, I could have used that name right in the **showAddresses** call. Since I didn't, I have to extract the address first. Anyway, once I have the address, I just invoke the map widget to show it. Then, I make the whole map box visible by setting the **visibility** attribute to **visible**.

If, on the other hand, the checkbox is *not* selected, my life is much easier. I just hide the box by setting **visibility** to **hidden**.

A piece of cake! To see the UI work, I first click the checkbox at the bottom of the user interface, as shown in Figure 7.34.

Figure 7.34: Click the box....

This invokes the doMap function, which will detect that the map checkbox (mapCB) is selected. It will then show the address in the GoogleMap and make the map visible. The result is shown in Figure 7.35.

Figure 7.35: ...The map appears!

One of the limitations with this approach is the Google API key. You have to sign on to Google and enter in the domain where you will be using the API. Google generates a huge string for you, which acts as the key. You need to then go back into the GoogleMap.js file and enter the key. Rather than make my key visible to all the readers of this book, I'm setting the value to null for the project. That means whenever I try to use a Google-Map, I get a screen like Figure 7.36.

You'll have to go to Google and sign up for a key of your own. I'm sorry, but that also means you have to set up a Gmail account. It's the price you pay if you want to take advantage of the Google APIs. I think it's a cheap price, but it depends on how much you hate creating Gmail accounts. Personally, I've probably created a dozen, most of which have long been forgotten, so I don't worry about it too much. I just don't give them any

Figure 7:36: The GoogleMap widget does this when you don't have a key.

personal information, so I don't feel like I'm being harvested for spam lists.

Section 5: Replacing a Synchronous Call with a Delegate

Oh my gosh, can we possibly be back to the architecture? I know, we just took something of a scenic route (seriously), but it's time well spent. However, it's time to get back to what this code was meant to do, which is communicate between multiple tiers to create a working business application. So, let's create that application, shall we?

This is the entire application, from head to toe:

```
package com.pbd.app;
import com.pbd.app.widget.*;
import com.ibm.egl.rui.widgets.*;
handler OrderInquiry type RUIhandler {
  initialUI = [ui],
  onConstructionFunction = initialization,
  cssFile="css/iRUI.css"}

// The UI consists of the prompt and the display
ui Box { columns = 1, children = [ promptBox, new Box ] };

// Prompt box - prompt for order number
promptBox Box = new Box { children = [
  new TextLabel {
    text = "Order Number: ",
    paddingRight = 10 },
  orderField,
  new Button { text = "Read", onClick ::= readOrder }
]};
orderField TextField { paddingLeft = 10 };
```

```
function initialization()
end

function readOrder(e event in)
  orderGrid OrderGrid{};
  orderGrid.showOrder(orderField.text);
  ui.removeChild(ui.children[2]);
  ui.appendChild(orderGrid.orderBox);
 end
end
```

The primary user interface is named "ui." It has two boxes as children. The first has three widgets: a prompt text, an enterable field, and a button. The second box is empty. When the user clicks the button, the readOrder function is invoked, which creates OrderGrid to read the order and then replaces the second element in ui with the newly read order.

These are the only two lines that might be a little tricky; while you can access widgets in a box through the children array, it's not a good idea to change widgets by just setting values in the array. Instead, use the **removeChild** and **appendChild** methods to remove children. The code here always removes the second widget and then adds a new one, presumably back into the second place. I'm obviously counting on there being exactly two widgets in ui.

The application works very well, as you can see in Figures 7.37 and 7.38.

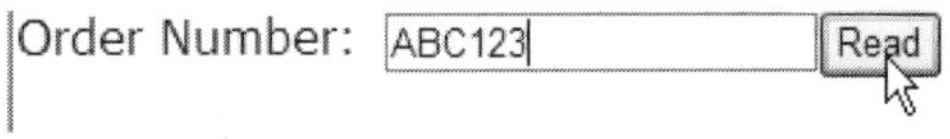

Order Number: `ABC123`   Read

Figure 7.37:The first time, only the prompt is displayed.

Order Number:	ABC123		Read		
Order Number	ABC123				
Customer Number	789				
Customer Name	Pluta Brothers Design, Inc.				
Item Number	Description	Quantity	Price	Extended
AS-1445	Squirt Guns	36	0.12	4.32
IIR-7728	Wading Pool	1	23.95	23.95
IIR-7243	Metal Ladder	1	9.45	9.45
		Tax		17.19
	Shipping and Handling			14.95
	Order Total			69.86

Ship To 542 E. Cunningham, Palatine, IL, 60074 Map: ☐

Figure 7.38: When I click the Read button, the order is displayed.

As you can see, now that I'm not having to explain each line of code, development just gets quicker and quicker. You'll find that to be true as you write more code, too. Creating Rich UI panels really is fast.

Now I've got a great working application, right? The problem, however, is that I'm using a synchronous call. As I explained at the beginning of the chapter, a synchronous call won't work in a multi-tiered environment. So, it's time to move to an asynchronous environment. The first step is to implement a delegate.

Two places need to be changed to implement a delegate. First, getOrder in OrderLib needs to be changed. Then, OrderGrid itself needs to be changed to accept a delegate. I'm going to show you these changes, but not spend a lot of time on them because, in reality, I would need even more listeners. Still, this allows me to implement the service and actually attach to the host, something we haven't done in quite some time.

The changes to OrderLib are tiny. I add a line defining the OrderListener delegate. When this delegate is invoked, it will be passed an **Order** record and an **Error** record:

```
Delegate OrderListener(order Order in, error Error in) end
(...)
 // Get an order
 function getOrder(
  orderNumber string in,
  orderListener OrderListener in)
  order Order = new Order { Header = new OrderHeader {
(...)
  orderListener(order, null);
 end
end
```

I didn't just pull these parameters out of the air. They match the parameters that will be received from the OrderService that I defined in the iEGL project. That service looks like this:

```
function getOrder(orderNumber string in, order Order inOut)
 returns (Error)
```

To determine the parameters that will be passed on a service call, just read through the parameters from left to right, and list the parameter of type **out** or **inOut**. If the function returns a parameter, add it to the end. In this case, the service will return two values, the first of type **Order** and the second of type **Error**. Note that I haven't been checking the error at all. Obviously, I'd need to do that in the production code.

The next modification is to change the getOrder function to have only input parameters. That's really the primary rule for this sort of delegation: any multi-tier function allows only input parameters, one of them being the delegate (the listener). The final modification is at the end of the function; rather than return the error code, I call the delegate with the new order and a null. The null is in place of an error code, since right now the code is doing no error checking. That will change shortly, but it's time to test the code.

The changes to OrderGrid are equally simple. In fact, it's really only one change, splitting apart the function that invokes the getOrder and moving the logic that updates the grid to a listener:

```
function showOrder(orderNumber string)
  OrderLib.getOrder(orderNumber, orderListener);
end

function orderListener(order Order in, error Error in)
  hbfOrderNumber.text = order.Header.OrderNumber;
```

The showOrder function is used to call getOrder to load the data into a local **Order** variable, and then execute some code to load data from the order into the widgets. All showOrder does is send the order number to getOrder, along with a reference to the orderListener function, where all the other logic exists. When orderListener is invoked, one of the parameters is the order, which is used to then load the widgets using *the exact same code as before*.

The fun part about this is that, if I've done this correctly, my test doesn't change at all! Since all I did was change the interaction among the various components of the application, and move from purely synchronous calls to a delegated architecture, the application works exactly the same way as before. The real reason I did this was to connect to the host.

As a side note, my little test program, Test1, also had to be changed to support the new getOrder function. Don't worry; that program is no longer needed, since we now have a much better testing framework in place.

Section 6: Attaching to the Service

Attaching to the service might be where EGL shines brightest at its intended purpose of removing complexity and hiding the plumbing. Think about what's necessary here: you have a client written in JavaScript that will use AJAX to communicate with a program written in Java running on the server. While there are obvious similarities, the two languages are quite different. Somehow, you have to pass complex structures of data between the two. Having done this sort of thing for most of my career, I can tell you that doing this manually would be at the very least a challenge, both in terms of design and coordination of programming. It would probably take several days to design, and maybe a week to implement.

With EGL, it takes a minute or two. I start back in the iEGL project (Tier 2). I go into the EGL source and right-click the service I want to call from Tier 1. I select EGL Services from the context menu and Extract EGL Interface from the resulting submenu, as shown in Figure 7.39.

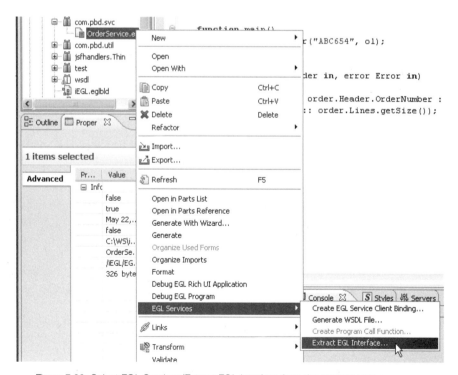

Figure 7.39: Select EGL Services/Extract EGL Interface from the context menu.

This option is designed to create an EGL interface part, which another EGL program can use to access the service. However, the default is to create the interface in the same project as the service, as shown in Figure 7.40. It might be a reasonable default, but it's the wrong default. I want to create the interface in the iRUI (Tier 1) project.

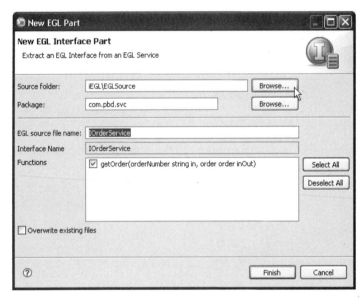

Figure 7.40: I'm ready to create the interface, but I don't want it in this project!

Because RDi-SOA allows me to create both sides of the project in the same workbench, it's a trivial task to correct the default behavior. First, I click the Browse button next to the Source folder field. That brings up the Folder Selection dialog, shown in Figure 7.41.

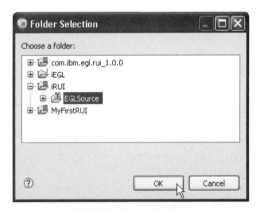

Figure 7.41: Now I can select the EGLSource folder in the iRUI project.

This dialog lets me select the target location for the extract. I expand the iRUI project, click the EGLSource folder, and click OK to continue.

The tool also wants to name the interface by putting the letter *I* in front of the service name, to stand for "Interface," I'm sure, and to avoid conflict with the actual service part. However, you might remember when I talked about creating the framework that I wanted to name the interface in Tier 1 the same as the service in Tier 2. So, I have to change that default as well. That's done in the New EGL Interface Part dialog, as shown in Figure 7.42.

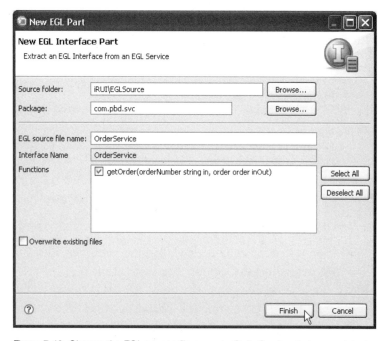

Figure 7.42: Change the EGL source file name to OrderService, to be consistent.

Basically, I just delete the letter *I* and click the Finish button. By default, all the functions in the service are selected. Since I only create pass-through functions in my services to expose business logic, I should always want all those pass-through functions to be exposed, so the default there is good.

Here's the generated interface:

```
package com.pbd.svc;
interface OrderService
 function getOrder(
  orderNumber string in,
  order com.pbd.data.order inOut)
 returns (com.pbd.util.error);  end
```

As you can see, the signature of the getOrder function in the OrderService interface matches the signature of the getOrder function in the OrderService service.

Okay, I've created the interface. Now, I have to modify my business logic proxy function to use that new interface. That involves two small tasks. First, I write the function that calls the service:

```
function getOrderRemote(
 orderNumber string in,
 orderListener OrderListener in)
 order Order;
 orderService OrderService { @RESTBinding
  {baseURI =
  "http://localhost:9080/iEGL/restservices/OrderService"}};
 call orderService.getOrder(orderNumber, order)
  returning to orderListener
  onException ServiceLib.serviceExceptionHandler;
end
```

You'll notice that the getOrderRemote function is very slim, just two lines. The first line defines the service. The **baseURI**, in particular, looks a little tricky, but it's not. You can pretty much copy it in this case; the only thing that should change (if anything) is the port number. (Refer back to Chapter 6, if necessary, to review how to determine the port number in your environment.) In case you want to know the other pieces, **http://localhost** identifies the workstation as the server, while **iEGL** specifies the iEGL (Tier 2) project. The **restservices** part is a special word reserved by EGL for REST service deployment, and of course **OrderService** is the service in iEGL.

The next line invokes the service. Services use callbacks. Usually, that would mean writing a callback here. However, I can pass to the service the listener that was passed to me. That's because back in Step 5, I was careful to make my orderListener signature (an order record and an error record) match the signature of the Order service. If I didn't do that—if I had to manipulate the values passed back from the service before calling the delegate—I'd have to do some additional (and unnecessary) work. I'd have to save the reference to the listener, and then write a callback proxy function here. That proxy function would accept the parameters from the service, extract the relevant bits, and then call the listener. It's definitely more messy than the technique shown here.

The second task is wholly optional, but it helps in the long term, for debugging. Note that I called my new function "getOrderRemote," rather than "getOrder." I will also rename the original getOrder to "getOrderLocal." That being done, I now write a new getOrder function:

```
useLocalGet boolean = true;

// Get an order based on the useLocal flag
function getOrder(
 orderNumber string in,
 orderListener OrderListener in)
 if (useLocalGet)
  getOrderLocal(orderNumber, orderListener);
 else
  getOrderRemote(orderNumber, orderListener);
 end
end
```

The point of this is simple: the **useLocalGet** flag can be set to either true or false to determine the access method for this library. If **useLocalGet** is true, it will create a dummy record, as it has in the past. This can be helpful in making major changes, where you don't want to worry about the additional complexities of invoking the host logic. All that being said, it's time to test the new service call.

There is a slight rub, though. When I set **useLocalGet** to true, I'll use the order data I create in OrderLib.getOrderLocal in iRUI (Tier 1). If I set that same flag to false, it should invoke the service, and then return the data from getOrder in OrderLib in iEGL. However, since one function is a clone of the other, I need to make a change, to make sure I'm using the correct function. I'm going to change getOrderRemote in iRUI to update the order number to append "(T1)" on the end:

```
OrderNumber = orderNumber :: "(T1)",
```

Then, I can test with **useLocalGet** set to true. I should see my local data. Indeed, in Figure 7.43, I do.

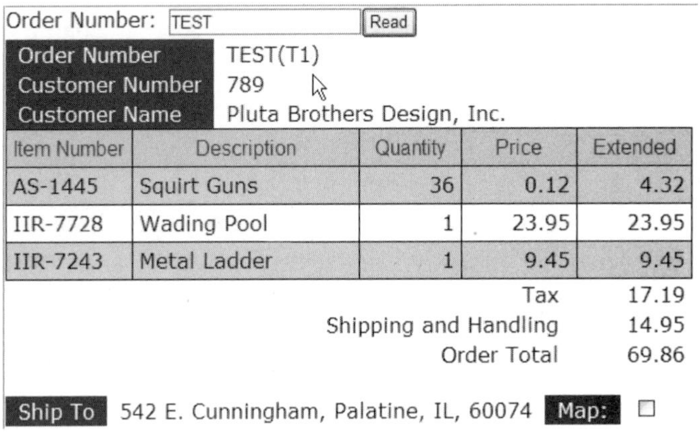

Order Number	TEST(T1)			
Customer Number	789			
Customer Name	Pluta Brothers Design, Inc.			

Order Number: TEST   Read

Item Number	Description	Quantity	Price	Extended
AS-1445	Squirt Guns	36	0.12	4.32
IIR-7728	Wading Pool	1	23.95	23.95
IIR-7243	Metal Ladder	1	9.45	9.45
			Tax	17.19
		Shipping and Handling		14.95
		Order Total		69.86

Ship To   542 E. Cunningham, Palatine, IL, 60074   Map: ☐

Figure 7.43: The "(T1)" marker comes through when the useLocalGet flag is set to true.

I will emulate that by changing the Tier 2 code (in iEGL) to return "(T2)." That's the getOrder function in OrderLib in com.pbd.svc in iEGL. I know it's not strictly necessary—if I change **useLocalGet** to false, and the data comes through without "(T1)," I can assume I went to iEGL—but there is a method to my madness. Besides, it's the very last test in this chapter, so I might as well do it right!

As you can see in Figure 7.44, the test works. I hope by now you would be more surprised if it *didn't* work!

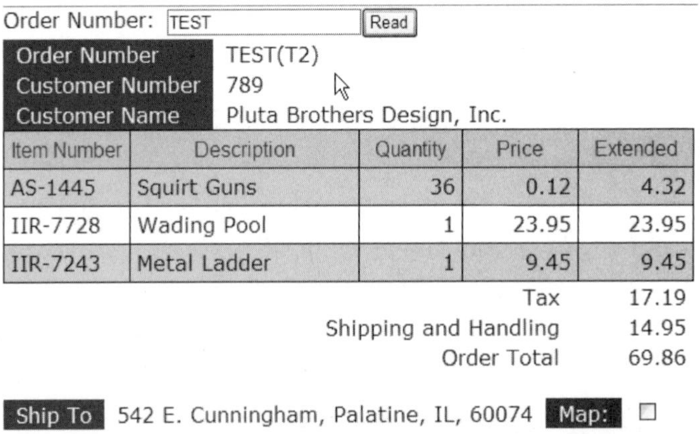

Order Number: TEST   Read

Order Number	TEST(T2)			
Customer Number	789			
Customer Name	Pluta Brothers Design, Inc.			

Item Number	Description	Quantity	Price	Extended
AS-1445	Squirt Guns	36	0.12	4.32
IIR-7728	Wading Pool	1	23.95	23.95
IIR-7243	Metal Ladder	1	9.45	9.45
			Tax	17.19
		Shipping and Handling		14.95
		Order Total		69.86

Ship To   542 E. Cunningham, Palatine, IL, 60074   Map: ☐

Figure 7.44: With useLocalGet set to false, the application does indeed go up to the iEGL tier.

The concept of delegates and callbacks works just like we wanted it to. Now, it's time to incorporate one of the biggest technological advances in EGL Rich UI, the Infobus.

Step 7: Getting on the Infobus

Steps 1 through 4 got us a basic user interface using synchronous calls, which corresponds to the architecture you saw back in Figure 7.1. Steps 5 and 6 attached that UI to the host using a REST service and delegates, mirroring Figure 7.2. Now, it's time to go for the gold, by implementing the Infobus, as shown in Figure 7.3. From a code standpoint, there's not much to change, but conceptually, it takes a little getting used to. First things first, however. I need to define my **InfobusMessage** record. Infobus supports an ID and an object that can contain pretty much anything. Someone subscribes to the Infobus with an ID, and any messages posted with that ID are sent to the subscriber. This is fine, except that I want a little more consistency in my framework. So, I create the **InfobusMessage** record:

```
package com.pbd.util;
record InfobusMessage
 src string;
 action string;
 data any;
end
```

The primary idea here is that I want a source ID (named "src" in my record), which would allow the listener to send a response back. So, if one component sent a message to another component and was expecting a response, the first component would subscribe to a specific ID and put that ID in the src field. Then, the second component would post its response to that ID. Simple, efficient, and easy to do.

After that, the only hard part is assigning specific IDs to each component. To do that, I first insert Infobus support into OrderGrid:

```
private id string;
private ibm InfobusMessage;
function setId(ibmSrc string in)
 id = ibmSrc;
 InfoBus.subscribe(id, listener);
end
```

```
function listener(eventName String in, eventData any in)
 ibm = eventData;
 showOrder(ibm.data);
end

function sendResponse(action string in, data any in)
  InfoBus.publish(ibm.src,
   new InfobusMessage {
   src = id,
   action = action,
   data = data });
end
```

The new code added here is very simple. First, the application controller has to call the setId function, to tell the widget which ID it should listen for. This is crucial because it allows multiple instances of the same widget to exist in the a single application. The widget saves that ID, and then subscribes to it and sits back and listens.

The listener function expects a message with an order number. When one is received, it calls the showOrder function to get the order and populate the widget. The third interface function is sendResponse, which sends a response back to the caller when the read is complete.

To enable responses, I just add a line at the end of the showOrder function to send a response:

```
sendResponse("SHOW", orderBox);
```

Now, I just need to update the application controller to use the Infobus. That's very easy. At the top of the application, I define the IDs for all components:

```
// InfoBus - One event per component
eidApp string = "com.pbd.OE0100";
eidOG string = "com.pbd.OE0100.OrderGrid";
```

In this case, there are only two components: the application itself, and the order widget. However, there could easily be many more.

Now that the widget needs to be initialized, I have to add the initialization code. This involves adding a couple of lines to the initialization function:

```
function initialization()
InfoBus.subscribe(eidApp, listener);
(new OrderGrid {}).setId(eidOG);
end
```

The first line subscribes the application, so that it will listen for responses. The eidApp string contains the value this listener will be keyed to; I then include that as the src field in any messages sent to the widget. That way, the widget knows to whom the response should be sent. The second line instantiates the OrderGrid widget and tells it the ID it should be listening to. In a larger application, I would execute one of these lines for each widget.

With the framework in place, I now just need to modify the program to use the Infobus, rather than the asynchronous call-and-delegate technique:

```
function readOrder(e event in)
InfoBus.publish(eidOG, new InfobusMessage {
  src = eidApp,
  action = "SHOW",
  data = orderField.text } );
end

function listener(eventName String in, object any in)
ibm InfobusMessage = object;
ui.removeChild(ui.children[2]);
ui.appendChild(ibm.data);
end
```

The new code is now completely segmented. The previous version of OrderInquiry instantiated the OrderGrid widget, and then stuffed that widget immediately into its own UI. From that point forward, whenever the widget changed itself, those changes would be reflected in the UI.

While that's all find and good for a fairly rigid interface, it doesn't help so much when you have widgets that can be moved, resized, hidden, and so on. So instead, I changed the code to send a **SHOW** command to the widget, and then wait for a response. When the response is received, it is assumed to be a box to display, and the listener stuffs it into the user interface just like the old code did.

It works perfectly, as you can see in Figure 7.45.

Order Number:	INFOBUS		Read	
Order Number	INFOBUS(T2)			
Customer Number	789			
Customer Name	Pluta Brothers Design, Inc.			

Item Number	Description	Quantity	Price	Extended
AS-1445	Squirt Guns	36	0.12	4.32
IIR-7728	Wading Pool	1	23.95	23.95
IIR-7243	Metal Ladder	1	9.45	9.45

		Tax	17.19
	Shipping and Handling		14.95
	Order Total		69.86

Ship To	542 E. Cunningham, Palatine, IL, 60074	Map:	☐

Figure 7.45: The Infobus version works just like the delegate version.

I'm not quite done with the Infobus, but that's all for this chapter. Next, it's time to finish the application by creating the back-end business logic. Once I've reviewed that portion, I'll return to debugging—an area where the Infobus can really come in handy.

Summary

In this chapter, you learned everything you need to know about using EGL Rich UI to create a business application designed to talk to a server. While the chapter itself is long, it highlights simplicity and productivity of EGL. Once you understand the architectural concepts and have a basic under-standing of the workbench, you will be able to run through these steps in an hour or so. In so doing, you will become proficient in EGL and its syntax.

I hope I've given you an insight into the sheer productivity of EGL. Remember, in Chapters 4 through 6, you learned how to create a complete, multi-tiered architecture on the host, including web services and thin-client interfaces. All of this can be done using a simple, basic syntax, without having to resort to writing a single line of Java or formatting a single XML file. Some other tools can provide some of this, but usually with more work and much less flexibility.

This chapter takes EGL to a new level. Using the same basic syntax, EGL Rich UI created a good-looking rich interface with very little code and no JavaScript. At the same time, any in-house JavaScript expertise can be leveraged through external types, as can third-party packages like the GoogleMap package.

For the first time since the browser became the interface of choice, application developers can focus on the creation of applications, rather than the minutiae of rapidly changing technology. Let's connect up the back end and take this hot rod out for a drive!

Implementing the Business Logic Tier

Here's something to think about: although this book is about building multi-tiered business applications using EGL and the IBM i, this is the first chapter specific to the i. That's because in a good multi-tier design, the UI and service tiers are server-agnostic; they can connect to any sort of business logic. This is truly the case here. You could finish the application from earlier chapters by writing pure EGL code that accessed relational data directly. You could also access logic from any platform, through services, stored procedures, or any of a number of other techniques. However, accessing the IBM i is the focus of this book, and that's what you'll learn about in this chapter.

The other odd thing is that, even though this chapter includes a full code review, it isn't particularly long. One reason for this is that RPG is a really good language for writing server code. It's a procedural language with tight integration to a relational database, which makes for really tight, efficient code. The other reason is that EGL is the only language with built-in support for the i. From implicit conversion between EBCDIC and Unicode to bidirectional parameters to stateful connections, EGL provides the best interface available.

Connecting EGL to the i connects the most efficient interface to the most productive business-logic platform available. Not only that, it's really simple. For this chapter, I created the data structures, wrote the server, and added the logic to the EGL in two hours. Thanks to the architecture, this two hours' worth of work simultaneously enabled ILE RPG business logic for my thin client, my SOAP service, *and* my Rich UI client.

Don't take my word for it, however. Read on, and see for yourself!

Multi-tiered Server Design

I've re-implemented client/server processing on more technologies than I care to remember. Whether it was between a Series/1 and a System/3 or between a PC and an AS/400, using async, bisync, or proprietary protocols, the business side of it was almost always the same. After a while, I didn't even think twice about the basic design, which looked something like Figure 8.1.

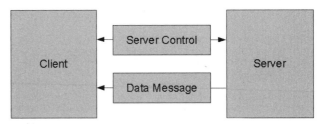

Figure 8.1: This is a standard multi-tier inquiry.

I nearly always used a two-parameter system, with one parameter being the control and the other being the data. The data parameters changed occasionally, but the control structure didn't. The same control structure could be used for any server that I needed to implement.

As my experience with this architecture grew, it turned out that, for the majority of cases, I only needed two basic types of servers: CRUD (Create, Read, Update, Delete) and query. For inquiry applications, I only needed a query server! The basic architecture of the query server is shown in Figure 8.1: the server control record tells the server what to do, and it returns the results in the data message. The server control identifies things like end-of-file and errors.

The CRUD architecture in Figure 8.2 is much the same, except that the data message is sent from the client to the server. For example, on a **write**, this data message is the information that needs to be posted to the database.

Over the years, I've refined this architecture so that I never start from scratch. I do, however, have to spend what is often a substantial amount of time figuring out the technical details of this sort of interface. For example,

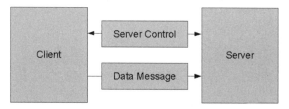

Figure 8.2: For the CRUD server, the data message is sent from the client to the server.

with JSP model II, I need to build the classes that support the call between the JVM and the ILE program. Not only do I have to identify each of the messages, but I have to write code to convert those messages from EBCDIC to ASCII. Then, I have to figure out how to pass that information to the user interface, get the results back, reformat the response for the server, and send it back. I also have to provide session support and a number of other technical pieces. And this is for one of the more technically advanced environments! It gets much worse for others.

That's where EGL comes in. With EGL, you just have to define the records that match your data structures (a very easy task). EGL does the rest of the work. As far as the actual program invocation, that's simply a matter of defining the program using the deployment description, and then adding a **call** opcode to the code.

The Messages

The best place to start is with the messages. The primary message, used in every server, is the server control. In RPG, we use an externally described data structure named DSSVRCTL:

```
R DSSVRCTL
    SCOPCD          2A          TEXT('Opcode')
    SCOPSC          2A          TEXT('Opsubcode')
    SCRTCD          2A          TEXT('Retcode')
    SCRTSC          2A          TEXT('Retsubcode')
    SCCNT           5S 0        TEXT('Count')
    SCMSG           80A         TEXT('Message')
    SCFLD           10A         TEXT('Field')
```

The record is simple enough, and even this is a bit of overkill. For example, I have Opcode and Opsubcode fields. This makes sense when I need dozens of operation codes; having the two values allows me to group similar opcodes for a little easier organization. The same is true of the two return-code values. Since this example only has a few opcodes and return codes, I don't really need the extra fields. Still, I want to show how you would extend the architecture. The Count field is also unused in this example, but it's a good place to return a count, whether of open orders or of currently attached sessions.

The Message and Field values are important. These are the primary vehicles for reporting business-logic errors to the user interface (and thus to the user). I'll discuss this issue later in this chapter.

You might have noticed that all of the fields in this record start with *SC*. That's because they're all defined right here in the message; they're not representing data from some other table. The following message shows the contrasting technique:

```
R DSORDHDR
   OHORDR      10A          TEXT('Order Number')
   OHCUST       6S 0        TEXT('Customer Number')
   CMNAME      50A          TEXT('Customer Name')
   W_ADDR      50A          TEXT('Shipping Address')
   OHSHIP       9S 2        TEXT('Shipping')
   OHTAX        9S 2        TEXT('Tax')
   W_TOTAL      9S 2        TEXT('Order Total')
```

While you can't see it directly in the document, if you went up to the IRUI library on your host and did a **DSPFFD** on the ORDHDR file, you would see the fields OHORDR, OHCUST, and so on, defined the same way as they are here. In fact, I could just as easily define them using the **REFFLD** keyword. However, then you wouldn't be able to see the exact layouts, and I want you to compare those to the EGL records I'll be defining shortly.

Not all of the fields come from the ORDHDR record, though. CMNAME is a foreign field. It's the customer name, and it comes from the CUSMAS file. Also, you'll note two fields whose names start with *W_*; that's my convention for a work field whose value is derived from other fields. You'll see how they're handled in the RPG code.

Here is the order detail message, which contains the order detail fields and one foreign field, the item description:

```
R DSORDDTL
  ODITEM        15A          TEXT('Item Number')
  ODQORD         9S 0        TEXT('Quantity Ordered')
  ODUPRC         9S 3        TEXT('Unit Price')
  ODXAMT         9S 2        TEXT('Extended Amount')
  IMDESC        30A          TEXT('Item Description')
```

While this is a pretty simple example, it covers most of the basic issues you'll see in client/server communication. As I said, this part of the architecture has been working for a long time.

You might be wondering, though, why I have *two* data message definitions. That's because I use a slightly different approach when querying data in one-to-many relationships. If I tried to create a single record that contained all of the data, I'd end up with a record that had both header and detail information, and the header information would be repeated for every detail record. This means unnecessary transmission overhead, the thing I dislike most about SQL result sets. To avoid this, I modify the server structure slightly for situations where I am querying master/detail data, as shown in Figure 8.3.

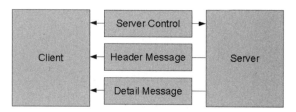

Figure 8.3: With complex data, I add additional parameters for the subsidiary types.

So, in the case of one-to-many relationships, I add an additional parameter for each relationship. I use one opcode to get the header record, and then I change the opcode to read each detail record. I want to emphasize that I only do this in the case of header/detail data. If I just need foreign data from another file (such as the customer name), I simply add that to the message.

Examples will help explain this, so it's time to walk through the RPG code. You should have already installed the IRUI library onto your IBM i using the save file provided. Once that's done, you'll also need a user ID and password that can access that library and the data within it. In my example, I use a user profile named "IRUITEST" with a password of "IRUITEST." In my hosts file on the workstation, I add an entry for IRUIHOST to point to the IP of the IBM i. If you have different values, I'll point out the places you need to change as you go through the first half of this chapter.

The RPG Program, ORDINQR

I name the server "ORDINQR." This is an inquiry server for the order files. The first three characters identify the file or files being queried, and *INQ* identifies a query server (as opposed to **SVR** for a CRUD server). The final *R* denotes this as an RPG program; this is just a long-standing convention.

Sometimes, the server is for multiple files, as it is in this case. The files are ORDHDR and ORDDTL. I start all my file names with the same three characters, which in turn become the first three characters of the server's name. I would use the same approach if this were a server for a single file, such as CUSMAS. In that case, I would name the server "CUSINQR."

The program itself is surprisingly compact, as you'll see. This is the header:

```
H OPTION(*NODEBUGIO : *SRCSTMT)
```

This program can run in the default activation group, so I'm letting it do so. However, I like to add the options above to aid in debugging.

Here are the files:

```
FORDHDR    IF   E          K DISK    EXTFILE(xFile) USROPN
FORDDTL    IF   E          K DISK    EXTFILE(xFile) USROPN
FCUSMAS    IF   E          K DISK    EXTFILE(xFile) USROPN
FITMMAS    IF   E          K DISK    EXTFILE(xFile) USROPN
D xFile          s            21
D xLib           s            11     varying

D               sds
D xsLib        81    90
```

ORDHDR and ORDDTL are the primary files (header and detail), and
CUSMAS and ITMMAS are related by foreign keys. Note that I specify
them all as **USROPN** with an **EXTFILE** keyword. This allows me to point the
files to a specific library without having to rely on the library list. You can
also do overrides, call a CL program to set the library list, or do whatever
you'd like. I like this technique, and you'll see how it works when you
read about the ***INZSR** routine, later in this chapter. The standalone fields
xFile and xLib and the program status data structure all play roles in the
initialization.

These data structures are used for file I/O:

```
    * File I/O Data Structures
D IOORDHDR      e ds                 extname(ORDHDR)
D IOORDDTL      e ds                 extname(ORDDTL)
D IOCUSMAS      e ds                 extname(CUSMAS)
D IOITMMAS      e ds                 extname(ITMMAS)
```

More specifically, they're used to enable the **eval-corr** opcodes later in
the program. Whenever a record is read from one of the database files, the
fields will be stored here.

The following data structures, on the other hand, define the messages that
will be passed between the EGL code and the RPG code:

```
    * Server Communication Data Structures (templates)
D DSSVRCTL      e ds                 qualified based(@)
D DSORDHDR      e ds                 qualified based(@)
D DSORDDTL      e ds                 qualified based(@)
```

These are the data structures I defined in the previous section. Note that all
are marked as qualified. This avoids the remote, but still possible, possibility of collisions between names in the server control message and the
data messages. Because they are based, and more precisely, are based on a
pointer that is never initialized, much less allocated, these structures take
no space. They're effectively just templates.

Next is the standard prototype information for an ILE RPG program:

```
D ORDINQR        pr                      EXTPGM('ORDINQR')
D   iDSSVRCTL                            likeds(DSSVRCTL)
D   iDSORDHDR                            likeds(DSORDHDR)
D   iDSORDDTL                            likeds(DSORDDTL)

D ORDINQR        pi
D   iDSSVRCTL                            likeds(DSSVRCTL)
D   iDSORDHDR                            likeds(DSORDHDR)
D   iDSORDDTL                            likeds(DSORDDTL)
```

The prototype matches the procedure interface. Both have the same name
as the program. The prototype has an **EXTPGM** keyword (required for programs in the default activation group), and each of the three parameters is
defined as like one of the communication data structures.

It is not clearly spelled out in the architecture, but since the sizes of the key
values are different for each type, it makes more sense to use the data message, rather than the generic server-control record, to pass those fields. The
general concept is simple: set the order number into the OHORDR field in
the order header parameter, put **GH** into the opcode of the server control
record, and call the server.

Now, it's time to begin the meat of the program:

```
/free

   // Execute specified command
   select;
```

A **select** statement is used to process the various possible operation codes.
In this case, there are only two: **GH** retrieves the header (and positions the
detail file), while **GD** returns the next detail record until end-of-file.

First, use the order number in the data message to attempt to retrieve the
ORDHDR record:

```
   // GH - Get order header
   when iDSSVRCTL.SCOPCD = 'GH';
      chain iDSORDHDR.OHORDR ORDHDR;
      if %found(ORDHDR);
```

If it's good, continue processing. Get any foreign records:

```
chain OHCUST CUSMAS;
```

Move data from the primary record into the data message:

```
// Primary fields
eval-corr iDSORDHDR = IOORDHDR;
```

The **eval-corr** will move all fields in IOORDHDR with a matching field in the iDSORDHDR data structure. Because this is done regardless of position, it is a nice way to move a subset of fields from one structure to another. (COBOL programmers are laughing because they've had this since sometime around the Civil War.) This is the main reason why I make sure the field names in my messages match their corresponding database fields.

The same concept is done with a different file to process the customer master:

```
// Foreign key fields
eval-corr iDSORDHDR = IOCUSMAS;
```

Yes, I know I'm only getting one field. However, if I need another field, I just add it to the iDSORDHDR data structure, and it gets handled automatically.

Next, the code does some magic, computing work fields. In this case, it formats the address fields into a single address string:

```
// Calculated fields
//   Shipping address
iDSORDHDR.W_ADDR =
  %trim(OHADR1) + ', ' +
  %trim(OHCITY) + ', ' +
  %trim(OHSTTE) + ' ' +
  %trim(OHPOST);
```

The code then calculates the order total:

```
//   Order total
setll OHORDR ORDDTL;
iDSORDHDR.W_TOTAL = OHSHIP + OHTAX;
reade OHORDR ORDDTL;
dow not %eof(ORDDTL);
  iDSORDHDR.W_TOTAL += ODXAMT;
  reade OHORDR ORDDTL;
enddo;
```

I start by adding freight and tax, and then accumulate the extended price of each line.

The following line of code is specific to the header/detail server; it positions the file pointer in the detail file to support the **GD** opcode:

```
// Position for first detail record
setll iDSORDHDR.OHORDR ORDDTL;
```

Indicate successful completion, and then fall through to the return:

```
iDSSVRCTL.SCRTCD = '00';
```

The following code is executed if the **CHAIN** to ORDHDR fails:

```
else;
  iDSSVRCTL.SCFLD = 'OHORDR';
  iDSSVRCTL.SCRTCD = '01';
endif;
```

While not strictly necessary, it indicates which field caused the failure and then sets a return code that isn't "00." The client and the server have to agree on the error codes; in this case, the value "01" indicates that the order was not found.

The get detail opcode, **GD**, is very similar to **GH**. The difference conceptually is that I assume multiple records, and use the **READE** to get the next record:

```
// GD - Get order detail
when iDSSVRCTL.SCOPCD = 'GD';
  reade OHORDR ORDDTL;
  if not %eof(ORDDTL);
    chain ODITEM ITMMAS;
```

The code reads the next record, and if found, gets the foreign item master record. Next, it moves the primary fields and the foreign fields:

```
// Primary fields
eval-corr iDSORDDTL = IOORDDTL;
// Foreign key fields
eval-corr iDSORDDTL = IOITMMAS;
```

Then, either indicate successful completion and fall through to the return, or return "01," meaning no record was found:

```
iDSSVRCTL.SCRTCD = '00';
else;
iDSSVRCTL.SCRTCD = '01';
endif;
```

If the opcode is not recognized, the following section of code returns error "99" as well as a message detailing the error and the opcode that triggered it:

```
// Bad opcode, fatal error
other;
iDSSVRCTL.SCRTCD = '99';
iDSSVRCTL.SCMSG =
'Invalid opcode ' + iDSSVRCTL.SCOPCD;
*inlr = *on;
endsl;
```

That's it for the server logic!

The last line of the mainline returns to the caller:

```
return;
```

Pretty simple, eh? Note that I don't turn on *INLR for any but the fatal errors. That makes multiple calls very, very fast.

The final section of code is a little bit of ILE RPG programming magic that allows me to easily support multiple environments:

```
// Open all files in correct library
begsr *inzsr;
  xLib = %trim(xsLib) + '/';
  xFile = xLib + 'ORDHDR';
  open ORDHDR;
  xFile = xLib + 'ORDDTL';
  open ORDDTL;
  xFile = xLib + 'CUSMAS';
  open CUSMAS;
  xFile = xLib + 'ITMMAS';
  open ITMMAS;
endsr;
/end-free
```

This code starts with the library from which the program was called, which it gets from the program status data structure. Since I'm calling this program from **IRUI**, xLib ends up with the value "**IRUI/**". Then, for each file, I take the library string and append the file name. For instance, the first time I compute xFile, I use the name "ORDHDR." Thus, xFile is "**IRUI/ORD-HDR**". Next, I open the ORDHDR file. Since it uses the **EXTFILE** keyword, the file specification will open ORDHDR in the library IRUI!

This is one of my favorite techniques.

Of course, it depends on the file residing in the same library as the program, which might or might not be the case. If it's not the case, you'll need whatever additional logic is necessary to determine the file library name from the program library name.

Configuring the Project to Talk to the RPG Program

The finish line is in sight for this example. There are two more tasks: specifying the program to call, and then adding the logic to the EGL library function. Today, you define programs in the deployment descriptor. Personally, I'm hoping that someday IBM will provide a program call stereotype that will allow you to define many of these values right in the EGL code. For now, though, you have to go through a tedious, but not too difficult, procedure.

Note that after this has been done once, a programmer with basic XML knowledge and more courage than brains (yes, I'm talking about myself) could go in and modify the Build Parts file (in this case, iEGl.eglbld) using a text editor. That would allow new programs to be added very quickly. However, that's an advanced topic for another day. For now, you need to go through the steps that follow to add a new ILE RPG server program to your application.

Start by right-clicking the iEGL.eglbld file in the EGLSource folder of the iEGL project, as shown in Figure 8.4. (By default, double-clicking does the same thing.)

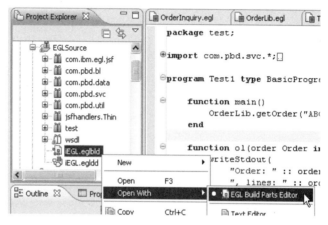

Figure 8.4: Open the EGL Build Parts file using the Build Parts Editor.

The Build Parts Editor opens to the panel shown in Figure 8.5. Unfortunately, you can't do what you need to do from here.

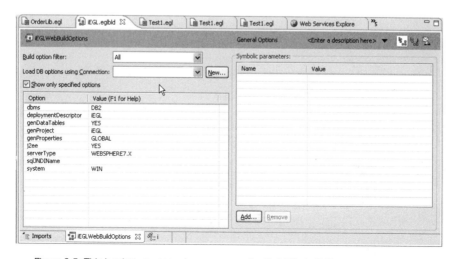

Figure 8.5: This is what you see when you open the Build Parts Editor.

Next, there is an operation that only needs to be done once per project. To put it as concisely as possible, you need to add some statements that define your RPG programs. While you can add multiple programs, they all must be part of a linkage part. The first step is to add that linkage part. The only way I know to do that is from the Outline view of the EGL Build Parts editor. So, I click the Outline tab, which brings up the outline shown in Figure 8.6.

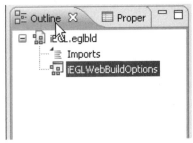

While the panel in Figure 8.5 allows me to modify parts that already exist (and I'll use it in a moment), only the Outline view allows me to add a completely new part to an EGL Build Parts object. I'm not sure why that is, but since it's not entirely intuitive, I'm going to go through the steps in some detail.

Figure 8.6: Click the Outline tab.

I right-click the top line, iEGL.eglbld, and select Add Part, as shown in Figure 8.7.

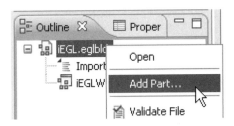

Figure 8.7: Add a new part.

The resulting dialog, shown in Figure 8.8, would allow me to add a number of different build components. However, the only one I'm interested in at this point is the linkage options part.

The linkage options part, shown in Figure 8.9, allows me to define the rest of my programs. As important as it is, the part itself has very little information: just a name and a description, and the description is optional!

I must admit that I don't know half of what this part can do. Just looking at the dozens of options makes me sure it can do a lot more than I use it for, but that's not important for this example. Right now, I just want to make a

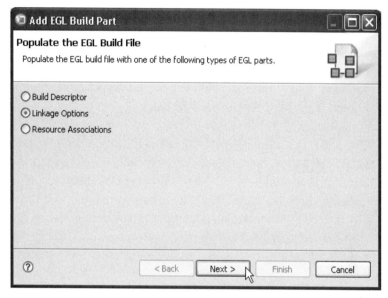

Figure 8.8: In order to add an RPG program, add a linkage part.

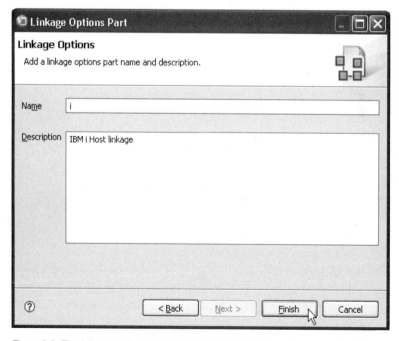

Figure 8.9: The linkage options part itself has only two fields, and one is optional!

linkage part that will allow me to call IBM i programs. To that end, I just call the part "i," and say it's my IBM i host linkage.

The idea behind the linkage part and the whole "build options" concept in general is quite powerful: you can have multiple sets of various options, and select them at build time to reconfigure your application as needed for a given deployment. In practice, I'd prefer a fast-path wizard to let me create these things, but since that's not available yet, let's continue the configuration required for our purpose here.

I've just added a linkage part, but while it's available to the build, it's not yet selected to be used. Selecting that particular linkage part is done on the EGL Web Build Options panel. However, by default, that panel only shows options that have already been configured (because there are literally dozens of them). Again by default, a new project has no linkage part configured. So, my next step is to de-select the checkbox marked "Show only specified options," as shown in Figure 8.10.

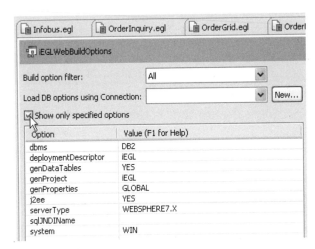

Figure 8.10: De-select the "Show only specified options" check-box to see all options, configured or not.

The resulting list, shown in Figure 8.11, has about a hundred options, but at least they're in alphabetical order. I scroll through the list until I see "linkage" (near the middle). Then, I use the interface to change the value.

Note that this interface is spreadsheet-like, meaning that the data is shown in columns, and you click a value to update it. Some values are simply text

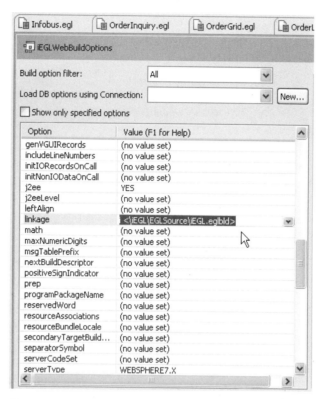

Figure 8.11: Now scroll through the alphabetical list to find the linkage option.

fields, while others are dropdowns. Some of the dropdowns are hardcoded lists of values, while others are populated by other things you've defined. The linkage field, for example, becomes a dropdown, and the only entry in it is the newly added "i" linkage part. I select it, and it appears in the linkage value, as shown in Figure 8.11.

Just to be clear: you cannot update a value in this particular interface by clicking the name in the left column. You must click the value in the right column. This holds true later, as well, when I actually configure the ORDINQR program.

The next step is to add components (called CallLink elements) to the i linkage part. Actually, I only need to add one component in this case, the definition of the ORDINQR program. It's simple enough; click the i component in the outline, and a panel like the one in Figure 8.12 will appear. There, I click the Add button.

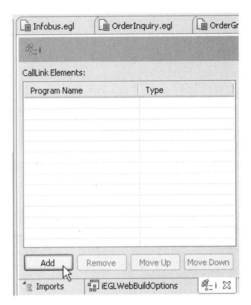

Figure 8.12: Add a new program to the i linkage part.

The left side of the panel lists the CallLink elements defined so far. When I click the Add button, a new line is added for me to modify. I click the new entry, change its program name to ORDINQR, and then change its type from **localCall** to **remoteCall**. Once that's done, a list of options is available on the right, as shown in Figure 8.13. (The list was shorter when the type was **localCall**.)

I don't have to update every value, just these:

- Change **conversionTable** to CSOE037. ("CSOE" is a string of alphabetic characters; "037" is numeric.)

- Change **javaWrapper** to YES.

- Change **library** to IRUI.

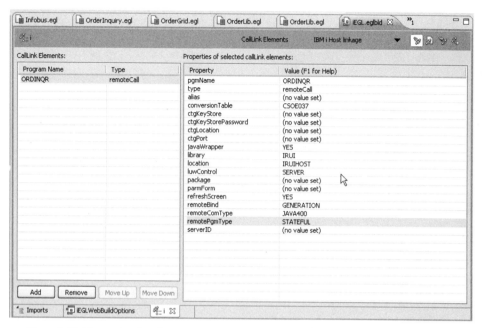

Figure 8.13: The updated attributes are required to define a CallLink element (AKA a program).

- Change **location** to IRUIHOST.

- Change **luwControl** to SERVER.

- Change **refreshScreen** to YES.

- Change **remoteBind** to GENERATION.

- Change **remoteComType** to JAVA400.

- Change **remotePgmType** to STATEFUL.

With those values entered, I'm done with the linkage part. However, take a look at the value for the **remoteComType** field. The value is JAVA400. That means I will be using the JT400 (or JTOpen) JAR file. This file is not included with RDi-SOA, so it needs to be copied from elsewhere. (It is available in the code for this book.)

Adding the JAR file is a copy and paste operation, as shown in Figures 8.14 and 8.15. Right-click the jt400.jar file in whatever Windows folder you have it, and then right-click and paste it into the iEGL project. All auxiliary JAR files like this one usually go in the same place: expand Web-Content, and then expand WEN-INF. You'll see a lib folder. That's where the jt400.jar file needs to be pasted.

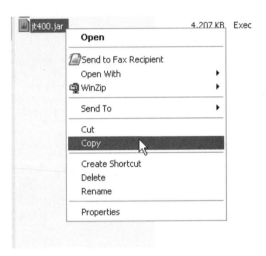

Figure 8.14: Find a copy of jt400.jar and use Windows Explorer to copy it.

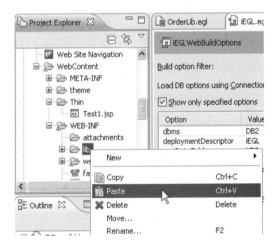

Figure 8.15: Paste the JAR into the lib folder under WebContent\WEB-INF in the iEGL project.

This might seem like a lot of work that isn't entirely intuitive. Honestly, I've stumbled on it on occasion. The good news is that you only have to do the steps shown in Figure 8.12 and 8.13 to add another program; the linkage part is done.

Adding the EGL Code

Finally, the moment we've all been waiting for: adding the EGL code! As you might imagine, there's a ton of code to be added...*not*!

First, I open up the OrderLib library. I rename the getOrder function to getOrderLocal, just as I did in the iRUI project. Then, I add the same sort of switch-selectable code:

```
useLocalGet boolean = false;

// Get order
function getOrder(
  orderNumber string in, order Order inOut)
  returns (Error)
  if (useLocalGet)
    return (getOrderLocal(orderNumber, order));
  else
    return (getOrderRemote(orderNumber, order));
  end
end
```

By setting userLocalGet true or false, I can switch between the local function that builds a dummy hardcoded order and the remote function that interfaces with RPG to get live data. Note that I always return a record of type **Error**, although that value may be null. This is for error processing later. Next, I add the two pieces that enable the remote logic, which are the message definitions and the code itself:

```
record DSSVRCTL
  10 SCOPCD char(2);
  10 SCOPSC char(2);
  10 SCRTCD char(2);
  10 SCRTSC char(2);
  10 SCCNT num (5,0);
  10 SCMSG char(80);
  10 SCFLD char(10);
end
record DSORDHDR
```

```
  10 OHORDR char(10);
  10 OHCUST num (6,0);
  10 CMNAME char(50);
  10 W_ADDR char(50);
  10 OHSHIP num (9,2);
  10 OHTAX num (9,2);
  10 W_TOTAL num (9,2);
end
record DSORDDTL
  10 ODITEM char(15);
  10 ODQORD num (9,0);
  10 ODUPRC num (9,3);
  10 ODXAMT num (9,2);
  10 IMDESC char(30);
end
```

I add the message definitions at the end of the OrderLib library. If you compare these record definitions to the data structures at the beginning of this chapter, you'll see that there is a one-to-one correspondence. Alphabetic fields are defined as **char**, while signed fields are defined as **num**. It's really quite simple. Actually, I think it would be a fun project for somebody to do programmatically. It would be even cooler to create a plug-in for RDi-SOA that would automatically create a record definition and add it to a source member. But I digress, as usual, when I should be focusing on the last piece of the puzzle:

```
// Get order remote
function getOrderRemote(
  orderNumber string in, order Order inOut)
  returns (Error)
```

The signature of the function is the same as getOrder (or getOrderLocal).

```
SysLib.setRemoteUser("IRUITEST", "IRUITEST");
```

This line of code defines the user ID and password to be used to connect to the host. Which user ID and password to use is actually a huge discussion. It depends on a wide variety of things, from the type of application to the authentication you have enabled. For example, there's currently a discussion and a Request For Enhancement regarding the use of Enterprise Identity Mapping (EIM) to provide this authentication. For the purposes of this exercise, however, a hardcoded user ID and password is plenty.

Here, I define the three parameters for the program, which are the server control, the order header, and the order detail records:

```
dsSvrCtl DSSVRCTL { SCOPCD = "GH" };
dsOrdHdr DSORDHDR { OHORDR = orderNumber };
dsOrdDtl DSORDDTL;
```

I love EGL's simplicity of syntax here: I define the server control and also initialize the subfields I need, which in this case is the single **GH** opcode. I create the order header the same way, this time initializing the key field, OHORDR, which will be used to get the data. The order detail record needs no initialization.

All it takes to call the program is a **call** opcode:

```
call "ORDINQR" (dsSvrCtl, dsOrdHDR, dsOrdDtl);
```

Here's the error processing:

```
if (dsSvrCtl.SCRTCD != "00")
  return (new Error {
    severity = dsSvrCtl.SCRTCD as int,
    message = "Error getting order " :: orderNumber
  });
```

If the record is found, the server returns "00" in SCRTCD. If not, it returns an error code. I return a new Error record, putting the SCRTCD into the severity field and hardcoding a little error message.

Otherwise, the server returned success, so it's time to create an order:

```
else
  order.Header = new OrderHeader {
    OrderNumber = clip(dsOrdHdr.OHORDR),
    CustomerNumber = dsOrdHdr.OHCUST,
    CustomerName = clip(dsOrdHdr.CMNAME),
    ShippingAddr = clip(dsOrdHdr.W_ADDR),
    Freight = dsOrdHdr.OHSHIP,
    Tax = dsOrdHdr.OHTAX,
    Total = dsOrdHdr.W_TOTAL
  };
```

Again, the simplicity of EGL is unparalleled. Remember, the caller passed in an Order record, but that record is actually two things: an order header and an array of order lines. The first thing I do is create a new header, using all the values from the DSORDHDR record. Alphabetic fields get clipped to remove leading and trailing blanks, and numeric fields just get assigned. Content-assist really helps here because it keeps track of which fields you've updated in the record you're creating (in this case, the Order-Header). It also makes sure you don't misspell things or modify fields that aren't in the record.

Next, I clear the array:

```
order.Lines = new OrderLine[];
```

Actually, I set the value to a new, empty array. That seems to work just fine.

I have to change the operation code to **GD** to start getting detail records:

```
dsSvrCtl.SCOPCD = "GD";
```

I loop, calling the program over and over as long as I get a successful return code:

```
call "ORDINQR" (dsSvrCtl, dsOrdHDR, dsOrdDtl);
while (dsSvrCtl.SCRTCD == "00")
```

For each success, I add a new OrderLine to the array. In EGL, the appendElement function is used to add an entry to an array:

```
order.Lines.appendElement(new OrderLine {
    ItemNumber = clip(dsOrdDtl.ODITEM),
    Description = clip(dsOrdDtl.IMDESC),
    Quantity = dsOrdDtl.ODQORD,
    Price = dsOrdDtl.ODUPRC,
    Extended = dsOrdDtl.ODXAMT
});
```

The rest of the code is the same type of logic, creating a new OrderLine record from the DSORDDTL message. Note that in this architecture, EGL doesn't have to do any calculations; all the computation is done on the host as the messages are being created. This makes the EGL code simple—there are less than 40 lines of code for a whole lot of functionality.

Finally, I call again, and loop until done:

```
    call "ORDINQR" (dsSvrCtl, dsOrdHDR, dsOrdDtl);
  end
 end
end
```

That's all the logic required to enable the RPG program. This is not a trivial example, either; it's a header/detail relationship with derived fields, totals, and foreign data. It might not be rocket science, but it's not "Introduction to Programming 101," either.

The Results

I suppose we should see what happens, eh? First, I make a little change to my test program, as shown in Figure 8.16. The order number QE-013321 is a large, 14-line order on the host that I can use to make sure my data is really getting through.

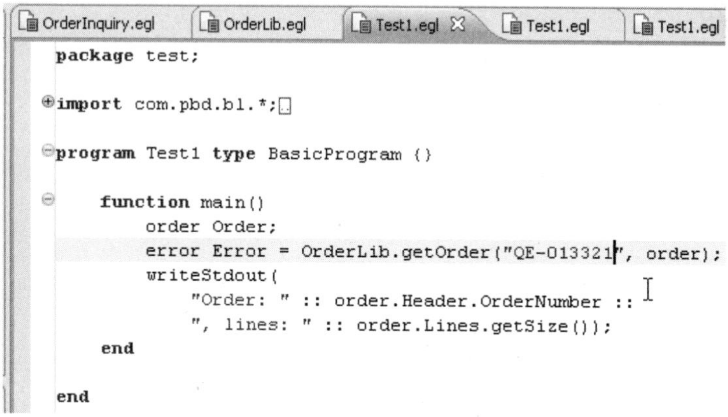

```
 OrderInquiry.egl    OrderLib.egl    Test1.egl ☒   Test1.egl    Test1.egl

   package test;

 ⊕import com.pbd.bl.*;□

 ⊖program Test1 type BasicProgram {}

 ⊖    function main()
           order Order;
           error Error = OrderLib.getOrder("QE-013321", order);
           writeStdout(
               "Order: " :: order.Header.OrderNumber :: I
               ", lines: " :: order.Lines.getSize());
        end

    end
```

Figure 8.16: Change the order number to QE-013321.

Then, I do the old right-click, and select Debug EGL Program. I get an error about not finding the source for ORDINQR. That's not surprising, since ORDINQR is an RPG program, not EGL. In the next chapter, you'll learn how to make this error go away. For now, though, I can just click the Yes button, as shown in Figure 8.17.

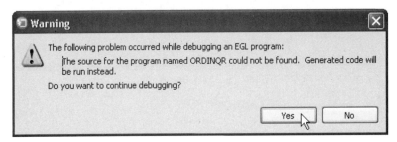

Figure 8.17: For now, clicking the Yes button works fine.

I get the result shown in Figure 8.18. You can go into the ORDDTL file and check it yourself, but there are, indeed, 14 lines.

```
<terminated> test.Test1 [EGL Program] C:\IBM
Order: QE-013321, lines: 14
```

Figure 8.18: The result is what I expected, 14 lines.

Now that I'm comfortable that the connection is working, it's time to check all the other pieces. This is the part that no other language can even come close to: the ability to affect all of your applications at the same time.

Next, let's check the thin client, as shown in Figure 8.19. I go to the page-handler code for the Test1 page and change the order number in the onPrerender function to attempt to read the same order, QE-013321. Then, it's a simple re-run by right-clicking Test1.jsp and selecting Run As/Run on Server from the context menu.

The result, shown in Figure 8.20, comes back very quickly, even though it had to recompile the page. Try it again by refreshing the page, and see how quickly it comes back the second time. (I can barely see the flash of the page on my workstation.)

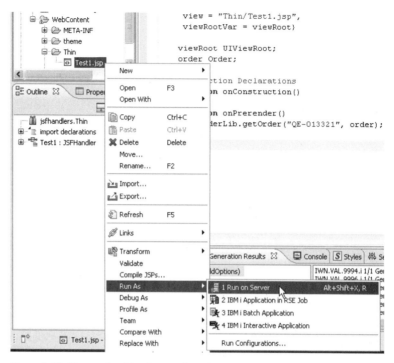

Figure 8.19: Change the thin client to show the same order.

http://localhost:9084/IEGL/Thin/Test1.faces

OrderNumber:	QE-013321
CustomerNumber:	654321
CustomerName:	Joe Pluta
ShippingAddr:	35 S. Wilmette, Westmont, IL 60559
Tax:	$7.25
Freight:	$13.25
Total:	$50,510.05

Lines:

ItemNumber	Description	Quantity	Price	Extended
CE333	Centrino (CE333)	12	$54.17	$650.04
CE366	Centrino (CE366)	14	$52.14	$729.96
CE500	Centrino (CE500)	25	$70.00	$1,750.00
CE600	Centrino (CE600)	35	$69.71	$2,439.85
P2350	Pentium 2 (P2350)	5	$24.00	$120.00
P2400	Pentium 2 (P2400)	5	$26.00	$130.00
P3750	Pentium 3 (P3750)	75	$78.13	$5,859.75
P3600	Pentium 3 (P3600)	120	$60.00	$7,200.00
XE500-1MB	Xeon (XE500-1MB)	5	$1,680.00	$8,400.00
XE550-2MB	Xeon (XE550-2MB)	3	$4,040.00	$12,120.00
AT700	AMD (AT700)	10	$196.00	$1,960.00
AT750	AMD (AT750)	15	$215.33	$3,229.95
AT800	AMD (AT800)	5	$350.00	$1,750.00
AT850	AMD (AT850)	10	$415.00	$4,150.00

Figure 8.20: And it works, automatically!

Okay, batch program, thin client. How about the web service? I'm glad you asked! The SOAP service automatically works just as well, as shown in Figure 8.21.

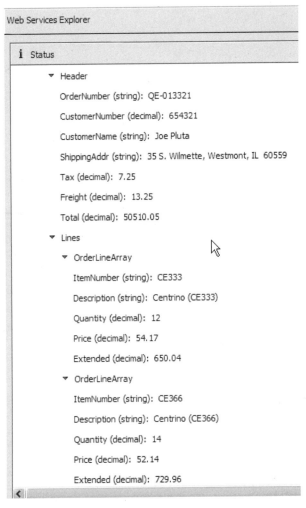

Figure 8.21: Another interface heard from!

Let's take a look at that rich interface, shall we? Remember, not one line of code was changed in the EGL Rich UI code to get the result in Figure 8.22.

And that, dear reader, is that. A complete, working business application using business logic and data on the host, and not one, but three different front-end interfaces: thin client, web service, and rich client. It took

Order Number:	QE-013321		Read		
Order Number		QE-013321			
Customer Number		654321			
Customer Name		Joe Pluta			

Item Number	Description	Quantity	Price	Extended
CE333	Centrino (CE333)	12	54.17	650.04
CE366	Centrino (CE366)	14	52.14	729.96
CE500	Centrino (CE500)	25	70.00	1750.00
CE600	Centrino (CE600)	35	69.71	2439.85
P2350	Pentium 2 (P2350)	5	24.00	120.00
P2400	Pentium 2 (P2400)	5	26.00	130.00
P3750	Pentium 3 (P3750)	75	78.13	5859.75
P3600	Pentium 3 (P3600)	120	60.00	7200.00
XE500-1MB	Xeon (XE500-1MB)	5	1680.00	8400.00
XE550-2MB	Xeon (XE550-2MB)	3	4040.00	12120.00
AT700	AMD (AT700)	10	196.00	1960.00
AT750	AMD (AT750)	15	215.33	3229.95
AT800	AMD (AT800)	5	350.00	1750.00
AT850	AMD (AT850)	10	415.00	4150.00

	Tax	7.25
	Shipping and Handling	13.25
	Order Total	50510.05

Ship To   35 S. Wilmette, Westmont, IL 60559   **Map:** ☐

Figure 8.22: The rich client gains the same capabilities as all the others.

about 100 lines of RPG on the host, and 100 lines of EGL in Tier 2 (which included the thin-client page handler). It also took about 300 lines of EGL Rich UI code, although to be fair, about a third of that code was the Rich UI equivalent of DDS, defining the widgets.

The generated code adheres to industry standards, such as JavaServer Faces, OpenAjax, and Cascading Style Sheets. Of course, RDi-SOA also provides you with superior WYSIWYG editors to get the work done quickly.

Summary

Are you seeing a trend here? Do you see how EGL lends itself to an architecture in which you can enable any interface required, and in which all the interfaces can use a central business-logic repository? You are not limited by technology. In fact, you are future-proofed, as you will see in Chapter 10.

Just as important, changes to the repository are instantly reflected through-out your entire application repertoire, regardless of the implementation style. Thin, rich, service—it doesn't matter; they all just work. This is what should get you excited. With a few hundred lines of code and a couple of extraordinary WYSIWYG tools, you can create a completely diverse appli-cation that perfectly complements the extraordinary power of the i.

For those who have long clamored for a GUI for the i, this is it. Never again is an i application limited by the green screen. Now, the only limit is your imagination!

Chapter 9

Error Handling, Logging, and Debugging

I find that the hard part of programming is not designing the architecture or writing the code. Don't get me wrong; those are difficult tasks, and it takes a long time to become proficient at them. Still, the part of programming that really separates the rookies from the gurus is debugging. Debugging actually has a number of components. It starts with a good architecture.

Your architecture needs to have solid error-handling built in from the ground up, not added as an afterthought. Next, you should have logging built in. Logging is so important, in fact, that Java, like other modern languages, has an entire package devoted to it. EGL makes it really easy either to incorporate external logging packages or to "roll your own." Where EGL really shines, though, especially RDi-SOA, is in debugging. Because the same workbench is used for every tier, you can set and manage breakpoints throughout the process, all from a central interface. This includes the client tier running in JavaScript, the web tier running in Java, and the business logic running in RPG. There's no comparable multi-language debugging tool on the market.

When Good Code Goes Bad

Let's start out by looking at the interface you've seen throughout this book. A three-line order is entered in this interface in Figure 9.1. As you can see, my application works wonderfully, at least when I enter good information and the order is found.

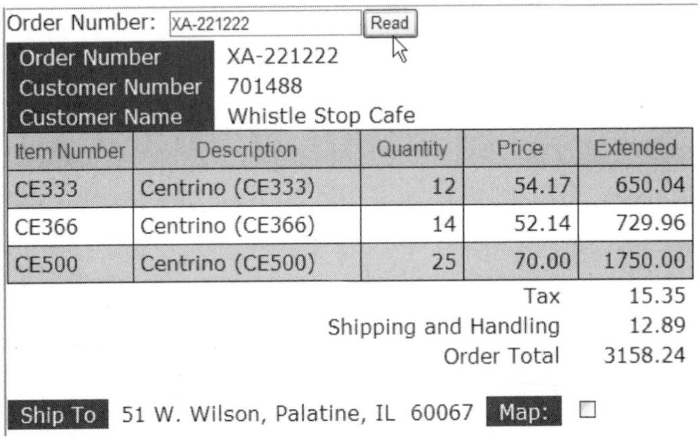

Figure 9.1: Here is the EGL Rich UI interface for a small order.

However, what happens when I enter a bad order number, or no order number at all? The interface doesn't work so well, and I get an error. I end up with what is basically computer gibberish, as shown in Figure 9.2.

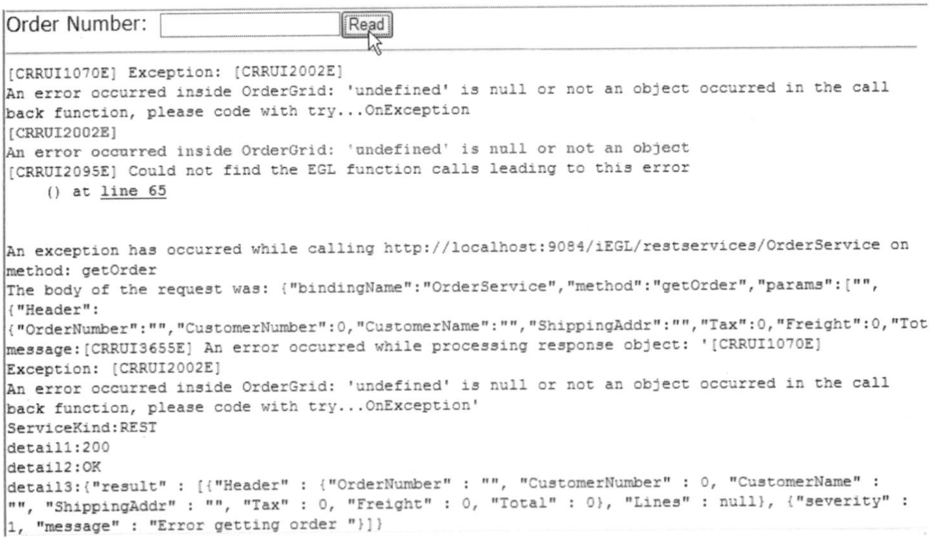

Figure 9.2: Entering an order without an order number causes the EGL to get ugly.

Actually, some of this might be relatively readable. I think I can even discern an error message near the bottom of Figure 9.2. Obviously, though, this isn't what you'd want users to see. They need to get a better error. The good news is that the error message is indeed being returned. It's just not being handled.

Handling Errors

You've seen my Error record in earlier chapters. Right now, it only has a severity and a message. That's enough for basic error-handling. Obviously, there are many ways you can show an error; for this first pass, I just want to display the message received from the business logic.

If you remember how the example application works, when things go well, the OrderGrid super-widget sends a box to the OrderInquiry application. That box contains all the order information, as shown in Figure 9.1, and everybody is thrilled. When an error occurs, I need to do something a little different. I'm going to send back a simple TextLabel, instead of the order box.

The message is in the Error record; I'll use it to create the TextLabel on the fly. This involves two simple modifications to the code from previous chapters:

```
function orderListener(order Order in, error Error in)
  if (error.severity > 0)
    sendResponse("SHOW", new TextLabel {
      text = error.message, class = "error"
    });
  else
    hbfOrderNumber.text = order.Header.OrderNumber;
(...)
    (shipping.children[2] as TextLabel).text =
      order.Header.ShippingAddr;
    sendResponse("SHOW", orderBox);
  end
end
```

Most of the code stays exactly the same. I've added a wrapper to the old code (from the line that sets **hbfOrder** to the call to **sendResponse**) in a big If/Else/End construct. The If tests for an error severity greater than zero, since zero means no error. If there is an error, it creates a new Text-

Label that's sent back, instead. You might note that I set the class to **error**. That allows me to do this in the CSS file (iRUI.css):

```
.error { color: red; font-weight: bold };
```

Thanks to that, I get the message in Figure 9.3 when I put in a bad order number. Although you can't see the color on this black-and-white page, the error message shows up in bold red letters.

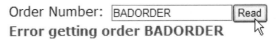

Figure 9.3: Basic error handling is done!

Also, notice that I didn't have to make a single change to the main application handler, OrderInquiry. (That's thanks, in large part, to the Infobus design.) How cool is that?

Visual Indicators

There is one thing I didn't do here: I didn't provide a visual indicator that identifies the field in error. That part of the application design is really a much larger one, but I want to address it, at least from a high level.

The reason it's a big issue is that people have varying opinions on what constitutes an appropriate visual response. I've seen things ranging from an asterisk next to the field, to changing the color of the field, to changing the color of the prompt text. In this case, I'm going to change the CSS class for the field itself, to bold white on red. That should show up even in a black-and-white image.

The high-level design point to take into account here is that OrderGrid (the embedded super-widget) is going to send an error indicator to the embedding component, which in this case is the application controller. The application controller will then determine what to do with the error.

This time, there is almost no change to the OrderGrid widget. Most of the change is in the OrderInquiry application. Here is OrderGrid:

```
if (error.severity > 0)
  sendResponse("ERROR", "");
  sendResponse("SHOW", new TextLabel {
    text = error.message, class = "error"
  });
else
```

It's pretty simple: I just add one line to send an **ERROR** response back to the caller. Now you can see the method to my madness in creating the sendResponse function in Chapter 8. It's really beginning to come in handy.

Next, I make the changes to the OrderInquiry application. There are two, a small change to readOrder, and a more substantial change to the listener function:

```
function readOrder(e event in)
  orderField.class = "";
  InfoBus.publish(eidOG, new InfobusMessage {
    src = eidApp,
    action = "SHOW",
    data = orderField.text } );
end

function listener(eventName String in, object any in)
  ibm InfobusMessage = object;
  case
    when (ibm.action == "ERROR")
      orderField.class = "inputerror";
    when (ibm.action == "SHOW")
      ui.removeChild(ui.children[2]);
      ui.appendChild(ibm.data);
  end
end
```

In readOrder, I just clear the class on the orderField before attempting to read the order. That's sort of like clearing the error indicator. In listener, I add the **case** construct. I could use have used an If/Else/End instead, but I like the idea that I could easily add more actions by just adding new **when** clauses. The old code executes when the action is **SHOW**.

The new code runs when an **ERROR** action is received. At that time, I set the orderField class to "inputerror." You've probably already guessed that I need a CSS statement to define the new class:

```
.inputerror { background-color: red; color: white};
```

That's all it takes to get the result in Figure 9.4.

Order Number: BADORDER [Read]
Error getting order BADORDER

Figure 9.4: Now I have a visual indicator on the order-number input field.

That does it. While it might be a little overkill not only to display an error message but also to change the color of the only field on the panel, it shows you the general idea. Consider a maintenance panel with a dozen fields on it; the ERROR message could easily identify the field in error, and the application could then set the class on the corresponding widget. The point is that it's very easy to do this—it's just as easy as turning on an indicator in a display-file DDS.

Logging

Logging is a simple way to take a look at your programs as they execute. It's easy to do in most development environments, and EGL is no exception. The problem is how to implement logging effectively. Logging for the web app tier is a little different than logging for the client tier, but the fundamentals are the same. I always keep two things in mind. First, I always use a Boolean flag to determine whether to log a given routine or not. Second, I always test the flag before I invoke the routine, rather than testing within the logging routine itself. (You'll see why shortly.)

Here's the code I added to OrderLib in iEGL (the web app tier):

```
logging boolean = true;

// Get order
function getOrder(
  orderNumber string in, order Order inOut)
  returns (Error)
  if (logging) log("gO:enter:" :: orderNumber); end
  if (useLocalGet)
    if (logging) log("gO:gOL:" :: orderNumber); end
    return (getOrderLocal(orderNumber, order));
  else
    if (logging) log("gO:gOR:" :: orderNumber); end
    return (getOrderRemote(orderNumber, order));
```

```
      end
end

// Get order remote
function getOrderRemote(
  orderNumber string in, order Order inOut)
  returns (Error)
  if (logging) log("gOR:enter:" :: orderNumber); end
(...)
  if (dsSvrCtl.SCRTCD != "00")
    if (logging) log("gOR:SCRTCD<>00"); end
(...)
  else
    if (logging) log("gOR:SCRTCD==00"); end
(...)
  end
  if (logging) log("gOR:exit:" :: orderNumber); end
end
function log (logEntry string in)
  writeStdout("OrderLib:" :: logEntry);
end
```

I added a Boolean flag that controls the logging for this library, and then at various points in the routine, I log a message. However, I only call the log function if the logging variable is true. I could test the logging variable inside the log function, but that would mean I would have to format the message before invoking the log function.

The messages here are pretty simple; sometimes there's just a constant, sometimes there's a constant and a variable concatenated. In other situations, however, you might want to log more complex data. In those cases, it doesn't make sense to format that data if you're not logging it.

The log function then uses **writeStdout** to write to the **stdout** for the web application server, which in RDi-SOA, then shows up in the console.

Here's the result of one of my logging runs on the big order:

```
[5/30/09 22:02:28:937 CDT] 00000026 SystemOut    0
OrderLib:gO:enter:QE-013321
[5/30/09 22:02:28:937 CDT] 00000026 SystemOut    0
OrderLib:gO:gOR:QE-013321
[5/30/09 22:02:28:937 CDT] 00000026 SystemOut    0
OrderLib:gOR:enter:QE-013321
[5/30/09 22:02:28:937 CDT] 00000026 SystemOut    0
OrderLib:gOR:SCRTCD==00
[5/30/09 22:02:28:968 CDT] 00000026 SystemOut    0
OrderLib:gOR:exit:QE-013321
```

Note the nice timestamps, and everything. This is good stuff. By the way, note that it took about 31 milliseconds to get the entire order (all 14 lines) from the server, using RPG calls. That included converting from EBCDIC data structures to EGL objects. I told you this was fast! There are, of course, other ways to log. You can embed one of the standard Java logging libraries, such as log4j, by creating an external type and then executing the logging features of that package. I personally find the console logging to be sufficient, but if you're using logging as a recording mechanism, as opposed to using it for problem determination, a more formal logger might be a better option.

JavaScript Logging and the External Type

So, what are these external types I speak of, grasshopper? You've already seen an example in the GoogleMap add-on, but I've got an opportunity here to show you in more detail. The **writeStdout** in the Rich UI doesn't have the same timestamping as the companion method in the web application tier. Not only that, but JavaScript doesn't have any easy way to format timestamp data the way Java does. The closest thing I've found was a post on a newsgroup by someone named "Evertjan" in the Netherlands. I encapsulated that code into my own JavaScript function, along with a hardcoded time-zone adjustment, and then exposed it as an EGL ExternalType.

The code is nothing earth-shattering:

```
egl.defineClass(
  'com.pbd.util', 'Fmt', // this class
{
  "constructor" : function() {
    this.ms = new Date().getTime();
  },

  "getNow" : function( ) {
    function two(x) {
      return ((x>9)?x:"0"+x)
    }
    function three(x) {
      return ((x>99)?x:"0"+two(x))
    }
    var sec = Math.floor(this.ms/1000);
    var msec  = this.ms % 1000;
    var min = Math.floor(sec/60);
    sec = sec % 60;
    var hr = Math.floor(min/60);
```

```
        min = min % 60;
        hr = (hr + 18) % 24;

        t = two(hr) + ":" + two(min) + ":" +
            two(sec) + "." + three(msec);

        return t;
    }
});
```

I create a new date object, and get the time in milliseconds. Then, I divide out the hours, minutes, seconds, and milliseconds, and format them into a string. This code is then placed in the WebContent folder. Since I'm using the package name com.pbd.util for this class, it makes sense (although it's not strictly required) to use the folder name com/pbd/util to store the JavaScript code.

The only other thing I have to do is write the EGL part that will provide access to this little gem, and that only takes a few lines of code. I separate the part that gets the time in milliseconds and the part that formats it, so that I can create a **Fmt** object once and get the (same) formatted time over and over.

The way to define functions here takes some getting used to: they're defined as keyword/value pairs, with the keyword being the name of the function as EGL sees it, and the value being an anonymous function that is called when EGL references that name. It's a little strange, but it works.

Once I've created the appropriate JavaScript code, I can then set up the ExternalType to reference it:

```
package com.pbd.util;

ExternalType Fmt type JavaScriptObject {
    relativePath = "com/pbd/util",
    javaScriptName = "Fmt"
  }
  function getNow() returns (string);
end
```

The code is very simple. First, I identify the name and location of the JavaScript file, and then define the functions I wish to expose. Note that in the JavaScript world, types are very fluid; it's up to me to make sure that the type I return in the JavaScript function matches the type specified in the ExternalType definition. Also, as a convention, I make sure that the folder name in the **relativePath** keyword is the same as the package name (with dots replaced by slashes), and the type name is the same as the JavaScript file name. This isn't required, but I can imagine the potential for disaster if I didn't do it that way. Besides, that seems to be the way IBM does it, and if it's good enough for them, it's good enough for me.

Now that I have my nice little time formatter, I can add the same sort of logging to my JavaScript client:

```
// Logging
logging boolean = true;
(...)
function showOrder(orderNumber string)
  if (logging) log("sO:" :: orderNumber); end
  OrderLib.getOrder(orderNumber, orderListener);
end
(...)
function log(message string in)
  writeStdout(
    new Fmt().getNow() ::
    " OrderGrid:" :: message);
end
```

The concept here is the same: I add a Boolean flag and then test it at various places throughout the code. If it's set, I format a message and call the log function. The log function writes the message out to the console, but with my nicely formatted timestamp prepended. In EGL Rich UI, the "console" is the web page itself. RUI outputs the HTML it would normally have generated, and then writes out a horizontal line, followed by any console output. The result is shown in Figure 9.5. According to that figure, processing took 312 milliseconds.

Here's another example:

```
21:56:13.171 OrderGrid:sO:XA-221222
21:56:13.296 OrderGrid:sO:oL:Enter
21:56:13.296 OrderGrid:sO:oL:Success
21:56:13.406 OrderGrid:sO:oL:Exit
```

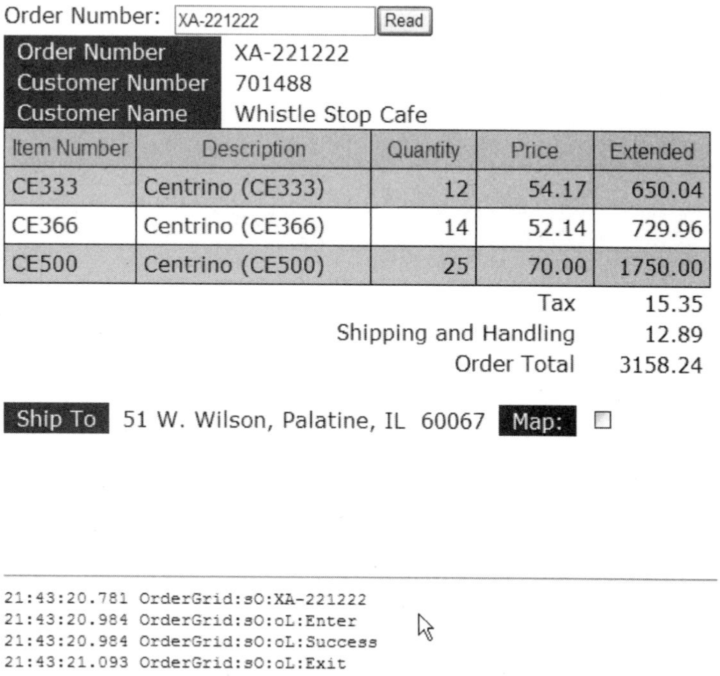

Order Number: | XA-221222 | | Read |

Order Number	XA-221222
Customer Number	701488
Customer Name	Whistle Stop Cafe

Item Number	Description	Quantity	Price	Extended
CE333	Centrino (CE333)	12	54.17	650.04
CE366	Centrino (CE366)	14	52.14	729.96
CE500	Centrino (CE500)	25	70.00	1750.00

Tax   15.35
Shipping and Handling   12.89
Order Total   3158.24

Ship To   51 W. Wilson, Palatine, IL 60067   Map: ☐

```
21:43:20.781 OrderGrid:sO:XA-221222
21:43:20.984 OrderGrid:sO:oL:Enter
21:43:20.984 OrderGrid:sO:oL:Success
21:43:21.093 OrderGrid:sO:oL:Exit
```

Figure 9.5: The console for EGL Rich UI is at the bottom of the rendered page.

In this run, it took about 230 milliseconds (about a quarter of a second) to render the entire order, including the actual service call. Broken down, it took about a tenth of a second (120 ms) to get the data, and about another tenth of a second (110 ms) to render it. It's not quite as fast as green screen, but a quarter of a second is a pretty decent response time!

Debugging, the Final Frontier

Logging is fine as far as it goes, but sometimes logging just isn't enough. In fact, for green-screen programmers like me, logging is the equivalent of **DEBUG PRINT** statements in our reports, or at best a trace dump. Debugging took a quantum leap forward with integrated debuggers like **STRDBG** and **STRISDB**. RDi-SOA has a set of tools that takes debugging to the next level.

Let's take a closer look at what happens with logging. In Figure 9.6, I'm trying to bring up an order.

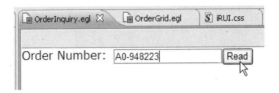

Figure 9.6: I'm trying to view another order.

The logs in Figures 9.7 and 9.8, however, tell me I'm getting an error. It looks like the error is all the way in the RPG code, but to be sure, I'll have to walk through the code.

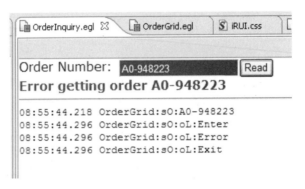

Figure 9.7: Here's the log from the client side.

```
[5/31/09 9:55:44:250 CDT]  00000022 SystemOut   O OrderLib:gO:enter:A0-948223
[5/31/09 9:55:44:250 CDT]  00000022 SystemOut   O OrderLib:gO:gOR:A0-948223
[5/31/09 9:55:44:250 CDT]  00000022 SystemOut   O OrderLib:gOR:enter:A0-948223
[5/31/09 9:55:44:250 CDT]  00000022 SystemOut   O OrderLib:gOR:SCRTCD<>00
```

Figure 9.8: Here's the log on the server.

Debugging JavaScript

JavaScript is notoriously difficult to debug. Although some tools exist, they're usually browser-specific. Even then, they're not particularly easy to use. Certainly, they're not integrated into whatever programming tool you're using. If you're using a code-generation tool like EGL, debugging the resulting JavaScript is a little bit like trying to debug the machine code generated by the RPG compiler. It's certainly not as productive as being able to debug at the 4GL level.

RDi-SOA lets you debug at that higher level. You can set breakpoints in your EGL Rich UI source code, and then launch the application in debug mode. Let me show you how I do that with the current application, shown in Figure 9.9.

```
    function orderListener(order Order in, error Error in)
            if (logging) log("sO:oL:Enter"); end
            if (error severity > 0)
  ✔ Show Quick Diff      Ctrl+Shift+Q   }) log("sO:oL:Error"); end
    Show Line Numbers                    se("ERROR", "");
    Folding                          ►   se("SHOW", new TextLabel {
                                          error.message, class = "error"
    Preferences...
    Add Breakpoint
    Disable Breakpoint                   }) log("sO:oL:Success"); end
                                         ber.text = order.Header.OrderNumber;
    Add Task...                          Number.text = order.Header.CustomerNumber;
    Add Bookmark...                      Name.text = order.Header.CustomerName;
```

Figure 9.9: Setting a breakpoint in EGL is the same as in any other language.

The editors in RDi-SOA all use the same technique for setting a breakpoint: right-click in the gray column to the left of the source, and select the Add Breakpoint option from the context menu. You can also double-click to add or remove a breakpoint. Once you've done that, it's time to debug the client.

To debug the client, you launch it into an external browser, using the Debug tool from the toolbar in the upper-right corner of the WYSIWYG designer's Preview tab. This is shown in Figure 9.10. You can also right-click the Rich UI Handler and select Debug EGL Rich UI Application from the context menu to start debugging.

Figure 9.10: Launch in debug mode in the external browser.

At that point, your external browser will be invoked, and the application will appear in that instance. Which external browser is launched depends on a Preferences setting.

If you leave the default setting, it will use whatever web browser you usually use. It's a good idea to use different browsers for testing purposes. For example, my default web browser is Firefox, but I would test in Internet Explorer if my preferences were set as shown in Figure 9.11.

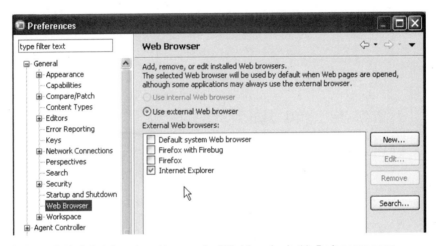

Figure 9.11: Select the external browser for RUI debugging in this Preferences page.

Once the browser has launched, I can invoke my application. In Figure 9.12, I enter the order number and click the Read button. This will start my application.

Figure 9.12: The browser comes up, and I can run my application.

If you remember how this application is written, the next thing that should happen is that I'll send an Infobus message to the OrderGrid widget. This will, in turn, cause OrderGrid to call the getOrder function in OrderService to attempt to retrieve the order.

When that happens, I get the error in Figure 9.13. In debugging mode, the system needs some more information about services. If I click the Cancel button here, the dialog will be skipped, and the debugging session will continue. This acts the same as selecting "generated" mode (called "source" mode is shown in Figure 9.13), and runs the generated code. Because it's running in generated mode, not source mode, I can't set a breakpoint in the EGL code for the service. I'm not debugging the middle tier right now, anyway, so that's okay. So, I click the Cancel button, as shown in the screen shot.

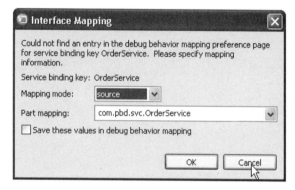

Figure 9.13: Running the application causes an Interface Mapping error.

Next, I get the Confirm Perspective Switch dialog shown in Figure 9.14. It's asking me if I want to switch to the Debug perspective. I absolutely do, because this perspective gives me all the tools I need to debug my application.

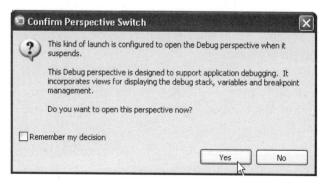

Figure 9.14: I switch to the Debug perspective.

As shown in Figure 9.15, the Debug perspective is complex. I don't have the room here to do it justice, but I will discuss a few of its more important features.

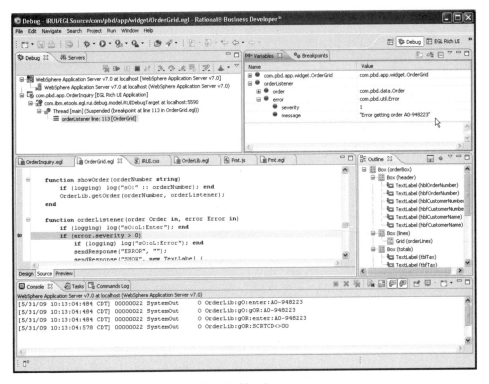

Figure 9.15: Here's the Debug perspective, in all its glory.

The Editor view is a major part of the workbench, taking up a good portion of the center of the panel. Here you'll see the source code of the interrupted part, with the currently executing line highlighted, as shown in Figure 9.16. This is a standard graphical debugger, with tools to step through your code as needed.

Another hugely important view is the Variables view. Here, you can look through all the variables currently available to your code. In EGL, you see the scopes, and then the variables visible within each of those scopes. Figure 9.17 shows that I've got two active scopes (the OrderGrid widget

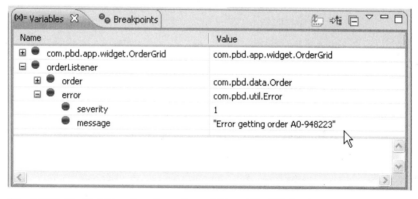

```
  OrderInquiry.egl      OrderGrid.egl  ⊠      iRUI.css         OrderLib.egl

  ⊖     function showOrder(orderNumber string)
               if (logging) log("sO:" :: orderNumber); end
               OrderLib.getOrder(orderNumber, orderListener);
          end


  ⊖     function orderListener(order Order in, error Error
               if (logging) log("sO:oL:Enter"); end
⇥Ð             if (error.severity > 0)
                   if (logging) log("sO:oL:Error"); end
                   sendResponse("ERROR", "");
                   sendResponse("SHOW", new TextLabel {

  Design Source Preview
```

Figure 9.16: The Editor view shows the code hitting a breakpoint.

```
(x)= Variables ⊠    ⊙⊙ Breakpoints                           🔃  ⇥🔳  🗎  ▽  ▭  🗆

Name                                        Value
⊞ ●  com.pbd.app.widget.OrderGrid           com.pbd.app.widget.OrderGrid
⊟ ●  orderListener
   ⊞ ●   order                              com.pbd.data.Order
   ⊟ ●   error                              com.pbd.util.Error
         ●  severity                        1
         ●  message                         "Error getting order A0-948223"
                                                                         ▷
```

Figure 9.17: The Variables view shows the variables at the EGL level.

and the currently executing function, orderListener). The orderListener function has a few local variables, specifically the parameters that were passed in on the call.

I've expanded the orderListener scope and the error variable within that scope, to show the values in the error message. It clearly shows that the JavaScript received an error message, and so I know now that the JavaScript is acting correctly, and that the error is somewhere farther upstream. Welcome to the world of forensic debugging!

Since I know the error is higher up, I just resume this program as shown in Figure 9.18. I get the error shown in Figure 9.19, and move on.

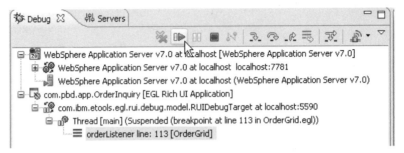

Figure 9.18: Click the "standard" Resume button to continue.

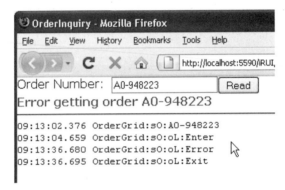

Figure 9.19: The error appears, just the way I saw it in the Variables view.

Debugging the Middle Tier

Next, I need to debug the middle tier. This turns out to be quite simple, thanks to the way my architecture is laid out, with a service being little more than a wrapper over a library function, First, I add the breakpoint.

The chunk of code that invokes the host program is the getOrderRemote function in the library OrderLib. So, I open the OrderLib source, as shown in Figure 9.20.

Breakpoint processing is consistent: find the line of code where execution should pause, right-click in the gray column to the left, and select Add Breakpoint. This is shown in Figure 9.21. With this done, I fire up the program again.

```
OrderInquiry.egl      OrderGrid.egl      iRUI.css      OrderLib.egl      Fmt.js

  import com.pbd.data.*;

  library OrderLib type BasicLibrary {}

      useLocalGet boolean = false;
      logging boolean = true;

      // Get order
      function getOrder(orderNumber string in, order Order inOut)
          returns (Error)
          if (logging) log("gO:enter:" :: orderNumber); end
          if (useLocalGet)
```

Figure 9.20: I open up the middle tier business-logic library, OrderLib.

```
SYSLIB.SECREMOCEUSEL("IRUIIESI", "IRUIIESI");
dsSvrCtl DSSVRCTL { SCOPCD = "GH" };
dsOrdHdr DSORDHDR { OHORDR = orderNumber };
dsOrdDtl DSORDDTL;
call "ORDINQR" (dsSvrCtl, dsOrdHDR, dsOrdDtl);
if (dsSvrCtl.SCRTCD != "00")
```

```
✔ Show Quick Diff    Ctrl+Shift+Q       ) log("gOR:SCRTCD<>00"); end
  Show Line Numbers                      Error {
  Folding                           ▶    y = dsSvrCtl.SCRTCD as int,
  Preferences...                          = "Error getting order " :: orderNumber
  Add Breakpoint
  Disable Breakpoint                     ) log("gOR:SCRTCD==00"); end
```

Figure 9.21: Setting a breakpoint in the middle tier is the same as in the client.

The result is the Interface Mapping dialog that you saw in Figure 9.13. This time, I definitely want to debug the service, so I make sure the Mapping mode is set to "source." Next, I make sure the "Save these values in debug behavior mapping" checkbox is checked, as shown in Figure 9.22. Then, I click the OK button.

```
┌─────────────────────────────────────────────────┐
│ 🔵 Interface Mapping                          [✕] │
├─────────────────────────────────────────────────┤
│ Could not find an entry in the debug behavior    │
│ mapping preference page for service binding key  │
│ OrderService. Please specify mapping information. │
│                                                   │
│ Service binding key: OrderService                 │
│                                                   │
│ Mapping mode:     [ source          ▼]            │
│                                                   │
│ Part mapping:     [ com.pbd.svc.OrderService  ▼]  │
│                                                   │
│ ☑ Save these values in debug behavior mapping     │
│                                                   │
│              [    OK    ]  [  Cancel  ]           │
└─────────────────────────────────────────────────┘
```

Figure 9.22: The first error I encounter is the OrderService error.

Figure 9.23 shows the next error I get. When EGL tries to start debugging an EGL part that calls an RPG program, it tries to find the source for the called program ORDINQR. However, since ORDINQR is an RPG program, there is no EGL source. That being the case, I have to tell EGL to skip ORDINQR. I can click the Yes button whenever this comes up, or I can fix it myself using the preferences.

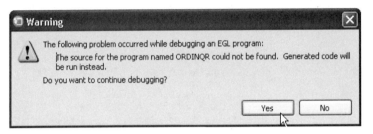

Figure 9.23: EGL can't find the source for an RPG program

Before talking about what happens after you click the Yes button, I want to show you the preference setting you need to stop the error in Figure 9.23 from reappearing every time you run a test. First, I go to the Preferences dialog. (Remember, select Window/Preferences from the main menu.) There, I can expand EGL and then expand Debug to see the Debug Behavior Mapping option. After making sure the Called Program tab is selected, I click the Add button, as shown in Figure 9.24.

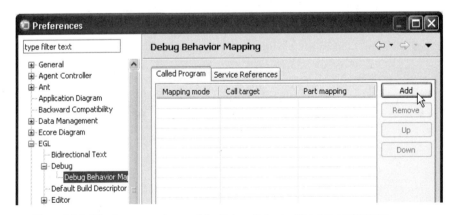

Figure 9.24: Skipping source is one of the Debug Behavior Mapping preferences.

There is no "direct" way to step into the RPG program from EGL, so I have to tell the EGL debugger to just use the generated version of

ORDINQR. As shown in Figure 9.25, I set the Mapping mode column to "generated" using the dropdown, and then type in ORDINQR for the Call target, and click the OK button. I can also use generics, so if my program-naming conventions are consistent, I wouldn't have to add every program here. Also, in an upcoming release, the error shown in Figure 9.23 will have an option to create this map automatically, similar to the one in Figure 9.22.

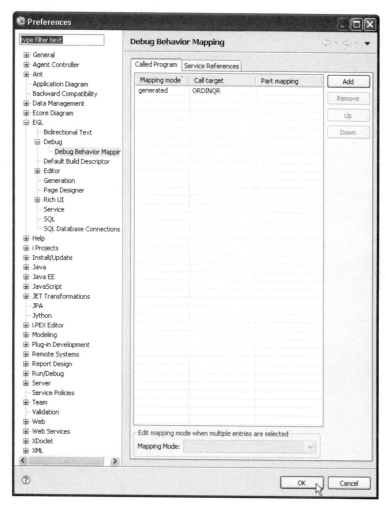

Figure 9.25: Map ORDINQR as a generated program.

The first time I stepped into the middle tier, I saw the error in Figure 9.26. Pay attention to the line outlined in dashes. It says I got a **NoClassDef-FoundError** on the AS400SecurityException class in the package com. ibm.as400.access. I recognize that package name as belonging to the jt400. jar file that I added to the middle tier project in Chapter 8. EGL's source debugger doesn't find that JAR file, so I have to tell it where to find it. Back to the preferences!

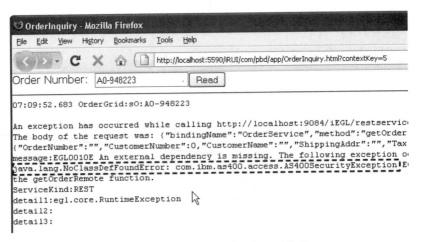

Figure 9.26: This error occurs when first stepping into the middle tier.

Once I'm back at the Preferences dialog, I select EGL/Debug from the navigator to see the dialog shown in Figure 9.27. On the right side, toward the bottom, there is a set of buttons. Click the second one, Add JARs.

Next, I use the Add JARs dialog, shown in Figure 9.28, to open the jt400. jar file added to the project in Chapter 8.

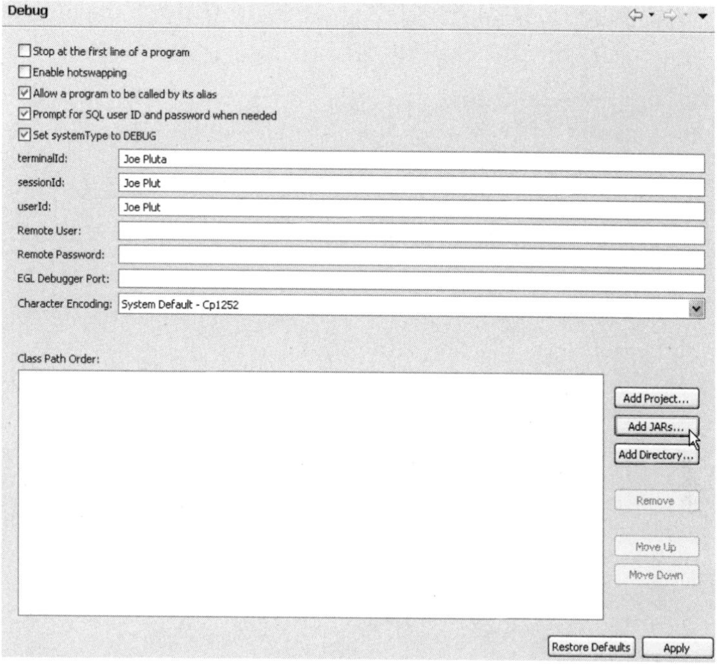

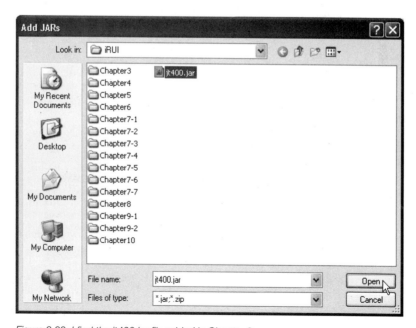

Figure 9.27: Here is the EGL Debug page of the Preferences dialog.

Figure 9.28: I find the jt400.jar file added in Chapter 8.

The JAR file appears in the Class Path Order list. I click the OK button, as shown in Figure 9.29.

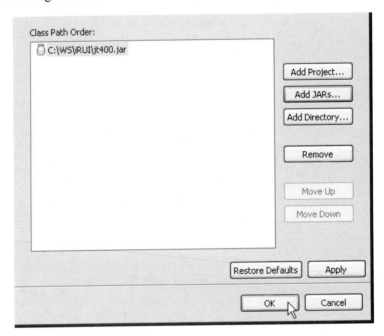

Figure 9.29: The JAR file appears in the list.

Now, I re-launch the application by clicking the Read button, as shown in Figure 9.30.

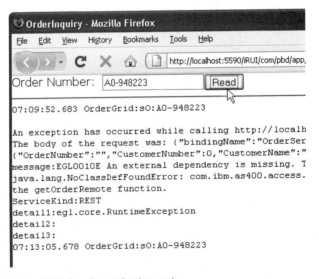

Figure 9.30: Run the application again.

Just like in the client debugging session, the middle tier is suspended at the breakpoint, as shown in Figure 9.31. I can view the variables as shown in Figure 9.32, and from this, I determine that the ORDINQR program, indeed, returned an error. It has a return code of 01, with the field OHORDR being the culprit. At this point, I've absolved both Tier 1 and Tier 2 of responsibility for the error. It's time to check Tier 3.

```
 OrderInquiry.egl    OrderGrid.egl    iRUI.css    OrderLib.egl ⊠    Fmt.js    Test1

        // Get order remote
 ⊖      function getOrderRemote(orderNumber string in, order Order inOut)
            returns (Error)
            if (logging) log("gOR:enter:" :: orderNumber); end
            SysLib.setRemoteUser("IRUITEST", "IRUITEST");
            dsSvrCtl DSSVRCTL { SCOPCD = "GH" };
            dsOrdHdr DSORDHDR { OHORDR = orderNumber };
            dsOrdDtl DSORDDTL;
            call "ORDINQR" (dsSvrCtl, dsOrdHDR, dsOrdDtl);
            if (dsSvrCtl.SCRTCD != "00")
                if (logging) log("gOR:SCRTCD<>00"); end
                return (new Error {
                    severity = dsSvrCtl.SCRTCD as int
```

Figure 9.31: The application stops at the breakpoint.

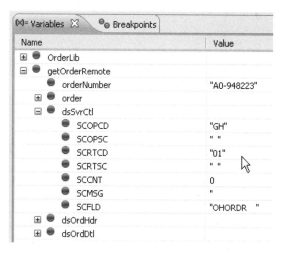

Figure 9.32: Indeed, an error was received.

Debugging the Host Program

The beauty of RDi-SOA is that you can debug your *entire* rich Internet application—the user interface, the middleware tier, and the business logic—all from the same workbench. There isn't a tool out there that allows this level of integration. In this section, you'll see just what that means.

Note that debugging a host job requires a slightly different setup, using something called a *service entry point (SEP)*. This is the way that host jobs can be suspended for debugging purposes.

I'll use the IBM i tools portion of RDi-SOA.

(It's interesting that we didn't even touch on the IBM i side of things until Chapter 8, and we haven't looked at an IBM i-specific tool until now. That just goes to show the flexibility of the EGL architecture.) First, I have to open the Remote Systems Explorer perspective. Then, I can select the Remote Systems Explorer, as shown in Figure 9.33.

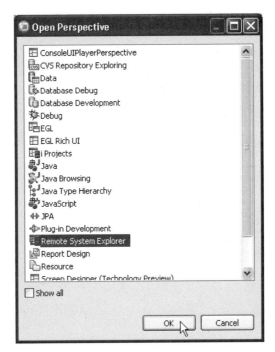

Figure 9.33: Open the Remote System Explorer perspective.

I click the New Connection tool on the toolbar, as shown in Figure 9.34, to create a new connection.

By selecting IBM i, as shown in Figure 9.35, I get the new Remote IBM i System Connection dialog.

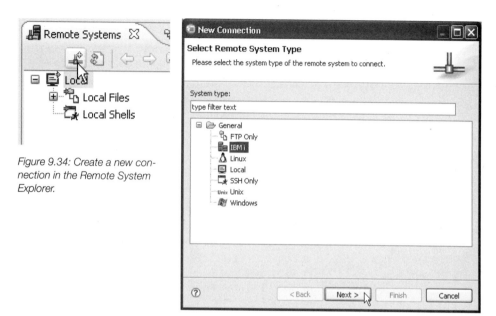

Figure 9.34: Create a new connection in the Remote System Explorer.

Figure 9.35: Create an IBM i connection.

As you can see in Figure 9.36, I use the name "IRUIHOST." I did this by setting up IRUIHOST in my hosts table, in the folder Windows/System32/

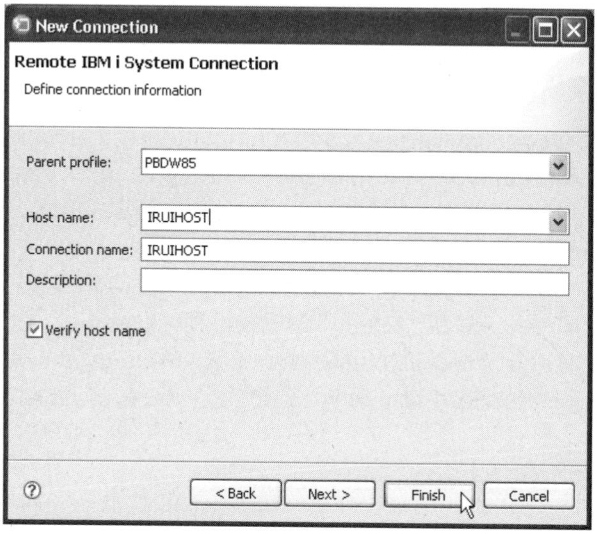

Figure 9.36: Enter the host name.

drivers/…etc. This is the same machine where I installed the IRUI library, and where I created a user profile on the host named "IRUITEST." All of this has to have already been done, or I wouldn't have been able to execute the program calls to ORDINQR.

The workbench won't actually try to connect to the host until I try to access host objects. The easiest way to do that is to open the library list, as shown in Figure 9.37. Obviously, the workbench won't have a library list unless it has an open job (a connection).

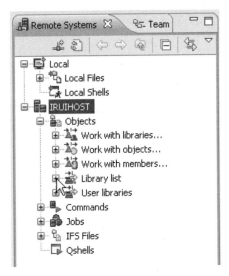

Figure 9.37 Expand the library list to force the connection to open.

At this point, the workbench is attempting to initiate a job, so it needs a user profile and password, as shown in Figure 9.38. I use the same user ID and password that I used when I invoked the ORDINQR program in Chapter 8.

Setting a service entry point is simple. I just right-click ORINQR in the library IRUI, select Debug Service Entry from the context menu, and then select Set Service Entry Point from the submenu. This is shown in Figure 9.39.

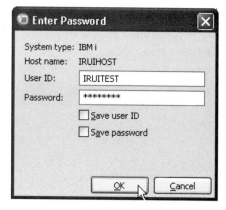

Figure 9.38: Now, enter the user ID and
password.

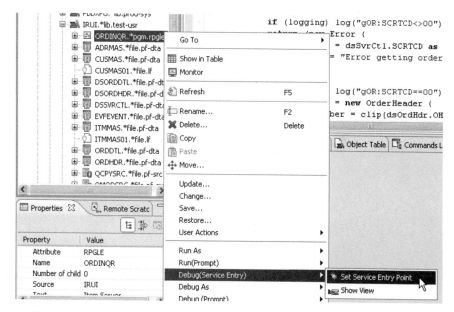

Figure 9.39: Set a service entry point.

The SEP is now set, as you can see in Figures 9.40 and 9.41. This will put the program into debug mode when I call it. However, if I want breakpoints, I have to set them.

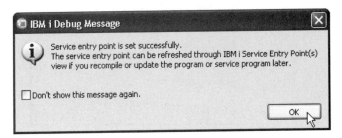

Figure 9.40: The dialog tells me I've set the SEP correctly.

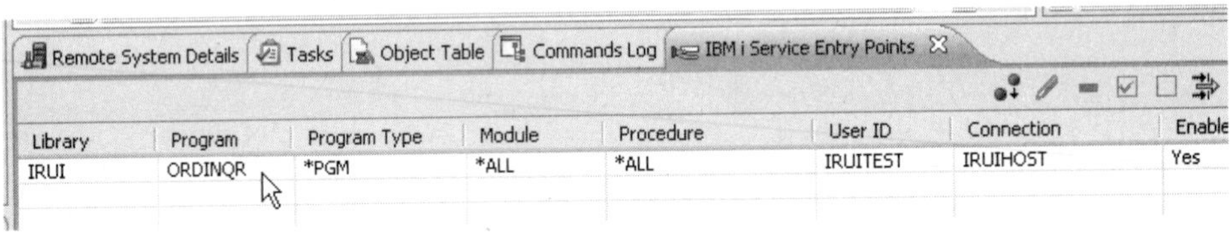

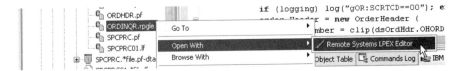

Figure 9.41: The view shows me the service entry point's details.

Setting a breakpoint in ILE RPG is much the same as setting one in any other language. First, open the source, as shown in Figure 9.42. Next, find the line, and add a breakpoint, as shown in Figure 9.43.

Figure 9.42: Open the source.

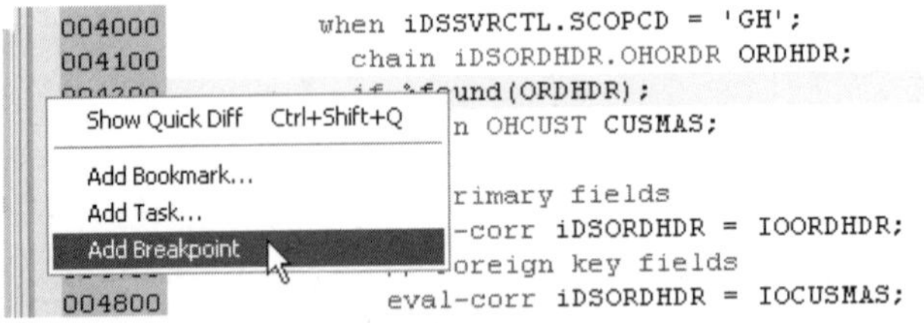

Figure 9.43: Find the line, and add the breakpoint.

That's all it takes. Now, I can continue running the application from either the rich client or the test program. It doesn't matter, but let's assume I'm running the test program because I don't have to enter the order number again. When I re-run the test program, I get the panel in Figure 9.44.

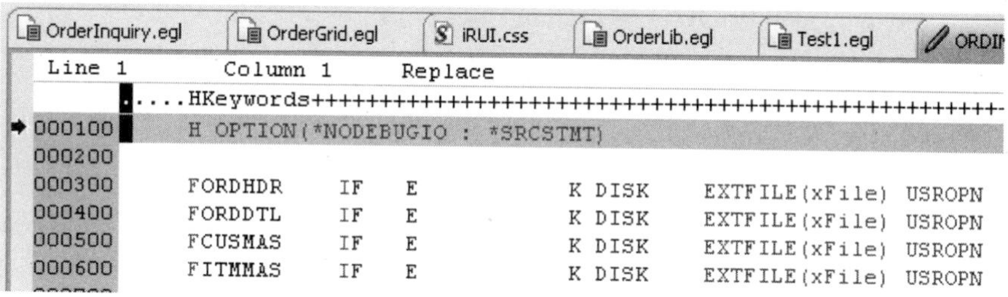

Figure 9.44: When a program with an SEP is called, this is the result.

The job on the host is suspended at the beginning of the call to the program, and control is transferred to the RDi-SOA workbench. RDi-SOA brings up the source and puts a dark blue arrow to the left of the line where execution is halted. The line is also highlighted with a light blue background. Since the program was just invoked, RDi-SOA highlights the first line of the code. Next, I want to get to my breakpoint, so I click the Resume tool. I see the results shown in Figure 9.45.

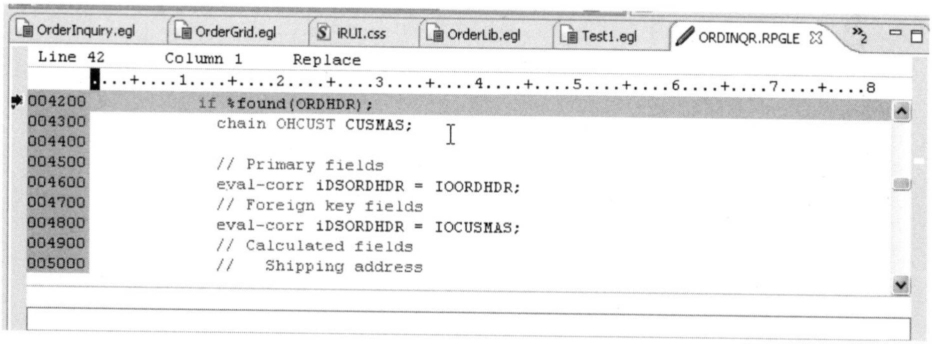

Figure 9.45: After resuming the program, the next thing I hit is the breakpoint.

The breakpoint I set at the **IF** opcode is next. Now, let's see if the record is found or not. If it is, the code will continue executing at line 4300. If not, it will jump to the **ELSE**. Note that there's no way to inspect the value of the **%found** built-in function via the debugger; you can only see the result indirectly, especially if the result is used in an If statement, like this. That's a painful shortcoming in the i tooling, as far as I'm concerned, but there's nothing to be done about it for now. All I can do is click the Resume tool as shown in Figure 9.46, and see what happens.

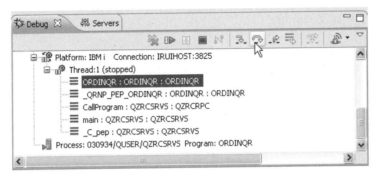

Figure 9.46: Click the Resume tool to see the next statement.

Figure 9.47 shows what happens. Since the program did get to the **ELSE** opcode, the **%found** BIF returned false. That means the **CHAIN** failed.

| OrderInquiry.egl | OrderGrid.egl | iRUI.css | OrderLib.egl |

```
    Line 69        Column 1      Replace
          ....+....1....+....2....+....3....+....4....+
► 006900              else;
  007000                  iDSSVRCTL.SCFLD = 'OHORDR';
  007100                  iDSSVRCTL.SCRTCD = '01';
  007200              endif;
  007300
  007400              // GD - Get order detail
  007500              when iDSSVRCTL.SCOPCD = 'GD';
  007600                  reade OHORDR ORDDTL;
  007700                  if not %eof(ORDDTL);
```

Figure 9.47: The next statement is the ELSE.

Now that I've determined the failure is, indeed, here in the RPG code, I can just let the program end. When I click the Resume tool, however, I hit my other breakpoint, as shown in Figure 9.48.

Oh, yeah—the other breakpoint. This is where RDi-SOA really shines, though. Remember when I mentioned that having all your languages integrated into a workbench is a real time-saver? Well, this is an example.

I open the Breakpoints view, as shown in Figure 9.49. I can see *all* of my breakpoints, regardless of the language, project, tier, or whatever. Not only

```
 OrderInquiry.egl    OrderGrid.egl    S iRUI.css    OrderLib.egl ⊠

        // Get order remote
⊖    function getOrderRemote(orderNumber string in, ord
        returns (Error)
        if (logging) log("gOR:enter:" :: orderNumber);
        SysLib.setRemoteUser("IRUITEST", "IRUITEST");
        dsSvrCtl DSSVRCTL { SCOPCD = "GH" };
        dsOrdHdr DSORDHDR { OHORDR = orderNumber };
        dsOrdDtl DSORDDTL;
        call "ORDINQR" (dsSvrCtl, dsOrdHDR, dsOrdDtl);
⇒       if (dsSvrCtl.SCRTCD != "00")
          if (logging) log("gOR:SCRTCD<>00"); end
          return (new Error {
            ⌐⌐⌐⌐⌐⌐⌐ ⌐⌐⌐ ⌐⌐⌐⌐⌐ ⌐⌐ int
```

Figure 9.48: I hit my middle-tier breakpoint.

that, but I can also manage them all from right here. That's what I do. I disable all breakpoints, except the one in the RPG. Also, note that this is reversible; the breakpoints still exist, they're just temporarily disabled. Oh, what I would have paid for this capability a few years ago!

I re-launch the test program. It gets to the first line of the RPG code, and now I want to take a closer look at the statement that's failing. I can do that without even setting a breakpoint, as shown in Figure 9.50.

I right-click on the line with the **CHAIN** opcode, and select Run To Location.

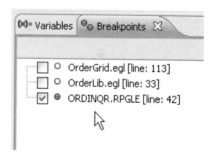

Figure 9.49: All breakpoints, at every tier, can be managed in one panel!

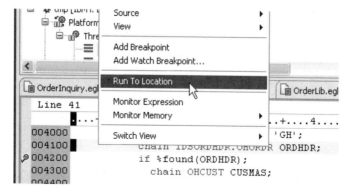

Figure 9.50: The Run To Location option is a great shortcut.

The debugger does just that. Now, I just need to take a closer look, perhaps at the OHORDR value I passed in.

This failed, as shown in Figure 9.51, but I know the value in the file exists. So what happened? Taking a closer look, I see that the value is "A0"—the letter *A* followed by the digit *0* (zero). Looking in the file again, I see that the key is actually the letter *A* followed by the letter *O* ("oh").

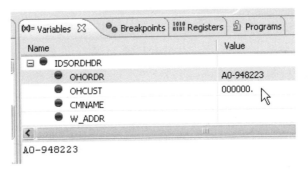

Figure 9.51: This failed. Why?

Could it just be a simple typo? Well, it's easy to test. I can change the value right in the Variables view, as shown in 9.52.

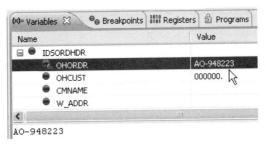

Figure 9.52: Change the value.

Now, I resume the program, and see the results shown in Figure 9.53. Amazing, isn't it? It works!

If I were to restart the application and enter the *correct* order number from the start, it would display Figure 9.53 again. Imagine that: I enter the correct input, and I get the correct output. The computer does exactly what I tell it to do!

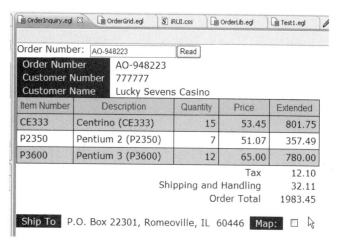

Figure 9.53: Life is grand!

Summary

We're nearing the end of this wonderful ride. I hope you've had as much fun as I have. EGL is an extraordinary language, and RDi-SOA is an incredible tool. Combine the raw power of RPG with the elegant philosophy of EGL, enable it with the sophisticated features of RDi-SOA, and I don't think there's ever been such a productive environment. I guarantee that if you take the time to learn the techniques I've outlined here, you'll never look at your business applications the same way.

I have one more surprise…read on.

10

The Future of EGL Rich UI

By the time you're reading this chapter, I hope you're excited about EGL Rich UI. It's a great technology, with a great pedigree. Application developers of all stripes can appreciate the general EGL philosophy of hiding technical details to allow the developer to concentrate on business design. At the same time, IBM i developers have to acknowledge the fact that EGL is the only modern language that really understands what the IBM i does best. Even without Rich UI, EGL has made serious inroads into being the best business language, period.

EGL Rich UI, however, is the component that really takes advantage of EGL's philosophy. The WYSIWYG designer lets you design widgets quickly and easily. The Infobus lets you encapsulate those widgets, so that you can easily combine them into larger widgets and eventually, into entire applications. The service part completely hides the details of your inter-tier communications, allowing you to invoke business logic in any form, from an external SOAP service to an internal REST service.

To do all of this, you don't need to write a single line of JavaScript. Similarly, you don't have to write a single line of Java to write the EGL code that provides the services used by the Rich UI.

Here's the real clincher: although EGL doesn't *require* JavaScript and Java skills, it allows you to *capitalize* on them, whether through something you commission from an outside consultant, something available from another in-house department, or something you create using your own current and future skills. Like Eclipse, EGL is built to be bigger than itself; it is built to embrace and encourage innovation.

Extending the Architecture

Let's take a moment to look at the extended version of the application you've seen throughout this book. In this extended version, I use the OrderGrid widget that I created in Chapter 7 as part of a larger "super-widget," which in turn is included in an even larger application UI. I can do this with a combination of careful widget design and the use of the Infobus, which you learned about in earlier chapters.

The extended example creates the Executive Dashboard panel shown in Figure 10.1. You can see the OrderGrid in the lower right. It has a few minor enhancements, which I'll point out shortly. Still, it's pretty much the same widget, embedded in a larger canvas that includes a bar graph and a grid.

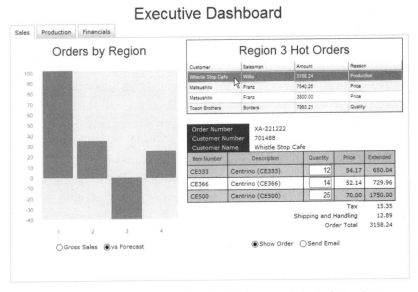

Figure 10.1: Here is the Executive Dashboard, which includes the OrderGrid widget.

The idea is that the bar graph is clickable, to get you a list of "hot" orders for the region. The grid is then clickable to get you the details for an order.

Just below the order detail is a radio button, letting you choose to either view the clicked order or send an email to the salesperson for that order.

If you click the Send Email button, the page changes, as shown in Figure 10.2. This happens instantaneously. Click the Show Order button, and the order detail returns. While not exactly the Taj Mahal of business application, it's a nice start.

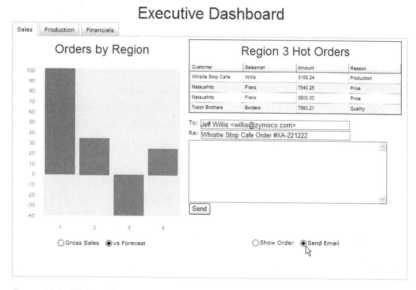

Figure 10.2: Click the Send Email button, and a pre-filled email widget instantly appears.

Incorporating Dojo

You might have noticed that the dashboard itself has three tabs: Sales, Production, and Financials. We're only looking at the sales widget in this example, but I'm sure you can imagine what those tabs (and others) might contain. The really cool thing is that the tabbed widget is part of the base Dojo widgets.

"What," you ask, "is Dojo?"

Dojo is one of the niftier Web 2.0 frameworks available today. Others include the Yahoo UI (YUI) and jQuery. These frameworks are self-contained libraries that can be included in your HTML documents to provide very fancy, rich-web client artifacts.

Dojo is a very powerful framework upon which a robust widget toolkit is layered. This toolkit, called Dijit, provides a wide variety of user-interface widgets, from simple things like buttons and checkboxes, to complex constructs like trees and grids. Dijit also provides a wide array of layout containers, including the tab container I take advantage of in Figures 10.1 and 10.2.

That's not all Dojo provides. It also has a library called DojoX, which provides an extensive array of graphical widgets, including 2D- and 3D-graphics. Again, I've taken advantage of these widgets in the dashboard example. The capabilities of these graphics are actually quite astonishing; they include event-handling, as well as something called "actions," which provide very sophisticated animation that can really put web applications on a par with thick clients. Actions such as **shake** and **highlight** actually visibly change graphical elements as you mouse over them. The effect is dramatic.

While you could write an entire book on Dojo (and people have!), its underlying idea is simple: to add functionality to your HTML pages through JavaScript. Dojo is interesting in that it allows you to add this functionality one of two ways: by adding simple HTML-like tags and attributes to your existing document, or by using JavaScript calls to its API. If you chose to learn Dojo, you could start with the tag-based syntax (which Dojo calls "declarative"), and then, as your skills at both Dojo and JavaScript grew, you could move on to the API (termed the "programmatic" interface).

Here's the cool part for EGL programmers, though: you don't have to do either.

That's right. The Dojo toolkit is encapsulated for you, and the EGL Rich UI interface is provided as an importable project. Currently, the toolkit is in an early state. The latest release I used was version 0.6, which reflects its status as a technology preview. Even in its infancy, Dojo is an exciting example of what EGL developers can expect as the tool evolves.

Getting My Dojo On

Here's the entire code for the Executive Dashboard panel:

```
package com.pbd.app;
import com.pbd.app.widget.*;
import com.pbd.util.*;
import com.ibm.egl.rui.widgets.*;
import com.ibm.egl.rui.infobus.*;
import dojo.widgets.*;
```

These are my imports. They let me access my application support, as well as the various IBM packages I need.

This is the standard RUIhandler definition:

```
handler Dashboard type RUIhandler {
  initialUI = [ui],
  onConstructionFunction = initialization,
  cssFile="css/iRUI.css"}
```

This is my Infobus setup:

```
// InfoBus - One event per component
eidApp string = "com.pbd.Dashboard";
eidST string = "com.pbd.Dashboard.SalesTab";
```

I specify the ID for the application, and the ID for any sub-widgets. In this case, the only one defined is SalesTab. As I developed additional tabs, I would add them here.

This is the entire layout of the application:

```
// The UI consists of the prompt and the display
ui Box {
  columns = 1, class = "ui",
  children = [ title, tabs ]};
```

As you can see, I have a title and a tab container. Here is the title, with a class so that I can play with the fonts and colors in CSS:

```
title TextLabel{
  text = "Executive Dashboard", class = "title" };
```

A DojoTabContainer is pretty simple to set up:

```
dataTab TabData[3] =[
  new TabData{title = "Sales", contents = tab1,
    selected = true },
  new TabData{title = "Production", contents = tab2},
  new TabData{title = "Financials", contents = tab3}
];
tabs DojoTabContainer{
  data = dataTab, position = "left",
  containerWidth = 800, containerHeight = 500 };
```

I specify the height and width, and an array of TabData elements. Each TabData element has a name and a content widget. The names are the text shown in the tabs; I also select the Sales tab to be the one visible.

The tabs must be boxes, but for the initial design, each box contains a single TextLabel as a placeholder:

```
tab1 Box { children =
  [ new TextLabel { text = "Sales", class = "title" } ] };
tab2 Box { children =
  [ new TextLabel { text = "Production", class = "title" } ] };
tab3 Box { children =
  [ new TextLabel { text = "Financials", class = "title" } ] };
```

This is the whole application:

```
function initialization()
  DojoLib.setTheme("tundra");
  InfoBus.subscribe(eidApp, listener);
  (new SalesTab {}).setId(eidST);
  InfoBus.publish(eidST, new InfobusMessage {
    src = eidApp,
    action = "SHOW" } );
end
```

First, I call a Dojo function to set the theme. Next, I set the application up to listen for messages and create the sub-widgets. Then, I tell them to render themselves.

After that, I just listen for events:

```
function listener(eventName String in, object any in)
  ibm InfobusMessage = object;
  case
    when (ibm.action == "SHOW" and ibm.src == eidST)
```

```
        dataTab[1].contents = ibm.data;
    end
  end
end
```

Typically, each sub-widget would tell me when it had been rendered, and I would then load its contents into the appropriate tab. In this example, I only have code for the SalesTab widget, but as I added new tabs, I would just extend the case structure. Also, I could conceivably get events other than simple render (**SHOW**) events; in a more complete example, I might set up logic for status messages and errors, but those would still fit right into this basic listener. This is the skeleton of every application you would ever write. (Actually, anybody who has written GUI applications using Windows or Java probably recognizes this structure—it's the event-loop processor.)

Notice that I've been able to take advantage of both the Dojo capabilities and the base EGL Rich UI widgets. Everything works together seamlessly, thanks to the Infobus. I can also continue to grow my application organically, extending and enhancing my widgets as needed.

Now, I've done some fudging with this. The data for the graph and for the "hot orders" grid is hardcoded. I've also made some changes to OrderGrid to provide input-capable fields, and reduced the column and font sizes to tighten up the widget a little, so that it fits within the larger application. But that's all! The base code remains the same. In fact, the original screen still works, as shown in Figure 10.3.

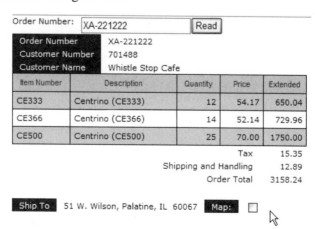

Figure 10.3: The original application still works!

I added some conditional processing to the widget. The setMap function determines whether the Ship To widget (the one that shows the Google-Map) displays, while the setEditQty function determines whether the quantity field is editable.

What I love is that I can focus on the problems at a business level, such as simply identifying which widgets to display. Here's an example:

```
function setMap(showMap boolean)
  orderBox.removeChildren();
  if (showMap)
    orderBox.appendChildren(
      [header, lines, totals, shipping, mapBox]);
  else
    orderBox.appendChildren(
      [header, lines, totals]);
  end
end
```

The setMap function has one parameter, a Boolean value that specifies whether the map section is shown or not. The map section includes the shipping box (which has the shipping address and the checkbox) and the map itself. The logic is simple: remove all the children, and then add back the ones that are appropriate. While this is a simple example, you can see how flexible it could be. You could literally redesign the entire interface, dynamically.

EGL Rich UI Futures

What's coming next? Well, while I'm writing this paragraph, I'm waiting for the latest release of Rational Business Developer. Version 7.5.1.3 contains a host of enhancements, which I'll touch on briefly in a moment. Even more exciting, however, is the recent announcement of the community edition of EGL Rich UI, whose current name is "To Be Determined Real Soon Now."

One of the impediments to the uptake of EGL has been its price tag. Rational Business Developer is not inexpensive, nor would you expect it to be with all the enterprise features it has built in. However, many of the other web technologies, such as PHP and .Net, provide some sort of free entry-level tooling. That not only allows early adopters to develop proof-of-concept applications, it also makes the language much more attractive to students, and thus to educational institutions.

The new free EGL Rich UI tooling will be a self-contained workbench supporting the creation of end-to-end Rich UI applications. You will be able to write both the EGL Rich UI client code and the EGL services code to support it. In contrast to the current design, where you first create a web project for the middle tier and then a Rich UI project for the client tier, with the new tooling, a single project will support both the web application and browser components of the application. It's a great feature, and you'll be able to test the whole application in the workbench without deploying to the server.

Back to the new features in RBD. The changes range from minor to major, and they affect the entire product, even including the Installation Manager (IM). IM will have a few cosmetic changes, but will work the same. As you might expect, there will also be a new release of the EGL Rich UI project. (The com.ibm.egl.rui_1.0.0 project will be upgraded to com.ibm. egl.rui_1.0.1.) You will be able to select either version; I can't wait to get my hands on the new stuff! It's this ongoing enhancement that really helps EGL developers. As the IBM folks make the widgets better, your applications will improve without you having to be a JavaScript expert.

Ease of use is high on the list. You should expect to see drag-and-drop capabilities within the Outline view, to help you more easily manipulate the components of your RUI handlers. I didn't spend any time on the Outline view in Chapter 3 because in version 7.5.1.2, it was a read-only review. The EGL developers, however, saw that it could be used as an alternative editing tool. I am really looking forward to this; it will be a great addition to the WYSIWYG designer.

The development team continues to streamline the process of writing code, as well. For example, suppose you want to write a handler for a widget event. The Events view will help you by suggesting a default name for the event (using the widget name and event name). Then, when you click the OK button to add the event handler, it will not only add the skeleton for the function, but it will take you right to the source, so you can enter your code. Nifty.

The EGL designers aren't just focusing on the quantity of code, but on its quality, as well. One of the little distractions I've had with the designer is that it always used fully qualified widget class names, such as "com.ibm. egl.rui.widget.Button," when defining the widgets in your code. Those definitions are now being replaced with non-qualified references and import statements, which greatly reduces the amount of clutter in the generated code.

Wrapping It All Up

I hope you've enjoyed this journey into EGL Rich UI. As you've seen, the EGL language is perfectly suited to create sophisticated business applications that take advantage of *all* of today's best technologies—from the IBM i for superior business logic and database performance, to the very latest in dynamic HTML and JavaScript frameworks. Perhaps even more important, EGL's fundamental underpinnings are designed to evolve.

By providing a simple, consistent syntax to access all of the best-of-breed technologies, EGL removes the guesswork of trying to determine which route to take. By allowing you the flexibility to extend syntax with your own expertise, EGL prevents you from being locked in as technologies change. And finally, for the IBM i developer, EGL is the only language that provides tools specifically designed to incorporate your existing business logic with the highest possible performance.

EGL and EGL Rich UI get you to the web faster than any other solution. At the same time, they protect your investment, by making your applications future-proof.

I hope you have much success with this powerful tool!

INDEX

J

JAR file
  business logic tier and, 205–206, **206**
  debugging and, 238–240, **239**, **240**
Java, 3, 9, 18, 19, 25, 26, 49, 167, 253
Java Toolbox, 26
JavaScript, 3, 15, 25, 26, 28, 97, 167, 253
  debugging and, 228–234
JavaScript Object Notation. *See* JSON
JavaServer Faces (JSF), 20
JavaServer Pages (JSP), 50, 100, 101, 189, 215
  multi-tiered application architecture and,
    13–14, **14**
JAX, 25, 26
jQuery, 255
JSON, 3, 4, 15, 16, 21, 28, 37
justification/alignment, 161, **161**

K

keywords, 90–91, 193, 194

L

labels, 24
Laffra, Chris, 158
libraries
  copying, 139–140, **140**
  proxy, 86, 124
library functions, EGL, 20–21, **20**, 117–118, **117**
Lines array, 106–108, **107**
linkage parts, 200–205, **200**, **201**, **203**, **204**, **205**
Linux, 9
listeners, 37–38, 135–136. *See also* delegates
  debugging and, 233
logging, 217, 222–224, 228, **228**. *See also*
  debugging; error handling

M

maximizing the view, 75, **75**, 109
messaging
  business logic tier and, 189–192, **191**
  Infobus and, 181–184, **184**
  record definition and, 29–32, **29**, **30**, **31**
  rich web client, 15–16

model-view-controller (MVC), 13–14, 51
modes in designer, 102, **102**
multi-tiered applications, architecture of. *See*
  architecture of multi-tiered applications
MyEclipse, 19, 26

N

naming conventions, 148
  EGL Rich UI Application and, 148
  packages, 85–87, 86*t*
  servers, 192
  widgets, 56, **57**, 60, **60**
nested boxes, 58, **58**, 60, **60**
Net, 260
.NET, 18, 22
NetBeans, 19
New EGL Data Variable wizard, 105–110, **105**
new project creation, 47–59, **47**
  defining tiers in, 81–82, **81**, **82**
  folder creation in, 52, **52**
  folder organization and, 98–99, **98**, **99**
  for Tier 2, 83–84, **84**
  framework for, 81–96
  package creation in, 52
  page handlers and, 50–51, **51**
  perspectives in, 48–50, **49**
  placeholders and, 87–89
  records to include in, 82–83, 83*t*
  rich UI application creation in, 50–54
  Rich UI handler in, 50–51, **51**, 52–54, **53**
  simple design prototyping for, 82–83
  type of project in, 47–48, **48**
non-EGL design of multi-tiered application,
  25–28, **25**
null values, 124, 130

O

onConstruction function, 110
onPrerender function, 110
OpenAjax, 137, 215
OpenAjaxHub, 4
ORDINQR program in RPG, 192–198
output of example application, **95**

NOTE: Boldface indicates illustrations and code; t indicates a table.

269

web service, *continued*

  Web Services Definition Language (WSDL) and, 28, 125–128, **125**, **126**, **127**, **128**

  Web Services Explorer and, 129–131, **129**

Web Services Definition Language (WSDL), 28, 125–128, **125**, **126**, **127**, **128**

Web Services Explorer, 129–131, **129**

WebSphere, 13, 18, 19

WebSphere Test Environment, 42, 44

widgets, 24–25

  adding to app, using WYSIWYG editor, 54–57, **55**, **56**, **57**, 62–67

  aligning/centering text in, 71–72, **72**

  boxes and, 57–59, **57**, **58**

  designer actions in, 69–70

  drop zones for, 55, **55**, 63–65, **64**, 69

  field editing in, 68–69, **69**

  formatting of, 152–162 **153**, **155**, **156**

  hierarchy popup for, 65–66, **66**, 69

  naming, 56, **57**, 60, **60**

  text added to, 66–67

  updating, 152

  width adjustment in, 72–73, **72**, **73**, 156–157, **157**

width adjustment, 72–73, **72**, **73**, 156–158, **157**

Windows, 9

Word, 23

Workbench, 45–47, **45–47**

workspaces, 45, **45**

WSDL. *See* Web Services Definition Language

WYSIWGY designer, 4, 14, 23, 26, 41–80, 253, 261

  absolute positioning in, 59

  adding EGL Rich UI code using, 78–80, **78**, **79**

  aligning/centering text in, 71–72, **72**

  box properties in, 61–62, **61**, **62**

  boxes in, 57–59, **57**, **58**

  button in, 59

  color codes and drop zones, in, 55, **55**, 63–64, **64**

  Design mode in, 103, **103**

  dotted line areas in, 56, **56**

  drag symbol in, **65**

  drop zones in, 55, **55**, 63–64, **64**, 65, 69

  editable fields and, 68

  EGL Rich UI Application and, 145–153

  events and, adding action to widgets in, 74–77, **75**, **76**, **77**

  fields and, 68–69, **69**

  folder creation in, 52, **52**

  hierarchy popup in, 65–66, **66**, 69

  maximizing the view in, 75, **75**, 109

  modes in, 102, **102**

  nesting boxes in, 58, **58**, 60, **60**

  new project creation in, 47–59, **47**

  package creation in, 52

  page handlers and, 50–51, **51**

  Palette, 55, **55**

  panning in, 56

  perspectives in, 46, 48–50, **49**

  Properties dialogs in, 61–62, **61**, **62**, 67–68, **67**, **68**, 71, **71**

  RDI-SOA installation for, 41–44, **42–44**

  Rich UI application creation with, 50–54

  Rich UI editor in, 54, **54**

  Rich UI handler in, 50–51, **51**, 52–54, **53**

  spanning boxes in, 58, **58**

  splash screen for, in RDI-SOA, 46, **46**

  split screen mode in, 102, **102**

  text added to widget in, 66–67

  TextLabel in, 59, 64–66, **64**

  type of project in, 47–48, **48**

  updates/saves in, 62

  views in, 46

  widgets added to app using, 54–57, **55**, **56**, **57**, 62–67

  width adjustment in, 72–73, **72**, **73**

  Workbench for, starting up, 45–47, **45–47**

  workspaces in, 45, **45**

X
XML, 15, 16, 28

X–Windows, 2

Y
Yahoo IU (YUI), 255

Z
Zend Studio, 19